Controlling Misconduct
in the Military

Controlling Misconduct in the Military

a study prepared for

the Commission

of Inquiry into

the Deployment of

Canadian Forces

to Somalia

Martin L. Friedland, O.C., Q.C.
Faculty of Law at
The University of Toronto

May 1996

© Minister of Public Works and Government Services Canada 1997
Printed and bound in Canada

Available in Canada through
your local bookseller or by mail from
Public Works and Government Services Canada — Publishing
Ottawa, Canada   K1A 0S9

Catalogue No. CP32-64/2-1997E
ISBN 0-660-168685

Canadian Cataloguing in Publication Data

Friedland, M. L. (Martin Lawrence), 1932-

Controlling misconduct in the military : a study

Issued also in French under title: Contrôle de
l'inconduite dans les forces armées.
ISBN 0-660-16868-5
Cat. no. CP32-64/2-1997E

1. Military discipline — Canada.
2. Military police — Canada.
3. Courts martial and courts of inquiry — Canada.
I. Commission of Inquiry into the Deployment of Canadian Forces to Somalia.
II. Title.

FC603.F74 1997   355.1'33'0971   C97-980055-2
F1028.F74 1997

Contents

Acknowledgements

I am indebted to five exceptionally able University of Toronto law students who helped produce this document. Caroline Ursulak, a recent graduate, assisted in the early stages of the project with the section on military justice. Robert Brush, completing third year, and Craig Martin, second year, worked closely with me over the summer and during the academic year in collecting material, helping me organize my thoughts, and assisting me in checking references. Elizabeth Evans and Rita Samson, both completing their third year, assisted with some specific tasks for part of the summer. Allyn Chudy provided excellent secretarial services. Very helpful comments on a preliminary draft of the study were received from a number of experts within and outside the Commission of Inquiry. I am indebted to the Commission Secretary, Stanley Cohen, for his comments and for his help in developing the framework of the study. Others within the Commission also willingly answered questions, supplied material, and provided detailed comments on a draft of the study and I would particularly like to thank Douglas Bland, François Lareau, David Pomerant, Jim Simpson, Jack Vance, and Donna Winslow. Incisive comments on the draft were also given by Charles Cotton, Deborah Harrison, Kent Roach, and Janet Walker. Linda Cameron, the librarian at the Commission, Shawn Goudge of the JAG library in Ottawa, Cathy Murphy of the Canadian Forces College library in Toronto, and the staff of the Faculty of Law library at the University of Toronto graciously supplied the author with requested material. To all these people I offer my sincere thanks. I am also grateful to the Faculty of Law and the Canadian Institute for Advanced Research for their continuing support and encouragement. The study is current as of May 1996.

M.L. Friedland

CHAPTER ONE

Introduction

On March 16, 1968, a company of U.S. soldiers in Vietnam was involved in slaughtering defenceless civilians in the hamlet of My Lai.[1] That event and its cover-up and investigation was a crucial defining moment for the American public and military and led to a determination to seek ways to control such misconduct in the military in the future.

Precisely 25 years to the day after the My Lai massacre — on March 16, 1993 — a young defenceless Somali was tortured and beaten to death by members of the Canadian Airborne Regiment in Somalia.[2] This event and its aftermath will also turn out to be a crucial defining moment for the Canadian public and the Canadian military. A number of Canadian practices have already been changed as a result of the Somalia affair, and no doubt more will change as a result of the investigation and report of the Commission of Inquiry into the Deployment of Canadian Forces to Somalia (the Somalia Inquiry).[3]

When researchers for the Somalia Inquiry met with senior U.S. Army officials in Washington in the summer of 1995, they were told that since the My Lai massacre, "the U.S. Army has now reached the stage where they are sure that a situation such as the conduct of 2 Commando at Belet Uen could not occur in the U.S. Army."[4] The task of the Somalia Inquiry, in my view, is to set the stage so that the Canadian military will be able to say the same.

I was asked by the Somalia Inquiry to prepare a background study examining various techniques used to control misconduct in the military.[5] No doubt my interest in sanctions and rewards in the legal system and my study of various institutions, such as my recent work on the judiciary, were responsible for the invitation.[6] (It was not because of my knowledge of the military, which before starting this project was based on three months in 400 Fighter Squadron one summer during high school.) The study looks at a range of military structures and institutions that provide controls on behaviour and analyzes how they can be improved to make members of the military more accountable for their conduct, without at the same time diminishing their effectiveness as a fighting force.

The project has been particularly interesting to me because of the light it sheds on ways to control conduct in non-military situations. There are many valuable aspects of military justice and other ways used by the military to control undesirable conduct. The military, like the academic world, uses rewards as a way of motivating desirable conduct (see Chapter 2), a technique that is not used to the extent it could be to control undesirable conduct in civilian society.[7] Further, the military, like the tax system, does not come in with its heavy guns of courts martial whenever wrongdoing is discovered.[8] As we will see, administrative sanctions are often used, as are summary proceedings. Summary trials constitute 98 per cent of military trials. There are about 4,000 summary trials (conducted by a commanding officer or a delegated officer) each year and only about 100 courts martial (see Chapter 6).

In civilian society, we give too much prominence to the criminal trial. We punish and stigmatize. The military generally tries to reintegrate the wayward soldier back into military society. Soldiers that cannot be reintegrated under any conditions, sociologist Lawrence Radine has written, "must be punished or expelled from the Army in such a way as to maintain the legitimacy of the Army in other soldiers' (and civilians') eyes."[9] Reintegrative shaming, such as occurs in summary proceedings before the commanding officer, is making a resurgence in criminological theory. As John Braithwaite states in his book, *Crime, Shame and Reintegration*, "Reintegrative shaming is superior to stigmatization because it minimizes risks of pushing those shamed into criminal subcultures, and because social disapproval is more effective when embedded in relationships overwhelmingly characterized by social approval." "Under the time-honored naval tradition of 'Captain's mast'", Braithwaite writes, giving an example of reintegrative shaming, "a seaman who fell asleep on watch...could be denounced by the captain in the presence of members of the ship's company assembled on deck for the purpose of shaming him."[10] In the civilian criminal justice system — this is particularly so in the United States — we tend to push wrongdoers into criminal subcultures by too harsh penalties.

The military is, of course, different from civilian society. There is what is referred to as "unlimited liability", that is, the obligation to risk one's life as a member of the military.[11] "Acceptance of this concept more than anything else," the military told the Somalia Inquiry at a policy hearing, "sets the service member apart from other members of society."[12] A member of the military may not simply quit when he or she wishes. Another significant difference is that members of the military may not "combine with other members for the purpose of bringing about alterations in existing regulations for the Canadian Forces"; may not sign or solicit signatures for "petitions or applications relating to the Canadian Forces"; and may not without authorization "enter into direct communication with any government department other than the Department of National Defence on subjects connected with the Canadian Forces."[13] Finally, unlike others in Canadian society, military members are governed by a Code of Military Discipline in addition to being subject to the regular civilian laws.

This chapter examines a number of introductory issues, looks at the available statistics on the extent of misconduct in the military, touches on the so-called mystique of the paratroopers, and outlines various possible techniques for controlling misconduct.

INSTITUTION OR OCCUPATION?

One of the questions much discussed in the military literature is whether the military can be classified as an institution or an occupation.[14] The more the military is cut off from society, the more it can be said to be an institution — or, in Erving Goffman's words, a "total institution", that is, "a place of residence and work where a large number of like-situated individuals, cut off from the wider society for an appreciable period of time, together lead an enclosed, formally administered round of life."[15] Goffman was writing in 1962 about mental institutions, which, like prisons and penitentiaries, have been moving away from being total institutions and moving slowly toward normal society.[16]

The same is true of military institutions.[17] Some military forces are consciously in the 'occupation' camp. Germany, for example, deliberately chose to create a civically integrated military.[18] Members of the military can join unions and run for parliament, and they are tried by civilian courts for the more serious military offences. Israel, on the other hand, has a permanent force that is closer to the institutional model. Reuven Gal, a former chief psychologist with the Israel Defence Force, notes that the Israeli military "is a professional organization that maintains its institutional characteristics, but these characteristics are not as pure and idealistic as they were initially."[19]

Not surprisingly, Canada, England, and the United States are somewhere between these two positions.[20] Charles Moskos and Frank Wood, two leading writers on the institution/occupation debate, think that "creeping occupationalism" makes a "real difference in military effectiveness... institutional identification fosters greater organizational commitment and performance than does occupational." Charles Moskos has shown that in the United States, at least, "the marked trend towards occupationalism in the 1970s has been countered somewhat by a renewed emphasis on institutionalism in the military in the 1980s."[21] One of the examples cited by Moskos is the 1987 U.S. Supreme Court case, *Solorio*[22] (discussed in Chapter 6), which overturned the 1969 decision in *O'Callahan* v. *Parker*,[23] which had required a "military nexus" between the crime committed by a member and military service. As a result of *Solorio*, a military tribunal may take jurisdiction in the United States for any offence allegedly committed by a military person, whether or not there is a military nexus.

Charles Cotton, a Canadian writer with a military background, does not think the Canadian military have done very well in solving the tension between the institutional and occupational models. The Canadian military, he wrote in 1988, "is a specialized federal bureaucracy with weak and ambiguous ties to society, while at the same time it exhibits internal dissent and strains. Its links to national values and social fabric and its internal cohesion have both suffered in recent decades." He points out that "an attempt to increase internal cohesion does not always imply a parallel decrease in the link with society."[24]

Trying to achieve internal cohesion, which is clearly important for a military organization, and yet at the same time avoid isolating the military from Canadian society and its values, including of course the *Canadian Charter of Rights and Freedoms*, is an objective that will not be easy to attain. The report of the Somalia Inquiry can, perhaps, offer some guidance. The Supreme Court of Canada provided some support to the institutional model in 1992 by upholding the concept of a separate system of military justice in *Généreux*,[25] but within the context of Charter values. Many members of the military had feared that the dissent by Chief Justice Laskin and Mr. Justice Estey in the 1980 case, *MacKay*,[26] who wanted military justice to be handled by the regular courts, would carry the day. As we will see in Chapter 6, there is still considerable uncertainty about the constitutionality of the system of summary justice. The view is expressed in a later discussion that the Supreme Court of Canada is likely to uphold the system of summary justice, particularly if some suggested changes are made. The system of summary justice has been upheld by the Supreme Court of the United States,[27] a fact that will carry weight in Canada because in both the law and military matters Canada is moving much closer to the United States than to the United Kingdom.[28]

MISCONDUCT IN THE MILITARY

In 1985, Major General C.W. Hewson led a study team investigating discipline infractions and antisocial behaviour in Mobile Command (i.e., the Army), with particular reference to the Special Service Force and the Canadian Airborne Regiment. That report is the latest that I have seen that attempts to compare military and civilian misconduct. The study points out difficulties in comparing civilian and military crime statistics. Military police investigations, for example, include dependents and civilian employees, but incidents involving military personnel dealt with exclusively by civilian authorities may not come to the attention of the military police.[29] Moreover, the comparison made was between the military population and the overall civilian population, which includes elderly people and children. The Hewson Report concluded:

Although a statistically valid comparison is not possible there appears to be a lower incidence of serious pathology and violent behaviour in the Canadian Forces than in the Canadian population at large. There is a relatively higher frequency of sexual offences which should be further investigated.[30]

All in all, it is difficult to base firm conclusions on the data collected, and the Somalia Inquiry may wish to gather current statistics on the subject. The figures from the 1980s do suggest, however, that criminal conduct in the military is not out of control. In the general population, the mean number of assaults per 100,000 population for the years 1979 to 1982 was 468, whereas for the military for the same period on military establishments (amounting to perhaps 100,000 persons including civilians and dependants) it was 133.[31]

Military personnel are, by the nature of their activity, aggressive. As Anthony Kellett states, "If an army is to fulfil its mission on the battlefield, it must be trained in aggression."[32] The wonder is that there is not more spillover[33] criminal activity by members of the military than there is.

One area of continuing concern identified by the Hewson Report is sexual assault.[34] As Clifton Bryant states in *Khaki-Collar Crime*, "Young males cut off from traditional informal controls, bolstered by a masculine and aggressive military subculture, and faced with a situation of relative unavailability and inaccessibility of females are prime candidates for sexual crimes against [the] person."[35] The Hewson Report identified this isolation as a particular problem at Petawawa (where the Airborne Regiment was stationed in Canada), leading to fights with the local male population. The Hewson Report states:

The young single soldiers in Petawawa are not greatly interested in base sponsored clubs, sports or activities. They prefer to spend most of their off-duty time in the limited number of local entertainment establishments, socializing and meeting girls. There is a limited number of girls in the local area and they are attracted to the soldier with his car, regular pay and job security. This antagonizes the local male population which is already frustrated by unemployment (particularly in Quebec). According to the local police, most incidents of violence involve disputes over girls.[36]

The Canadian Airborne at Petawawa, the Hewson Report found, experienced a higher number of assault cases than other units, indeed, twice the number of any other unit.[37]

There is also concern about domestic violence in the military. As was stated by two American authors:

Many characteristics of military life affect the risk for violence. Perhaps the most significant is the removal of the military family, usually young and inexperienced, from the support systems of the extended family and family friends. They are distanced from parents, grandparents, uncles, aunts, siblings, cousins, friends, and neighbors who usually provide support, instruction, companionship, and a sense of perspective to young couples. Frequently, military couples have to live in quarters assigned according to rank. Their neighbors, therefore, are also young people with little more experience in marriage and parenting than they have.[38]

Canadian authors Deborah Harrison and Lucie Laliberté, who analyzed the literature and conducted interviews with Canadian military personnel, also reached the conclusion that wife abuse was high. Writing in 1994, they quote the Adjutant of one Canadian army unit who recently speculated: "I think there are 93 married people [in the] unit. You could talk to every one of the wives, and you would possibly find a dozen wives that have been beaten [in the last two months]." Their explanation is that this could be a spillover into personal lives of violence used for legitimate purposes and that this reflects "a subculture in which physical aggressiveness is positively valued."[39]

PARATROOPERS

Physical aggressiveness is particularly valued for paratroopers. They are volunteers from other units who have passed the formal parachute course and have met higher physical fitness standards than in other infantry units.[40] Because of helicopters, parachuting — although still important — may not in fact be needed for military purposes to the extent that it was required in the past, but it has been continued, some maintain, "as a means of identifying action-oriented individuals."[41] It encourages aggressive behaviour. In an article published in 1975, a Canadian major states: "Jumping encourages self-confidence, determination, self-reliance, masterful activity, aggression, courage, and other items symptomatic of the Phallic-narcissistic type, all of which are very important in the military setting, especially in paratroop commando units, which rely heavily on individual action and are aggressive in nature."[42] Paratroopers, one American writer states, "consider themselves superior to all other such groups — not only in their military virtues but in their vices as well. A paratrooper is supposed to be able to outdrink, outbrawl, and outwhore any other member of the armed forces."[43]

Members of airborne units consider themselves an elite, with a special beret and a distinctive uniform. The Hewson Report states, however, that "in Canada, the reality is that they are no more than highly-spirited dismounted infantry." The mystique of the airborne, Hewson continues, does "enhance group cohesion and morale", and the "perceived elitism attracts young men who associate the 'airborne mystique' with the essentially fictitious content of military/paramilitary television programs, movies and magazines."[44]

Selection of an airborne unit for certain types of activities may be counterproductive. The U.S. military had to remove the airborne as occupation troops from Yokohama after the Second World War because of alleged rapes, robberies and murders. One American writer states that it is "troublesome, if not impossible, to convert finely honed combat soldiers into nonaggressive occupation troops."[45] It was parachutists (the 'paras') who killed 13 Catholics in Northern Ireland on Bloody Sunday in 1972, leading Henry Stanhope to write that "the affair led a number of people to question whether the paras were the right kind of troops to carry out peacekeeping operations, where restraint was called for."[46] Nevertheless, the Board of Inquiry on Somalia concluded that it was "quite appropriate" to send the Airborne to Somalia because of the very difficult and unpredictable conditions there. The Airborne had apparently performed well in Cyprus.[47] One of the tasks of the Somalia Inquiry will be, of course, to determine the appropriateness of sending the Airborne to Somalia.

ALCOHOL ABUSE

The use of alcohol can increase the incidence of violent behaviour. As the Hewson Report stated in 1985, "higher intake of alcohol reduces the threshold for potential violence and acts of antisocial behaviour."[48] The report found that drinking was high in Petawawa, although they did not compare this with the level at other bases.[49] "One reason for the military's high alcoholism rate," Deborah Harrison and Lucie Laliberté point out, "is the easy access to cheap alcohol on most bases, especially those overseas."[50] Drinking was accentuated at Petawawa because much of the drinking took place on the Quebec side where the bars stayed open later than in Ontario.[51] The problem at Petawawa obviously continued after 1985. The 1993 Board of Inquiry suggested a relationship between "incidents of insubordination by 2 Commando personnel and the heavy use of alcohol." In 1992, alcohol was banned from the quarters of 2 Commando.[52]

The Board of Inquiry noted that "military authorities throughout the Canadian Forces have instituted guidelines for drinking on National Defence premises that are consistent with national norms and even more strict rules were instituted for operational theatres such as Somalia." They found that "there is no evidence that drinking or drugs were a problem during operations in Somalia."[53] This is a matter that the Somalia Inquiry will want to explore carefully, because the videotapes of soldiers drinking beer in their quarters in Somalia suggest that drinking in Somalia was not in fact carefully controlled.

The U.S. Forces, in contrast, did not permit their troops to use alcohol in Somalia, a policy that had been adopted during the Gulf War.[54] This is also a matter that the Somalia Inquiry will wish to explore. The Canadian military has adopted a number of fairly recent rules and regulations relating to alcohol and drugs,[55] including various forms of drug testing and apparently strict rules relating to the mission in Bosnia,[56] but nothing goes as far as the U.S. rule prohibiting drinking (and, of course, drugs) while on foreign missions like Somalia.

Alcohol and drugs have been a serious problem in the U.S. Army, and it would be surprising if they were not also a problem in the Canadian military. Many writers have documented the widespread use of alcohol and drugs in military forces. "Their use is infinitely more widespread than bland official histories might suggest," states one military writer. Giving liquor to the troops was, in some cases in the past, official policy. Rum, for example, was given to British troops during the First World War. In some battalions a double ration of rum was given in coffee before troops went over the top.[57]

Drinking has also been considered important in the small group bonding process. Deborah Harrison and Lucie Laliberté surveyed Canadian military personnel for their book, *No Life Like It*, published in 1994, and they concluded that "most members still believe that units who drink together will bond more effectively."[58] Another writer suggests other reasons why alcohol may be tolerated or even encouraged: "From the standpoint of the authorities, alcohol serves to help solve the problem of morale and boredom and helps prevent the build up of potentially disruptive frustrations."[59]

During the Vietnam War, as is well known, drug use was a serious problem. By 1971, for example, a little over 50 per cent of U.S. Army personnel in Vietnam had smoked marijuana and over a quarter had taken heroin or opium.[60] Gabriel states that as many as 600,000 soldiers became addicted during their tours of duty.[61] The problem continued after the war. Alcohol has also been a serious problem. In a 1980 survey, more than a quarter of the 15,000 active U.S. military personnel surveyed reported work impairment resulting directly from alcohol misuse.[62] The pattern with respect to alcohol appeared to be somewhat the same in Canada at the time. At one Canadian Forces base, 15.3 per cent of the members reported that they considered themselves dangerous drinkers, according to a 1978 survey.[63]

More recent Canadian surveys continue to show widespread alcohol problems in the Canadian military, although they appear to have declined in the early 1990s.[64] In a survey in 1989, almost half the respondents reported being sick as a result of alcohol use, and about one-third had had blackouts during the past year. A 1994 random survey of almost 2,000 Regular Force members concluded that "a fifth of members had been drunk four or more times in the last three months and one in twenty-five show evidence of significant problems related to their alcohol use."[65] It may be getting better, but it is still serious. Controlling alcohol abuse is therefore an important ingredient in controlling undesirable conduct.

SELECTION

Selection of military personnel is the starting point in controlling misconduct. With full conscription, the military will roughly reflect the general population. But with an all-volunteer army, as Canada has, this is not necessarily so, because economic necessity will be a strong factor for those seeking a military career. One study of the 2,500 applicants to the Canadian Forces in the summer of 1975 showed that about 50 per cent were unemployed.[66] Although the Maritime provinces are home to only 10 per cent of the population, the region represents 20 to 35 per cent of recruits, no doubt partly because of high regional unemployment.[67] The minimum qualification for recruits is still grade 10 education, even though for civilian police it is normally at least completion of high school.

The quality of the intake will therefore vary with economic conditions. During the depression, the military more or less reflected the general population,[68] as a very high percentage of the population was unemployed. In the good times of the mid-1980s, recruiting was likely much more difficult and the quality of the applicants correspondingly lower. The U.S. military found a marked drop in quality when conscription was abolished in the early 1970s. As retired U.S. Vice-Admiral J.B. Stockdale stated: "With the closing down of obligatory military service, the armed forces lost the strength of a cross-section of the nation's youth. Now they must make do with the least highly qualified segment of the nation's young people. They have to deal with illiteracy, drug abuse, alcoholism, as well as with an increasing rate of desertion and criminality."[69] Richard Gabriel cites data showing that in the U.S. military "the reading level of the average soldier dropped from the twelfth-grade level in 1973 to the fifth-grade level in 1980."[70] This problem may be particularly acute in less specialized units. Anthony Kellett points out that today "the tendency to specialization in modern armies has led to a perception among combat arms that they receive the marginal applicant, with low technical skills and mental classification scores."[71]

This writer has not examined military recruitment in any depth, and it may not reflect the U.S. experience. (Recruitment is the subject of a separate study for the Somalia Inquiry.)[72] The 1985 Hewson study contained some disturbing facts, however. One was that inadequate checks were made on the recruit's prior criminal record. A 1985 study of more than

500 members of the Airborne Regiment found 34 cases of undisclosed serious crimes, including 12 cases where civilian police files were marked "violent" or "extremely violent".[73] The Somalia Inquiry will wish to ensure that adequate background checks on prior criminal records are now made.

Another issue discussed by the Hewson Report is psychological testing. It was not done then in the Canadian military, although it is apparently done for certain purposes in the U.S. military.[74] The Hewson Report recommended against it on the basis that it might violate human rights and would not be cost-effective, stating on the latter point: "The sheer volume of tests, added screening procedures and increased staff requirements would make added psychological fitness testing of questionable value." Again, this is a matter that the Inquiry may wish to explore. Although the present system can probably spot those with very serious mental problems, persons with personality disorders can slip more easily through the cracks. One of the studies done for the Hewson Report showed that although the incidence of serious mental illness was lower in the military than in the general population, there was a higher rate of personality disorders.[75]

A further question that might be explored is whether it would be desirable to select more women for peacekeeping operations. Female children are not normally socialized to be as aggressive as males.[76] "The very presence of women in military units," Clifton Bryant observes, "may well foster better conduct among the men." Bryant notes that the integration of male and female inmates in some correctional institutions tends to promote good behaviour.[77] The same effect occurs with female prison guards and female police officers.[78] For standard peacekeeping operations, greater integration may produce a very desirable moderating influence on conduct.

A recent article by Laura Miller and Charles Moskos shows that this was probably the effect of having women as part of the U.S. contingent in Somalia. Unlike the virtually all-male Canadian force, 12 per cent of the 25,000-member U.S. contingent was female. Two Somalis died as a result of the use of excessive force by U.S. military personnel between December 1992 and May 1993 — fewer than were killed by the 1,000-member Canadian force. The analysis by Miller and Moskos shows that "women were less likely than men...to view the locals negatively." They found that "the strategy of creating negative stereotypes, rejecting the humanitarian role, and treating the Somalis as enemies was objectionable...to most women soldiers." They contrast this approach with the exclusively (by military policy) male combat troops who tended to adopt a "warrior strategy" and "construct negative stereotypes of Somalis and perceive them as the enemy." This may be understandable in wartime because, as Miller and Moskos state, "Combat soldiers must be emotionally detached from their enemies in order to kill them, a task assisted by negative racial and cultural stereotypes."[79] It is not, however, applicable to a humanitarian mission. There was therefore a danger that many of the combat-ready Canadian Airborne forces approached their task as "warriors" rather than as humanitarians. Having women in the contingent might have had a beneficial effect on the behaviour of the Canadian troops.

TECHNIQUES OF CONTROL

Careful selection of personnel for the armed forces is therefore the first, but very crucial, technique for controlling misconduct. In this section we review a range of other techniques. Some are more applicable to combat situations, but all seek to have the soldier obey lawful rules and commands and meet military objectives.

Training is also of major importance in influencing behaviour, although no attempt to survey that vast subject will be attempted here. The repetitive basic training of the recruit is designed in part to produce an almost conditioned reflex of obedience, clearly necessary in battle.[80] Training also instills in members of the military their lawful duties and obligations. The U.S. Army, for example, teaches the following nine minimum principles as part of its initial entry training. The basic law of war rules, referred to as "The Soldier's Rules", are as follows:

1. Soldiers fight only enemy combatants.
2. Soldiers do not harm enemies who surrender. Disarm them and turn them over to your superior.
3. Soldiers do not kill or torture enemy prisoners of war.
4. Soldiers collect and care for the wounded, whether friend or foe.
5. Soldiers do not attack medical personnel, facilities, or equipment.
6. Soldiers destroy no more than the mission requires.
7. Soldiers treat all civilians humanely.
8. Soldiers do not steal. Soldiers respect private property and possessions.
9. Soldiers should do their best to prevent violations of the law of war. Soldiers report all violations of the law of war to their superior.[81]

Internalization of such rules by Canadian forces members would perhaps have been helpful in Somalia.

Sensitivity training with respect to gender and racial issues is also important. The use of derogatory racial labels in Vietnam probably contributed to the My Lai massacre. Recent commentators on the twenty-fifth anniversary of My Lai noted the "tendency by some of the members of Charlie Company to view the Vietnamese people as almost subhuman."[82] Clifton Bryant, writing in the 1970s, noted the risk of atrocities in future "police actions" in Third World countries because of the relative ease of "conceptualiz[ing] the enemy and the local civilian population as inferior, backward, or even subhuman."[83] The 1993 Board of Inquiry on Somalia noted the use of derogatory names by Canadian soldiers in Somalia.[84] In 1994, the Canadian military issued a Canadian Forces Administrative Order with respect to racist conduct and it includes policies on education and training.[85] The Somalia Inquiry will no doubt explore the issue carefully in relation to events in Somalia.

Leadership is also a vast subject, which will not be explored in depth here. Leadership is particularly important when military operations are undertaken. The military brief to the Somalia Inquiry defines leadership as "the art of influencing human behaviour so as to accomplish a mission in the manner desired by the leader." The military brief points out that "leadership styles vary with individual personality and what works for one person in a specific situation may not be effective for another person or another circumstance."[86] Leadership for wartime, for example, may require different characteristics than leadership in peacetime.[87] A leading military encyclopedia correctly notes that "the 'secret' of good leadership continues to elude explanation."[88] The Canadian Forces Military Training Manual, *Leadership in Land Combat*, states:

This manual is addressed to the combat leader who must be a manager, a commander and a leader. The combat leader is a manager by virtue of the fact that he must plan his mission, organize his men, and ensure that they are fit, equipped and provided with the necessities to carry out a mission in battle. He is a commander by virtue of the legal authority he holds. He becomes a leader, however, only when his men accept him as such. For leadership requires much more than management skills or legal authority. The leader is the vital member of the unit team; for he is the person who motivates the other members. He is personally responsible for seeing that his men are prepared for their tasks; that they are cared for if sick or wounded; comforted if dying; buried, when dead. He shares their lives — the discomforts, the risks, the joys and the victories. In this sharing, the combat leader, whether corporal or general, is set apart. Leadership is a twenty-four hour a day responsibility. "The commander is responsible for all that his men do or fail to do" is an old army truism.[89]

Leadership by example also is of importance. One much-discussed factor in leadership is the extent to which an officer is willing to risk his life in battle. British officers represented a greater proportion of those killed or wounded during the First World War than their percentage of the total force. The percentage of Canadian officers killed or wounded appears to have been even higher.[90] German officers in the Second World War, considered good leaders, also died in disproportionate numbers.[91] The Israeli Army is noted for the sacrifices made by its officers. In the 1967 Six-Day War, almost half the 1967 Israeli fatalities were officers. "There is no doubt," one study of the Israeli Army concluded, "that the fact that so many commanders, proportionately, fell in battle had a salutary effect on the morale of the troops... they were not being asked to give their lives for something for which the commander would not give his own."[92]

Both the 1985 Hewson Report and the 1993 Board of Inquiry discussed leadership. The Hewson Report emphasized the important role of junior leaders, particularly lieutenants and master-corporals. "In the last 10 years," the report states, "this relationship between the men and their immediate leaders has been increasingly eroded." One of the primary reasons for this, in their view, was the temporary absence of personnel from the unit to undertake other tasks or to attend courses. "In the absence of constant and effective leadership," they observed, "prolonged stress may lead to low morale and disciplinary infractions."[93] The Board of Inquiry also noted the relationship between leadership and discipline, stating: "Good discipline depends on good leadership. Discipline is established and maintained by officers and non-commissioned officers." They concluded that "discipline was somehow flawed within 2 Commando."[94] Obviously, this is a question that will be explored in depth by the Somalia Inquiry.

In the case of Israel, a high level of patriotism has been a strong motivating force. Patriotism is used as a motivating factor in all wars, particularly in the early stages of a war. The First World War poster stating that "England expects every man to do his duty" achieved the desired response.[95] But, as Robert Graves has written, the troops in the trenches in the First World War were less interested in King and Country than in their regiment and their fellow soldiers.[96]

Anthony Kellett has shown in various writings that regimental pride is a very important element in motivating troops in Commonwealth armies.[97] The U.S. Army, however, uses larger units; it experimented with a regimental system in the early 1980s but did not adopt it.[98]

Loyalty to a very small fighting unit, such as a platoon, a squad, or the soldier's "buddies" is probably the most important motivating force.[99] General S.L.A. Marshall stated in 1947 that "the thing which enables an infantry soldier to keep going with his weapons is the near presence or presumed presence of a comrade."[100] In Barry Broadfoot's oral history of Canadians in the Second World War, one person is quoted as stating that you fought for "your outfit, the guys in your company, but especially your platoon."[101] This small-unit cohesion[102] is obviously very important in combat motivation, although as the Americans discovered in Vietnam, it can also operate negatively. A large number of officers were deliberately killed by their own men (so-called fragging),[103] and in the great majority of these cases it was a group rather than an individual act.[104] Leadership and group cohesion are not discussed further in this paper, despite their enormous importance.

The use of rewards is also an important technique for controlling behaviour. As discussed in Chapter 2, no major institution in society makes such a display of rewards as the military does. Janowitz and Little rightly anticipated in 1965 that "military authority must shift from reliance on practices based on *domination* to a wider utilization of *manipulation*."[105] The use of rewards is a deliberate process of manipulation. Unfortunately, as Anthony Kellett has observed, "little consistent thought appears to have been given to the question of material and psychological rewards, despite the fact that psychological learning principles demonstrate that positive reward is more effective in producing desirable behavior than punishment is in eliminating undesirable behavior."[106]

In Chapter 3, we look at the various duties imposed on military personnel to report wrongdoing. The Queen's Regulations and Orders contain a provision requiring all members of the military to "report to the proper authority any infringement of the pertinent statutes, regulations, orders and instructions governing the conduct of any person subject to the Code of Service Discipline,"[107] although an officer has to do so only if he or she "cannot deal adequately with the matter."

Administrative and informal sanctions are extremely important in controlling conduct in the military. These are normally applied to redirect less serious undesirable conduct before more formal disciplinary proceedings are used. For example, a non-commissioned member may be

given a Verbal Warning or a Recorded Warning, be subject to Counselling and Probation, or be given a Compulsory Release. An officer may
also be given what is called a Reproof. These mechanisms are described
in some detail in Chapter 4.

In civilian society great reliance is placed on the police as means of
controlling conduct. The same is true in the military. Unfortunately, as
we will see in Chapter 5, the number of military police sent to Somalia
was far less than was required. The U.S. military operates with a greater
concentration of military police. A restructuring of the Canadian military
police is now taking place, and I argue later that it would probably be
unwise to reduce their numbers significantly.

A lengthy chapter is devoted to military justice, a crucial technique for
controlling misconduct in the military (see Chapter 6). The Somalia Inquiry will wish to explore carefully whether the decline in the use of
military justice in the 10 years preceding the events in Somalia may have
contributed to the lack of discipline that was evident in the Airborne Regiment in Somalia. The most important part of the military justice system
is the system of summary justice, and the Supreme Court of Canada is
likely to uphold its constitutionality, particularly if some changes related
to effective waiver of the right to a court martial and the amount of punishment a commanding officer can impose are introduced.

Another form of deterrence, which may become increasingly important in world affairs, is the international criminal tribunal, such as is now
operating under United Nations auspices with respect to events in Yugo-
slavia and Rwanda.[108] Such courts are considered part of international
law.[109] These tribunals go beyond those in Nuremberg and Tokyo following the Second World War, which can be categorized as victors' courts.[110]
The International Law Commission has produced a draft statute for a
permanent international tribunal,[111] and it is possible that one will be set
up in the next few years. The search for a permanent court has a long
history. The Red Cross suggested one in 1895, as did the League of Nations in 1937.[112] Further, many countries, including Canada,[113] permit
domestic prosecutions of war crimes and crimes against humanity. These
tribunals — domestic and international — will probably have an increasing effect on military conduct.

In Chapter 7 we consider civil control of the military, integration, and
various forms of oversight, noting that Canada does not have a military
ombudsman or a general ombudsman with jurisdiction over the military.
Nor does it have an Inspector General for the military, as in the United
States. Nor does it have a civilian complaints tribunal, as is applicable to

the RCMP. The Somalia Inquiry will wish to explore carefully whether some such body could be an important additional technique for controlling improper conduct in the military.

An earlier study by the author, along with colleagues Michael Trebilcock and Kent Roach, into methods of regulating traffic safety placed much emphasis on what is termed an epidemiological approach.[114] "In a traditional legal framework," the study stated, "much energy is devoted to isolating and punishing blameworthy behaviour, whereas in the epidemiological framework, attention is devoted to whatever source will be most effective in reducing injuries and their harmful consequences."[115] In the context of the events in Somalia, an epidemiological approach would focus, for example, on ways to control the use of alcohol and drugs, how best to prevent infiltration into military compounds, the use of non-lethal weapons, and how to ensure that persons taken prisoner are immediately given into the custody of the military police. Controlling conduct in such a way is obviously better than prosecuting persons after the fact.

THE RULES GUIDING THE MILITARY

An obviously fundamental ingredient in securing compliance with military rules is to make persons aware of the rules. This section looks at the various rules guiding the military. What are the rules and how are they made known?

The military does reasonably well in making their rules accessible to their members — certainly much better than civilian society.[116] Civilian society can learn much from the military about how to make the law more accessible.

The *National Defence Act* is the basic law governing the military.[117] It is as dense and difficult to read as most other statutes. At a second, more readable, level are the Queen's Regulations and Orders (QR&Os). This four-volume set of rules repeats, where applicable, parts of the *National Defence Act* and contains regulations and orders authorized to be made under the Act.[118] The QR&OS also contain helpful notes fleshing out the sections of the QR&Os.[119] At a further level of detail are Canadian Forces Administrative Orders (CFAOs), issued by the Minister of National Defence or the Chief of the Defence Staff, and "contain administrative policy, procedures and information of continuing effect" which "supplement and amplify the Queen's Regulations and Orders."[120]

There are also Canadian Forces Organizational Orders (CFOOs) dealing with the organization of various units. For example, CFOO 1.327, issued on 10 February 1993, was the original order dealing with the Canadian Joint Forces in Somalia. Further, there are command orders, standing orders for bases and units, routine orders, and oral and written commands or orders.[121] Thus, there are myriad regulations and orders, and many other official publications are issued under the authority of the Chief of Defence Staff,[122] such as training manuals and military police procedures.[123] Rules of Engagement, which loom large in the Somalia Inquiry, are also issued by the Chief of Defence Staff.

The QR&OS impose duties on military personnel to "become acquainted with, observe and enforce" the *National Defence Act*, QR&OS and "all other regulations, rules, orders and instructions that pertain to the performance" of the officer's or member's duties.[124] The QR&OS also impose duties on commanding officers to give publicity to the various regulations, rules, orders and instructions. QR&O 1.12 states that "a commanding officer shall cause regulations and orders issued in implementation of the *National Defence Act* to be readily available to all members whom they concern." And QR&O 4.26 provides that "a commanding officer shall ensure that all regulations, orders, instructions, correspondence and publications affecting members, whether in the performance of their duties or in the conditions of their service, are given such publicity as will enable those members to study them and become acquainted with the contents."[125]

The *National Defence Act* and the QR&Os contain provisions stating that a member will be deemed to have knowledge of regulations or orders in certain cases. Section 51 of the act provides that "all regulations and all orders and instructions issued to the Canadian Forces shall be held to be sufficiently notified to any person whom they may concern by their publication, in the manner prescribed in regulations...". Further, QR&O 1.21 provides that:

...all regulations, orders and instructions issued to the Canadian Forces shall be held to be published and sufficiently notified to any person whom they may concern if:
(a) they are received at the base, unit or element at which that person is serving; and
(b) the commanding officer of the base, unit or element takes such measures as may seem practical to ensure that the regulations, orders and instructions are drawn to the attention of and made available to those whom they may concern.

This appears to take away a mistake of law defence that might otherwise be applicable with respect to regulations not published in the *Canada Gazette*,[126] but some commentators argue that there is still scope for such a defence in relation to orders issued by bases and other units.[127]

Both the *National Defence Act* and the regulations make it an offence to disobey a lawful command of a superior officer.[128] Section 83 of the act makes a person who so disobeys liable to imprisonment for life by a court martial. Notes to the regulations accurately state that a member should not obey a "manifestly unlawful order."[129] "A manifestly unlawful command or order," a note states, "is one that would appear to a person of ordinary sense and understanding to be clearly illegal; for example, a command by an officer or non-commissioned member to shoot a member for only having used disrespectful words or a command to shoot an unarmed child." Section 129 of the act makes it an offence prejudicing good order or discipline to contravene the act, or any regulations, orders, instructions, or general or standing orders. A note to the QR&Os states that the section covers duties imposed "by law, practice or custom and of which the accused knew or ought to have known."[130]

How does a breach of a rule of engagement fit into the picture?[131] Rules of engagement are defined by Canada, the United States, and NATO as "directions issued by competent military authority which delineate the circumstances and limitations within which armed force may be applied to achieve military objectives in furtherance of national policy."[132] Rules of engagement (ROE) are a relatively recent concept. They first appeared in relation to air combat by the Americans in the Korean War[133] and were later adopted by the Navy and Army. Canada began its own development of a rules of engagement system in the late 1970s when it adopted the NATO maritime ROE for national use by Canada's Maritime Command. Canada's Air Command adopted its ROE system from NORAD, while the Land Force Command, until recently, employed ROE on an ad hoc basis.[134] The Canadian military issued rules of engagement for Somalia in December 1992[135] — very late in the day for an operation that was about to commence — and in June 1995 issued an official manual specifically on rules of engagement.[136]

What is the status of rules of engagement? The recent *Mathieu* decision of the Court Martial Appeal Court held that the rules of engagement under which Lieutenant-Colonel Carol Mathieu (the commanding officer of the Airborne Regiment in Somalia) operated constituted lawful orders and not mere guidelines. The Court also held that Mathieu could be prosecuted under section 124 of the *National Defence Act* for "negligently perform[ing] a military duty imposed on that person" and that negligent conduct was to be judged by an objective test.[137] The Court Martial Appeal Court in *Brocklebank* subsequently took the same approach.[138] Canadian law appears to differ from that of the United States and England, where rules of engagement are said to constitute guidelines only and have no legal force of their own.[139]

An article by Major Mark Martins of the U.S. Army Judge Advocate General (JAG) argues persuasively that there is too much reliance on a legislative approach to rules of engagement. It would be preferable, he argues, to indoctrinate soldiers with respect to rules of engagement using a training-based approach.[140] No doubt the Somalia Inquiry will consider this issue carefully, because the 1993 Board of Inquiry found that "during training, the overall criteria of minimum and graduated escalation of force was not well understood in all sub-units."[141]

A CODE OF ETHICS?

A further issue is whether a code of ethics would be helpful. The author has recently argued in favour of a code of conduct for the judiciary.[142] Would such a code be useful for the military? Many writers favour adopting one.[143] Richard Gabriel, for example, states that "one needs a very clear statement of the ethical obligations that one ought to observe if one is to be expected to behave ethically." He sets out a suggested one-page code of ethics, containing provisions such as these: "A soldier will never require his men to endure hardships or suffer dangers to which he is unwilling to expose himself. Every soldier must openly share the burden of risk and sacrifice to which his fellow soldiers are exposed" and "No soldier will punish, allow the punishment of, or in any way harm or discriminate against a subordinate or peer for telling the truth about any matter."[144]

An even shorter, more general code was proposed by Lt. Colonel C.A. Cotton:

A Canadian Military Ethos

Having freely joined Canada's military community, members of the Canadian Forces are expected to serve their nation with:

Pride

in its political, social, cultural and military institutions;

Concern

for the welfare and integrity of all citizens, both in and out of uniform;

Commitment

to place the performance of their military duties and the operational effectiveness of the Canadian Forces above their own concerns;

for selfless acceptance of the unlimited liability of military service is the essence of a free society's defence capability.[145]

To give another example, in a staff college paper in 1992, Major A.G. Hines set out his proposal as follows:

Having enrolled in the Canadian Forces of my own free will, I recognize the unique sense of purpose and commitment I have to all Canadians.

I believe in a strong and free Canada and accept the Canadian Forces exist for the preservation of an acceptable way of life for all Canadians.

I have been charged with and accept the responsibility to maintain the security and sovereignty of Canada through the use of military force if necessary.

I will discharge my duties to the best of my ability, upholding the values of integrity, honesty, loyalty and courage in all undertakings.

I will perform all of my duties with the good of my country, superiors and subordinates, in that order, foremost in my mind.

I will act in accordance with all laws, regulations and orders.

I will uphold the values espoused by the Canadian Constitution and Charter of Rights and Freedoms.

I will conduct myself in a manner to reflect credit on the Canadian Forces and Canada.

I will not become engaged in any activities which would use my position in the Canadian Forces for personal benefit or gratification.

I accept the unlimited liability of military service as an obligation of my membership in the Canadian Forces.[146]

Hines argues that having a code "can bring the topic [of unethical behaviour] to the forefront and get people talking about right and wrong." "It may not help," he rightly concludes, "but it can't hurt!"[147]

CIVIL LIABILITY[148]

There is some potential for controlling undesirable conduct through civil lawsuits. It should be noted that the Canadian military in Somalia paid $15,000 U.S. (said to be the equivalent of 100 camels) to the family of Shidane Arone, the murdered Somali teenager, for a complete release from civil liability.[149] It is not at all clear, as we will see, whether a civil suit brought in Canada by the family of the deceased would have been successful.

It is difficult to say whether the threat of liability has very much effect on the conduct of Canadian military personnel. There are, in fact, very few reported cases involving members of the military. There are a number of reasons for the paucity of cases. One important reason is that under Canadian costs rules, unsuccessful plaintiffs have to pay not only their own costs, but also a significant portion of the defendants' costs.[150] Another factor is that the military person who caused the damage is usually without substantial funds and so would not be able to satisfy a judgement awarded.[151] The lawsuit would therefore be aimed at the government.[152] But under the rules of vicarious liability, an employer is liable only for torts committed in the course of the wrongdoer's employment, which is often not the case.[153] It is likely, however, that a court would hold that the harm done to Shidane Arone was done in the course of the members' employment. Moreover, it is necessary under the law governing Crown liability to be able to hold an individual responsible before the Crown is liable,[154] "a costly and difficult (if not an impossible) task in large organizations."[155] Further, members of the military or their estates cannot sue the Crown if they are receiving compensation from the government "in respect of the death, injury, damage or loss in respect of which the claim is made."[156] Some of these rules could be changed, which would make civil liability easier to achieve, but it is not likely that the government will wish to go very much further to expose itself to more liability than it has at present. There is also a legitimate fear that civil liability may "overdeter" the conduct of officials and prevent them from vigorously pursuing their duties in the public interest.[157] One change that should be considered, however, is to amend the *Crown Liability and Proceedings Act* to make the Crown liable even if a specific individual may not be liable, where it is shown that one or more employees were in fact responsible for the damage, even if the person responsible cannot be pinpointed.

One section of the *Crown Liability and Proceedings Act* relates specifically to the military. Section 8 provides that nothing in the previous sections "makes the Crown liable in respect of anything done or omitted in the exercise of any power or authority exercisable by the Crown, whether in time of peace or of war, for the purpose of the defence of Canada or of training or maintaining the efficiency of, the Canadian Forces." Peter Hogg has commented that this "is a sweeping immunity for military activity, drawing no distinction between war and peace; between combat, training and discipline; or between injured civilians and injured members of the forces."[158] He points out that "the United Kingdom, Australia, New Zealand and the United States have not enacted any such blanket immunity, leaving the courts to adapt the common law to the unique characteristics of military activity."[159] Hogg advocates a less categorical and more liberal approach in which the public interest in the particular military activity would be considered in determining the reasonableness of the impugned conduct.[160] This seems to be an appropriate solution that would prevent the military from being held liable for necessary damage caused by its legitimate operations. At the same time, however, the military would know that it could always be held civilly liable for unreasonable conduct.

Section 8 might not have been a barrier to a civil suit by the Arone family, however, because its language refers to "the defence of Canada", and a humanitarian mission does not seem to fit that language, although it could be argued that the activity was "for the purpose of...maintaining the efficiency of the Canadian Forces." Moreover, a Federal Court trial judge held in a 1981 case that "the immunity conferred by [section 8] only applies inasmuch as the power exercised is exercised in a normal and reasonable manner"[161] — and clearly in the Arone case it was not. The ruling is a sensible one and should be built into the legislation.

A further hurdle is the questionable act of state doctrine which prohibits an action brought by an alien in certain cases for an act committed outside the country. But this is a bar to a civil suit only if the act complained of was "committed on the orders of the Crown or was subsequently ratified by the Crown." Peter Hogg ventures the opinion that "the decision to command or ratify must have been taken by cabinet or at least by an individual minister."[162] The doctrine would not therefore have been a bar to a suit by the Arone family.

This brief survey suggests that civil liability has some potential for controlling improper conduct in the military but appears not to be as potent a force as other techniques. It is to these techniques that we turn now.

CHAPTER TWO

Rewards

The military uses rewards as an important technique for controlling behaviour. No other major institution in society makes such a display of rewards. Military personnel wear their rewards on their sleeves and chests, and the rewards system permeates all aspects of military life.

Rewards are used widely in other institutions as well. Universities rely extensively on rewards for both faculty and students — marks, ranking, reference letters, employment, tenure, professorial ranks, publications, honours, merit pay, and so on. Because of their importance, misstatement of academic qualifications is taken as seriously as wearing undeserved military medals.[1] Business and industry also use rewards to motivate employees. A behavioural organization psychologist, Hugh Arnold, has observed that although "there is no doubt that punishment can and does have an impact on employee behaviour...there is emerging consensus that the effects of punishment on performance are not as strong as the influences of reward."[2] The problem with punishment, he points out, is that it "has a tendency to create resentment, anger, and hard feelings toward the punishing agent and the organization in general", and it is effective only as long as the potential punishing agent or some independent monitoring device is present to observe behaviour.[3] There is also a growing trend toward the use of incentives in the area of public regulation.[4]

In combat situations, discipline is becoming a less crucial control technique because of the changing nature of warfare. The massing of armies characteristic of military operations up to and including the First World War required great discipline. The Second World War changed the focus. As S.L.A. Marshall wrote shortly after the war, "The philosophy of discipline has adjusted to changing conditions. As more and more impact has gone into the hitting power of weapons, necessitating ever-widening deployments in the forces of battle, the quality of the initiative in the individual has become the most praised of the military virtues."[5] "In combat," Janowitz and Little wrote in 1965, "the maintenance of initiative has become a requirement of greater importance than the rigid enforcement of discipline... The technology of warfare is so complex that the coordination of a group of specialists cannot be guaranteed simply by authoritarian discipline... Improvisation is the keynote of the individual fighter or combat group." The authors believe that "military authority must shift from reliance on practices based on *domination* to a wider utilization of *manipulation*. Traditional or ascriptive authority relies heavily on domination, while manipulation is more appropriate for authority based on achievement."[6]

HISTORY OF MILITARY REWARDS

In earlier periods, the rewards of battle were the opportunities for plunder, prize money, and ransoming prisoners.[7] Medals and rewards for bravery were not used widely until the nineteenth century. Only one British soldier, for example, received an award for gallantry during the American War of Independence.[8] A medal for those who fought against Napoleon in the Peninsular War was not approved until 1848, and the Victoria Cross was not instituted until 1856, during the Crimean War. Napoleon, on the other hand, had created the highly sought after Legion of Honour in 1802. Apparently Napoleon expressed surprise at the absence of medals on the seasoned British troops aboard the ship taking him into exile and noted: "Such is not the way to excite or cherish military virtues."[9]

During the 1800s the British started to issue campaign, long service, and good conduct medals in greater numbers, in some cases accompanied with a small annuity. The writings of Winston Churchill, as Anthony Kellett points out, indicate his strong desire for medals and being mentioned in dispatches. When his period in India was over in 1898, Churchill tried to join Kitchener's army in the Sudan and told his mother: "It would mean another medal — perhaps two — and I have applied to wear my Cuban decoration so that with a little luck I might return quite ornamented. Now do stir up all your influence."[10]

In earlier times U.S. troops had even less chance than the British of winning medals. Although the Purple Heart was instituted in 1782 as a reward for conspicuous military service, a negligible number were awarded during the War of Independence. The decoration was revived in 1932 and given to all those wounded in the First World War or any other campaign. The Confederate forces did not award medals for bravery but adopted the perhaps equally desirable reward of recording names on a roll of honour and publishing it in newspapers.[11]

During the Vietnam War, military medals were awarded in significant numbers. There was considerable criticism of the number of medals awarded and questions about the merit of those who received them. By early 1971, one and a quarter million medals for bravery had been awarded, compared with one and three-quarter million medals awarded to U.S. soldiers in all of the Second World War.[12]

The writings of soldiers show the importance of medals, although few are as openly covetous as Churchill was. One soldier, for example, wrote that "a ribbon is the only prize in war for the ordinary soldier. It is the outward visible proof to bring home to his people that he has done his job well."[13] Another wrote: "Civilians may think it's a little juvenile to worry about ribbons, but a civilian has a house and a bankroll to show what he's done for the past four years." One knowledgeable person who conducted research on motivation in the military recently stated: "whatever men might say in public about decorations, in private they were eager to discuss them at length, and my notes on decorations eventually came to fill more index-cards than those for any other single subject."[14] Let us turn to examine the various rewards in the Canadian military.

REWARDS AND INCENTIVES IN THE CANADIAN MILITARY

Chapter 18 of the Queen's Regulations and Orders, as well as various Canadian Forces Administrative Orders, contain much material on rewards and incentives. Perhaps the most substantial incentive is promotion to a higher rank, which also brings higher pay and greater status.[15] This affects even such things as the number of rounds fired at the individual's military funeral.[16] Even within the same rank there are several categories; individuals who meet "performance standards" are paid at the "next higher incentive pay category."[17] For a captain, for example, there are 10 incremental categories.[18] Yearly performance evaluation reports sent to National Defence Headquarters affect all aspects of a person's career progression.[19] Reports on officers are done by the immediate superior in the chain of command. The officer being evaluated reads and signs the evaluation. "Outstanding" and "adverse" reports are reviewed at all higher levels of command.[20] No mention of having the opportunity to read a report done on a person below the rank of officer is mentioned in the applicable CFAO,[21] although the practice is to allow members to read a portion of the report. Only NDHQ keeps copies of these evaluation reports. All duplicates and drafts are to be destroyed.[22] Further, recommendations by one's superiors in the chain of command also control to a great extent whether individuals have access to particular training courses,[23] often an important prerequisite for career advancement. Similarly, the views of superiors affect such things as future postings.

Conduct sheets are kept for all non-commissioned members.[24] Conduct sheets for officers are set up only when an entry is necessary. Conduct sheets contain records of convictions as well as special acts of gallantry and commendation. These follow the individual and are not confined to NDHQ. The CFAO provides an incentive to have certain Service Code convictions (i.e., where the punishment was a fine of $200 or less or a minor punishment) wiped out within a certain period (e.g., 12 months during which no other conviction has been entered). In such a case a new conduct sheet is prepared, containing all the other entries.[25] Further, a commanding officer can in certain cases later change a punishment awarded in a summary proceeding, for example, by remitting in whole or in part the fine paid.[26] Having a good military record also affects career prospects after discharge from the military, although perhaps less so in Canada than in Israel, where potential employers apparently take military records very seriously.[27] Finally, pensions are seriously affected if members are forced to take compulsory release.[28] In short, incentives are found in most aspects of military life.[29]

There are medals for campaigns and deployments, medals for bravery,[30] the Meritorious Service Cross,[31] and the Chief of Defence Staff Commendation.[32] A service medal for service in Somalia has been officially proposed, designed, and minted under the authority of the Chief of Defence Staff, but still awaits the approval of the Minister. Honours and awards have already been given, however, for individual acts of note.[33] The United Nations has issued a number of medals that Canadian personnel are entitled to wear "if they have not been convicted of any serious offence during their period of assignment with the U.N."[34] In addition, military personnel are eligible to be nominated for the Order of Canada.[35] Further, 12 years' good conduct in the military lead to a decoration and the right to use the initials C.D. (Canadian Forces' Decoration) after one's name.[36]

There are also awards for candidates taking leadership, trade, and classification training courses. In addition, some honours are awarded to a unit rather than individual members.[37] This puts peer pressure on all members of the group to perform well.[38] In wartime, having the unit mentioned in dispatches is a much-sought goal.[39]

Even military detention entails specific and elaborate incentives.[40] Detention is in two stages. During the first stage, which cannot be less than

14 days and can be much longer, the inmate is not entitled to "a communication period", "a smoking period", or "visitors, other than official visitors." When an inmate is promoted to the second stage, the person is "entitled to the prescribed privileges" and commences to earn remission of punishment. Second-stage privileges are 30 minutes a day to communicate with other inmates, 30 minutes for smoking, the use of the library, and permission to receive visitors. Each day the inmate may earn up to 8 marks and cannot be promoted to the next stage unless 112 marks (i.e., 14 days at 8 marks a day) have been earned. There is an elaborate system of earning remission during the second stage. Marks earned in the first stage do not count. An inmate can gain a remission of two-fifths of the remaining time by earning the maximum of eight marks a day. Fewer marks mean less remission. Combined with this reward system are the following possible corrective measures for misbehaviour: "close confinement; No. 1 diet; No. 2 diet; loss of privileges; and forfeiture of marks earned for remission." Number 1 diet, for example, when applied for a period of three days or less, consists of 14 ounces of bread a day and unrestricted quantities of water."

CONCLUSION

A 1989 study by the Bureau of Management Consulting on "Career Progression and Rewards System in the Canadian Forces" contained statistical analysis of how military personnel viewed various rewards in the military. Of the 7,500 questionnaires sent out, more than 7,000 completed responses were received. Of all the factors considered important by non-commissioned members, pay ranked highest. Other rewards, such as "more status (e.g., mess privileges, marks of respect)" were rated the lowest of the various categories. In all ranks, 65 per cent rated "more pay" as very important, but only 19 per cent rated "more status" as very important ("higher rank" was in a different category). Not surprisingly, the higher the rank of the member, the more that status was valued. Whereas only 17 per cent of those in the low ranks of non-commissioned members ranked status as very important, 30 per cent of those in the high ranks did so. Responses to another question showed, however, that status in the form of recognition of rank is very important. When asked questions about designation of rank on one's uniform, 71 per cent of those of low rank thought it was very important and 95 per cent of those of high rank thought so. So rewards in the form of rank are very important to most military personnel independent of salary considerations. Surprisingly, only about

25 per cent thought that unit or command affiliation was very important. The item that was least important on the list was years of service in a rank, because this tells the world that one had been passed over for promotion.[41]

More work should be done to assess the value of rewards as a motivating force in the military. As Anthony Kellett states, "little consistent thought appears to have been given to the question of material and psychological rewards, despite the fact that psychological learning principles demonstrate that positive reward is more effective in producing desirable behavior than punishment is in eliminating undesirable behavior." He goes on to argue that lack of recognition "can often have very detrimental and lasting effects" and that "seemingly arbitrary and capricious rewards policies are potentially counterproductive."[42] This is clearly an area where further studies are warranted to find the appropriate balance between the use of sanctions and the use of rewards.

CHAPTER THREE

Reporting Wrongdoing

In contrast to civilian law, military regulations and orders impose a great many duties on military personnel to report wrongdoing. There is no general duty on civilians to report even very serious offences. The old offence of misprision of felony has not survived,[1] and the law imposes a duty to take positive steps to prevent or report harm in only a handful of cases.[2]

In the military, it is important for those higher up the chain of command to be aware of serious misconduct by persons lower in the chain, so they can ensure that problems are dealt with adequately. There is also a desire on the part of the government and senior military officials to be kept abreast of issues so as to be able to respond to events. Thus, there are detailed reporting requirements. There may, however, be reluctance to bring an incident to the attention of those higher up, because of the possibility that a report will reflect poorly on those who allowed the incident to occur. Seymour Hersh makes this point in *Cover-Up*, his analysis of the My Lai disaster:

Koster [a very senior officer in Vietnam] could, of course, have court-martialed some violators of international law for their crimes. This might have limited the number of such violations, but it also would have signaled to higher headquarters that such infractions of law did occur. Koster's efficacy as a commander would have been questioned and the name of the division sullied by the inevitable press reports. That this difficult situation exists is well known to officers throughout the Army, but the theme rarely emerges in public.[3]

Let us look at the duties to report in the Canadian military. It is military regulations and orders, rather than the *National Defence Act*, that impose the various duties to report. A breach of regulations, orders, or instructions constitutes "an act, conduct, disorder or neglect to the prejudice of good order or discipline", which is an offence under section 129 of the *National Defence Act*. The only duty to report mentioned in the *National*

Defence Act is section 89(a), which makes it an offence for a person to fail to report a known desertion: "being aware of the desertion of a person from any of Her Majesty's Forces, does not without reasonable excuse inform his superior officer forthwith."[4]

The Queen's Regulations and Orders contain a number of reporting provisions. Under QR&O 4.02(e), officers are required to "report to the proper authority any infringement of the pertinent statutes, regulations, rules, orders and instructions governing the conduct of any person subject to the Code of Service Discipline when the officer cannot deal adequately with the matter." QR&O 5.01(e) relating to non-commissioned members does not include the qualification about not being able to deal adequately with the matter. It states: "A non-commissioned member shall...report to the proper authority any infringement of the pertinent statutes, regulations, rules, orders and instructions governing the conduct of any person subject to the Code of Service Discipline."[5] QR&O 105.14 provides that reports be sent to National Defence Headquarters "where an officer or non-commissioned member above the rank of sergeant is arrested." These two QR&Os therefore cover a wide area. There are more. QR&O 202.01(2) imposes a duty on an accounting officer of any rank to report immediately "to his commanding officer any shortage or surplus of public funds." Further, QR&O 36.10 states that "Any officer or non-commissioned member who discovers the loss of or damage to materiel shall immediately report the circumstances to the commanding officer." And QR&O 19.56 requires a member of the military to report his or her arrest by civil authorities to the member's commanding officer.

The QR&Os also contain a duty by an officer commanding a command to report unusual incidents. QR&O 4.11 states: "An officer commanding a command shall report immediately to National Defence Headquarters and to the Regional Headquarters concerned any serious or unusual incident that occurs in or affects any base, unit or element in the command, which is not required to be reported by any other regulations or orders, has a military significance, and is likely to be the subject of questions to National Defence Headquarters."

QR&O 4.11 relating to reporting unusual incidents is extended in the Canadian Forces Administrative Orders. CFAO 4-13 "Reporting of Significant Incidents" was issued in April 1995. It clarified the earlier CFAO 4-13, which was entitled "Unusual Incidents", but dealt with both "unusual" and "significant" incidents. The replacement CFAO does not use the word "unusual" except in the first paragraph outlining the purpose of the CFAO: "This order outlines the procedures for reporting unusual occurrences that happen in, or affect, any base, station, unit or other element of the Canadian Forces (CF), and that may engender public interest or that might otherwise come to the notice of senior departmental officials by means outside the normal military reporting chain." "Significant incident" is defined as "any occurrence, major or minor, including news reports, that will, or may create public interest, or is likely to be the subject of questions to the Minister or other senior departmental officials."[6] The object therefore is to enable the military and the Department of National Defence to be aware of matters that will be the subject of news reports or questions to the DND or in the House of Commons. The CFAO states that significant incidents "must be assessed against the criterion: Is it possible that this incident will arouse the interest of the public or the media and be the subject of questions to the Department of National Defence?" The CFAO goes on to state: "It is inappropriate for ministers, or other senior departmental officials, to learn of Department of National Defence (DND) related events through questions from the news media, or through press reports, public queries, or questions in the House of Commons." The object of the CFAO would seem to be to give the military and the minister time to respond to questions and to exercise some damage control.

The reporting is "to the officer commanding the command, with a copy to the Land Force Area commander and to the local DND Public Affairs (DNDPA) office." The CFAO goes on to provide — no doubt influenced by the Somalia affair — that "a Canadian contingent commander of a United Nations (UN) contingent or other international command shall report incidents of national interest directly to NDHQ/NDOC (National Defence Operations Centre) with a copy to the commander commanding the command who is the office of primary interest (OPI) in addition to meeting UN or international reporting requirements."

There are many other duties set out in the CFAOs to report incidents. CFAO 4-13, "Reporting of Significant Incidents", states specifically that "A report of an incident as 'significant' does not preclude the requirement to report it through other means and other channels in accordance with current regulations and orders." Some of these other reporting requirements are to report any "injury except a minor injury such as a superficial cut or bruise" to a "higher authority no later than seven days after the event."[7] Another CFAO requires that NDHQ be notified when a person above the rank of sergeant is proceeded against under the Code of Service Discipline or is suspended from duty.[8] Air infractions — to give an example — must be reported by any member of the military: "Members of the Canadian Forces (CF) shall report all incidents that appear to contravene air regulations, flying orders or air traffic control orders."[9] There is also a CFAO dealing with "the action to be taken by her Majesty's Canadian (HMC) Ships in reporting an accident or serious incident"[10] and another dealing with the reporting of "objects that are found or sighted, which by their unusual nature or circumstances may be of intelligence interest to the Canadian Forces (CF) and the Department of National Defence (DND)."[11]

Other CFAOs do not spell out what should be done with respect to certain incidents, but require that the standing orders deal with the matter. So, for example, CFAO 71-4 provides that "commanding officers shall ensure that...a reliable and efficient system of processing ammunition accident, incident, defect and malfunction reports is established."[12] And CFAO 30-2, dealing with fires, provides that "local standing orders shall contain an instruction requiring that the person discovering a fire must report it immediately to the designated authority."[13] Breaches of standing orders are, as we have seen, violations of section 129 of the "good order and discipline" section of the *National Defence Act.*

There were, of course, orders for the Somalia operation, which also contained reporting requirements on top of the requirements already mentioned. "Operation Deliverance Operations Orders 01 of December 12, 1992, for example, provided in paragraph 4C: "(1) Daily SITREPs will be sent to HQ CJFS by HMCS PRESERVER and Cdn AB Regt BG accurate as at 0300Z to arrive NLT 0600Z commencing 15 Dec 92. (2) A consolidated SITREP will be sent to NDHQ/J3 Ops by HQ CJFS accurate as at 0600Z to arrive NLT 1100Z commencing 15 Dec 92."[14]

The military police have special reporting obligations set out in CFAO 22-4 and in volume 4 of Police Procedures.[15] CFAO 22-4 provides that "significant or unusual incidents having criminal, service or security implications and involving the CF or DND will be reported forthwith by the military police via a Military Police Unusual Incident Report (MPUIR)...directly to DG Secur."[16] The submission of such a report, the section goes on to state, "does not absolve commanders of the requirement to submit a Significant Incident Report (SIR) in accordance with CFAO 4-13, Unusual Incidents." A commanding officer also has a duty under CFAO 22-10 to notify the military police "When loss of or damage to public or non-public property is suspected to be the result of a criminal offence."[17] If there are no military police in the locality, they should notify the civilian police and then "report immediately the theft or loss" to the base Security Officer and to the Director of Police Operations NDHQ.[18]

Chapter 48 of volume 4 of Police Procedures deals with the Military Police Unusual Incident Reports.[19] Reports are sent directly to NDHQ/ Police Operations. "The Military Police (MP) Unusual Incident Report (MPUIR)", the document states, "is a means of providing early notification of important security and police related events directly to National Defence Headquarters". The report "shall be used to advise NDHQ/D Police Ops, commanders, security advisers and other staff as appropriate, of unusual incidents, involving DND, which come to the attention of MP. MPUIRs are used each working day morning by DG Secur to brief CIS (Chief of Intelligence and Security) and principal staff at NDHQ on incidents which require the attention of the Chief of the Defence Staff and/or the Deputy Minister."[20] The reports, a later section states, "allow rapid advice to be provided to formation commanders and to NDHQ for the appropriate staff actions. MPUIRs may also assist in the preparation of press releases by DND."[21] So there is the "damage control" aspect of reporting, but there is, of course, also an advice and supervision aspect.

The document gives examples of "unusual incidents" that are to be reported, which include "serious injuries or death when there are criminal or security implications...theft, loss or recovery of all types of weapons...theft or fraudulent use of public property...other criminal or serious service offences involving DND establishments or personnel that may come to the attention of media as newsworthy, or may result in questions to NDHQ by the Ministers, Parliamentarians, commanders or the public."[22]

A new police policy, Bulletin 14.0/94, published in 1994, deals with the reporting requirements of Canadian military police employed as part of a Multi-National Force.[23] As noted in Chapter 5, no doubt the experience in Somalia caused a tightening up of military police procedures. The policy makes it clear that "all incidents involving Canadian Contingent members which would be reportable if they had occurred in Canada, must be reported to D Police Ops" (paragraph 9) and that a copy of all reportable incidents that have been investigated be sent to D Police Ops (paragraph 10). This was probably already a requirement, but the new policy now makes it clear.[24]

The Somalia Inquiry will no doubt carefully explore compliance with these various reporting requirements in relation to events in Somalia. Were reports of the various incidents appropriately sent to NDHQ by the military police and the commanding officers?

The Inquiry will also wish to explore the techniques used by the U.S. inspectors general. In Chapter 7, the U.S. system of internal military inspectors general and the more recently established statutory civilian Inspector General for the Department of Defense are explored in detail. Both the internal and external statutory inspectors general receive complaints from civilians as well as the military, provide anonymity to persons, protect whistleblowers[25] and have a toll-free hotline. No such formal system exists in Canada. The Canadian regulations and orders do not contemplate anonymous complaints, although undoubtedly many are submitted. The U.S. system would not only help bring matters to the attention of senior military personnel, but it would help ensure that the normal reporting mechanisms are followed because of fear of later exposure through anonymous channels.

Protecting whistleblowers — by providing anonymity and preventing reprisals[26] — may also be an effective deterrent against improper conduct in the first place. In a recent study of corporate behaviour in Canada, whistleblowers were seen as an important technique for controlling undesirable conduct.[27] The authors of one of the chapters in the study rightly state: "one of the most generally held tenets of contemporary criminology is that increasing the likelihood of detection and prosecution tends to be a more effective means of strengthening deterrence than making sanctions more severe." They recommend that "whistleblowing bounties" be considered, as are now available in the United States.[28] The military is, in effect, a giant corporation. The position of the whistleblower in the Canadian military should clearly be enhanced by giving anonymity, where possible, and by preventing reprisals, even if the next step, rewarding whistleblowers, is not taken.

A great variety of reporting provisions for the military are set out in this chapter. As stated at the beginning of the chapter, reporting is required in part to ensure that problems are dealt with adequately and in part to enable the military and the government to keep on top of issues and respond as necessitated by events. Both purposes are important, but one senses that the latter, being able to respond to issues, often tends to be the dominant consideration. Discouraging and dealing appropriately with improper conduct through reporting and protecting whistleblowers are at least as important, and many would say more important. A considerable amount of loyalty to fellow soldiers and to one's unit is desirable for cohesion. The question the Somalia Inquiry will want to answer is whether this protective philosophy has gone further than it should in Canada.

CHAPTER FOUR

Administrative and Informal Sanctions[1]

It is helpful to conceptualize the system of mechanisms, processes, and institutions that function to control improper behaviour within the military as lying along a continuum. The more formal and severe forms of control, considered later, can be seen as lying at the upper range of the continuum. The spectrum continues down through administrative actions to non-legalistic forms of control, those rooted in custom and tradition. These latter forms are much more difficult to bring into clear focus. One of the difficulties arises from the fact that the controls at the lower end of the continuum are seldom set out in statutes, regulations or orders, but rather flow from tacit understandings, long-established custom, and less formal standard operating procedures.

Much of what is done in the military is founded in its organizational culture. What distinguishes the military perhaps from other organizations is two opposing functional requirements: strict maintenance of control and discipline on the one hand, and maximum flexibility for the leadership in the field on the other. The tension between these two imperatives effectively drives the exercise of control down the scale, to invest a great deal of authority that is exercised at the discretion of individual leaders, guided by unwritten codes that form a highly developed organizational culture, and one that has become cloaked in custom and tradition over time.

This, of course, makes it somewhat difficult to draw an analogy between the lower end of the spectrum and the civilian experience, or at least civilian society broadly conceived. It is easier to do so with the system of summary trials and courts martial, as a judicial system designed to enforce compliance with law, regulations, and orders, supported by police and prosecutorial institutions. In civilian society, however, such institutional mechanisms would normally constitute virtually the entire range of state mechanisms to control deviant behaviour. In the military, these mechanisms and institutions form only the upper end of the spectrum, the lower end of which is also well developed and subtle in its operation. The difficulty of grasping clearly the functioning of the lower end makes it easy to overlook. But this lower end is in fact crucial to the operations of the military, a vital element in the matrix of controls designed to mould and shape individual talents into a cohesive disciplined force. The corollary of harnessing "the good" for collective effort, however, is that lower-end mechanisms also serve to check deviation from the desired norm, and so serve to control misconduct as well. Seen one way, such mechanisms are a positive element in shaping the best possible fighting force; seen another way, the operation of lower-level controls is very important in maintaining order and discipline within the military.

It is not possible here to provide an in-depth examination of this more ephemeral aspect of the military sub-culture. However, two features of the lower end of the scale — or perhaps more precisely, aspects that fall outside the formal disciplinary system of control mechanisms — should be highlighted. The first is the nature of administrative sanctions, as contrasted with disciplinary action under the Code of Service Discipline. Administrative action, as will become clear, can well be viewed as extending into the upper extremes of the spectrum, with release from the service being part of the array of possible sanctions. Administrative action is also quite clearly authorized in regulations and orders and so is not part of our concept of the informal sanctions imbedded in organizational culture. The second feature is the informal or non-legally authorized application of disciplinary action within the military.

ADMINISTRATIVE ACTION

Two avenues can be pursued in applying sanctions or attempting to apply negative controls against individuals in the military: the administrative system and the disciplinary system. A commanding officer has a choice of taking administrative action, disciplinary action, or both. CFAO 19-21 on drug control programs, for example, provides that a member is "liable to administrative action or disciplinary action, or both."[2]

The aims of the two systems are different. It is often said that the administrative system is remedial in nature and that it constitutes action taken to correct or improve a member's performance rather than punish bad conduct. Nonetheless, as the following illustrates, administrative action can have a very negative impact on a member's career and is certainly a mechanism for shaping behaviour. The system that encompasses the summary trial process, up to and including the court martial process, is strictly part of the disciplinary system, and the punishments listed in QR&O 104.02 as being punishments that can be applied under that system are purely disciplinary sanctions. A decision to pursue the avenue of disciplinary sanctions involving a summary trial or court martial thus involves a presumption of innocence as well as certain evidentiary, procedural fairness, and levels-of-proof considerations. The other avenue, avoiding many of these considerations, is to apply administrative sanctions or, as it is often called, "take career action" as a means of controlling undesirable behaviour.[3]

Such action typically moves through several increasingly serious stages, ending with release if the undesirable behaviour persists. The process is similar for officers and non-commissioned members, though the specifics differ. The procedure for non-commissioned members is as follows:

(i)   Verbal Warning
(ii)   Recorded Warning[4]
(iii) Counselling & Probation
(iv)   Suspension from Duty[5]
(v)   Compulsory Release.[6]

The verbal warning stage can be omitted or merged with the recorded warning, but the recorded warning is usually considered a necessary precondition to moving on to Counselling and Probation.[7] The Recorded Warning does not have any effect on promotion, training, posting or pay, though it stays permanently on the member's file. By contrast, Counselling and Probation, which is considered "the final attempt to salvage a member's career",[8] does affect eligibility for training selection and promotion, as well as eligibility for incentive pay.[9] Counselling and Probation effectively places the member on probation for a six-month period, during which he can be released at any time, under QR&O 15.01, "unless there is notable and continuous improvement and the shortcomings are corrected."[10]

The process for officers is similar. The interesting difference is that rather than a Recorded Warning, the lower-level mechanism is a "reproof". A reproof can also be given to a non-commissioned member of warrant officer rank or above. The reproof appears to be something of a hybrid mechanism, in that it is promulgated in the disciplinary volume of QR&Os and has a more disciplinary character than the Recorded Warning; yet the

QR&O states clearly that a reproof "is not a punishment and shall not be referred to as such."[11] The reproof is effective for a 12-month period, after which the record of reproof is supposed to be destroyed.[12]

Instead of Counselling and Probation, officers are subject to a Report of Shortcomings, which is also "considered as a final attempt to salvage the career of an officer of the Regular Force or Reserve Force."[13] A reproof is not considered a necessary condition precedent to placing an officer on Report of Shortcomings. All that is required by the CFAO is that the commanding officer personally have informed the officer of his shortcomings, counselled him on ways and means to overcome the shortcomings, and stipulated a period in which the officer must improve to avoid being the subject of a Report of Shortcomings.[14] As in the case of Counselling and Probation, the Report of Shortcomings is effective for a period of only six months, though it can be extended for one three-month term, after which a decision is made on the retention or release of the officer. That decision is made at NDHQ. Also, a record of the report remains on the officer's file.[15]

Administrative action is not subject to the burdens of proof or fairly high requirements for procedural fairness that disciplinary action is. This is illustrated in a letter from Brigadier General Dallaire, dated 23 September 1992, that is one of the exhibits before the Somalia Inquiry. The letter is an Official Incident Report involving a junior officer; in it General Dallaire points out that the Judge Advocate General's office had advised that in situations involving the violation of certain orders or regulations, it must be shown that such orders or regulations both existed and had been published in such a way as to have been sufficiently available to the accused before the alleged offence was committed. Specifically, the Judge Advocate General's office had not advised that it would be possible to prove the culpability of the officer in question beyond a reasonable doubt. General Dallaire had therefore concluded that the Incident Report should be placed in the officer's personal file and that further administrative action be taken. In response to the Incident Report, the officer was issued with what was termed a Verbal Warning, but given the manner in which it was recorded, it would have to be classified as something akin to a Recorded Warning — only two steps away from release — for an incident for which it was determined there were insufficient grounds to proceed by way of discipline.[16]

In applying administrative action there is no need to prove culpability or to adduce any evidence in any formal way, so there is no opportunity for the impugned party to respond in any meaningful way to the case against him or her or to present a counter-argument. Yet the results of such action can later be adduced as evidence of culpability in a disciplinary hearing. An instance of this is the court martial of Major Seward in the Somalia affair. Major Seward had received a reproof for three specific perceived shortcomings in his leadership of 2 Commando in the field in Somalia in January 1993. The court challenged both the reproof's legal existence (because it was more than 12 months old) and its admissibility under the rules of evidence regarding character evidence. At the end of the *voire dire*, having heard testimony undermining the relevance of the reproof, the prosecution abandoned the attempt to use it as evidence. Nevertheless, the prosecution had clearly sought to rely on an administrative action — which required no proof and attracted no evidentiary burden or presumption of innocence when it was executed — as evidence to support an inference of wrongdoing in a disciplinary proceeding.[17]

To be fair, the use of administrative action as a substitute for disciplinary action is discouraged, at least on paper. For example, the CFAO on Report of Shortcomings states that "A Report shall not be considered a substitute for disciplinary action. A CO shall consider taking action under the Code of Service Discipline with respect to shortcomings attributable to misconduct which may, by their seriousness or repetition, result in a Report of Shortcomings."[18] However, to take another example, the CFAO on Personal Relationships states that, with respect to conduct between service 'couples' in violation of this CFAO, "Disciplinary action is to be considered when the conduct is so unacceptable that disciplinary action is more appropriate than administrative action, *or when administrative action has failed to correct the inappropriate conduct*."[19] This would seem to suggest that the application of administrative action has a lower threshold, despite the fact that it has potentially more extreme career ramifications. Further, taken in conjunction with the incidents described above, it is possible to infer that administrative action may be deemed more "appropriate" when the circumstances simply make it difficult to apply the disciplinary process.

In terms of procedural fairness requirements in accordance with principles of administrative law, the mechanisms include a process for giving the subject 'notice' of the action taken and a theoretical opportunity to respond, albeit in a very limited way.[20] Also, the Redress of Grievance process provides for any member to make formal submissions in response to perceived unfair treatment of either a disciplinary or an administrative nature.[21] There is apparently a very strong perception within the system, however, that availing oneself of the Redress of Grievance process is likely to attract reactions unfavourable to career progression and be counter-productive in the long term. It is therefore a process that is resorted to only in the most egregious or serious cases of perceived injustice.

The ease with which these sanctions or controls can be applied, coupled with their potentially serious impact on the member's or officer's career progression, makes them an important element in the military system of controls.

INFORMAL SANCTIONS

Control is also exercised through less formal means used to maintain discipline and good order. To make clearer just what is meant by "informal" or "non-legally authorized", we start with a look at the regulations. QR&O 104.02 details the "Scale of Punishments", in accordance with the *National Defence Act*:

> The following punishments may be imposed in respect of service offences:
> (a) death,
> (b) imprisonment for two years or more,
> (c) dismissal with disgrace from Her Majesty's service,
> (d) imprisonment for less than two years,
> (e) dismissal from Her Majesty's service,
> (f) detention,
> (g) reduction in rank,
> (h) forfeiture of seniority,
> (i) severe reprimand,
> (j) reprimand,
> (k) fine, and
> (l) minor punishments,
> and each of the punishments set out in paragraphs (b) to (l) shall be deemed to be a punishment less than every punishment preceding it.[22]

With respect to "minor punishments", the QR&OS go on to amplify section 146 of the *National Defence Act* as follows:

> the following minor punishments may be imposed in respect of service offences:
> (a) confinement to ship or barracks;

(b) extra work and drill;

(c) stoppage of leave;

(d) extra work and drill not exceeding two hours a day; and

(e) caution. (article 104.13(2))

In a note to the article, the QR&Os continue with "the punishments prescribed in paragraph (2) *may only be imposed at summary trials* held
under Chapter 108 (Summary Trials by Delegated Officers and Commanding Officers)" (emphasis added). This would seem to imply that the
lower end of the spectrum of disciplinary sanctions are these "minor punishments", which can be imposed only as a result of a summary trial
conviction. Yet it appears that anyone who has served any time in the
military is fully aware that there are circumstances under which almost
the entire array of the minor punishments listed here can be and are applied in normal daily operations.[23] They are imposed utterly independent
of any summary trial process; indeed, they can be imposed in a manner
that appears, to the outside observer, divorced from any process at all. If
these minor punishments are to continue — and no doubt they will —
there is much to be said in favour of recognizing and regularizing the
practice in the QR&Os.

It is the imposition of "minor punishments" without benefit of summary trial that is referred to here as "informal". And it is in this apparent
contradiction or inconsistency between rules and regulations and practice that we find the notion of tacitly understood rules and operating procedures, of unwritten codes and collective understandings of how things
are done. In short, it is the operation of an organizational culture. This is
not unlike the informal operating procedures and organizational culture
of any large organization.

Before examining the concept in more abstract terms, we should first
explore the actual operation and range of such authority and how it is
understood by members of the military. When long-serving officers were
asked what authority they had to impose informal sanctions, they were
somewhat nonplussed — unable to point to official authority empower-
ing them to impose sanctions — but clearly quite confident of the legitimacy of their exercise of such authority. The application of these sanctions
is not grounded in any formal authority, but nor are they meted out as
arbitrarily as might first appear. The authority rests on a tacit understanding that permeates the organization: a cultural or corporate perception of
authority legitimately vested in both rank and position. Furthermore, the
manner in which this authority is to be exercised is understood quite clearly,

and there are also well understood limitations and boundaries to both the range and application of such authority.

An example may make this clearer. On a ship (as one example of an operational unit), senior officers, particularly the executive officer and the combat officer (and of course the commanding officer through the executive officer) feel quite free to impose such sanctions as additional duty, denial of leave, or withdrawal of wardroom privileges on junior officers. The authority to impose such punishment is tacitly accepted (although there must still be a reasonable relationship between the seriousness of the transgression and the sanction). However, officers certainly do not act in such an "arbitrary" fashion with regard to enlisted men, and greater consideration is given to maintaining the forms of "due process". This is done, for instance, by exercising authority through the chain of command, possibly even giving a non-commissioned member's direct superior discretion to determine what sanction to apply and how best to apply it. Here too there is an informal system — no less complex for being informal — for moulding behaviour.

There are also mechanisms to check perceived abuses of this authority and prevent the crossing of the understood boundaries for its exercise. The formal routes include the Redress of Grievance procedure, but informal checks and balances are also essential features for smooth operation of the organizational culture, serving to legitimize and reinforce informally exercised authority and thus enhance the effectiveness of this form of behaviour control. An example will help to clarify how these mechanisms function.

Returning to the example of the ship, suppose that a junior officer, in his capacity as divisional officer, begins to impose punishments in a way that is seen as arbitrary or heavyhanded. This perception would begin to circulate informally, eventually reaching other officers. They would likely exercise some influence to bring the 'offender' back into line. If the conduct persisted, however, discontent would increase. Acting perhaps on a personal complaint (or simply responding to general perceptions), the coxswain (the senior non-commissioned officer aboard ship) would likely approach the executive officer. The 'rogue' officer would then find his behaviour the subject of possible administrative action by the executive officer. In this manner, the officer's conduct would either be brought back in line with tacit and formal norms of behaviour, or he would become the subject of formal sanctions.[24]

This complex system of checks and balances, often functioning through informal and semi-formal communication networks, extends beyond the operational unit. The coxswain has the ear of the command chief (the highest non-commissioned officer in the Navy) at Maritime Command Headquarters and so can advise the admiral informally of problems in the exercise of a commanding officer's authority. Such links outside the formal chain of command are not only recognized but are accepted as essential (again, within tacitly understood limits) and are therefore fostered and encouraged.[25]

Finally, the boundaries and limits on the exercise of informal authority — the character of the organizational culture — can vary with circumstances and from one operational unit to another. In training situations, for example, sanctions might range from push-ups to denial of leave or withdrawal of mess privileges, and punishments might even extend to sanctions that would be considered unique, if not bizarre, with little or no serious questioning of the authority to impose them. In an operational unit such actions would be less apparent. At NDHQ, attempts to exercise informal authority in this way would be seen as utterly inappropriate, and the imposition of sanctions would not likely escape challenge on the spot by the recipient. This point is important in the context of the sub-cultures of isolated units, which can become infused with norms and attitudes that begin to deviate from the broader culture of the Canadian Forces as a whole.

The tendency to function on the basis of the informal dictates of organizational culture is no different in the military than in large civilian organizations. The difference is one of degree, and the reason for that lies in the inherent tension referred to earlier: the tension that arises from the traditional need for strict discipline and the exercise of authoritarian leadership on the one hand, and the need to maintain maximum flexibility for leaders in the operational theatre on the other. The need for flexibility in battle, and the inability to foresee and regulate for all likely scenarios, creates pressure to allow a considerable degree of discretion in the exercise of leadership and leads to reliance on informal standard operating procedures. Yet the extreme conditions for which members of the military must be trained, the precision demanded in operations, and the dire consequences of failure, not to mention the aggressive temperament required of the organization — all speak to the need for a well developed and somewhat rigid system of control, implemented unsparingly and rigorously enforced. Means of balancing these conflicting needs is therefore needed — and it is reliance on the informal exercise of authority and implementation of disciplinary controls in accordance with tacitly understood organizational norms rather than rigidly defined rules and regulations that provide this balance.

This equilibrium is often unstable, however. This is where differences in organizational culture between units become important. Sometimes organizational culture is corrupted or distorted in such a way as to destroy the equilibrium. This is particularly so in small, isolated units and units where informal norms have become exaggerated to the point of elevating traditions and customs to sacred status — in short, in so-called elite units. As Lieutenant-Colonel (Ret'd) Charles Cotton recently put it in relation to events in Somalia:

Members tend to identify themselves with their warrior tribe and to reject the standards expected from the more general military population. Simply put, their cohesive spirit is a threat to the chain of command and wider cohesion... It is with the concept of an elite unit itself, a unit ideal which nourishes and makes possible an 'above-the-law' outlook among its members.[26]

In other words, it is the discretion and latitude to exercise authority informally — so essential for general operations and for maintaining discipline and good order — that paradoxically create the potential for corruption of the system. This must not be confused with *informal leadership*, a very different phenomenon. Informal leadership is the influence wielded by members of an organization in whom little or no formal authority has been vested. This too manifested itself in problematic ways in 2 Commando, but that is not the focus here. Of concern here is the *informal exercise of authority* within the duly authorized chain of command.

CONCLUSION

It has not been possible to convey fully in this chapter the intricate nature or the importance of mechanisms at the lower end of the spectrum of control mechanisms. What should be understood, however, is that although the functioning of lower-end processes is more difficult to grasp or bring into sharp focus, their significance should not be overlooked as a result.

CHAPTER FIVE

Military Police

Military police play a very important role in controlling misconduct in the Canadian military. There are now about 1,300 authorized Security and Military Police (SAMP) positions in the Canadian Forces,[1] out of a total regular force of about 65,000 persons[2] — that is, about one military police position for every 50 members of the military. Some military police are attached to bases, some to units, some are stationed at NDHQ, and some form platoons in each of the brigades that could be deployed as a unit.

Outside the military, the figure is about one police officer per 500 persons.[3] But the figures for military police are not as dramatic as they first appear. A number are involved in policing Canadian embassies around the world, more than a hundred are seconded to the United Nations forces, and about two dozen are on loan to NATO. Moreover, the military police staff the detention barracks and the service prison in Edmonton.[4] Further, a significant proportion of military personnel is made up of younger males who, in the general population, account for a significant proportion of criminal activity. (In addition, spouses, children, and the elderly are not included in the figure of 65,000 military personnel, yet if they live on a base, they are subject to military discipline.)

Military police nevertheless account for about two per cent of military personnel. In the U.S. army, however, they make up three to four per cent of the force.[5] As we will see, the U.S. army military police also play a modest combat role.

HISTORY OF THE MILITARY POLICE

Military police have been part of the military for many centuries, from ancient Rome through the Crusades to the present. Military leaders have found military police a valuable component of military campaigns. George

Washington appointed a Provost Marshall in 1776, and Congress established a Provost Corps in 1778.[6] Napoleon is quoted as saying, "Two or three hundred cavalrymen more or less, do not mean much. Two hundred more policemen ensures serenity in the army and good order."[7]

The *International Military and Defense Encyclopedia* states that "military police originated from the need to ensure that stragglers on the battlefield were put under military control and returned to the battle and that prisoners were taken into custody." The military police also help control the movement of traffic in a battlefield. This function was very important in both world wars and, almost half a century later, in the Gulf War:

Complex movements, such as the flanking manoeuver of U.S. and coalition forces for Operation Desert Storm in February 1991, require close coordination of military convoys to ensure that units arrive on time where they are needed. The movement plan is based on route reconnaissance performed by the MP units.[8]

In recent overseas operations, controlling the flow of refugees has been another important military police task.[9]

There is apparently no record of military police in Canada until late in the First World War.[10] In April 1918 the Canadian Corps of Military Police was created by order in council, and in November of that year the first Provost Marshall was appointed. Further research would no doubt show that in earlier periods the military police role was filled by others. The Corps of Military Police ceased to exist in early 1920, and until 1939 there were only garrison-level police within the Canadian military. With the onset of the Second World War, a new Canadian Provost Corps was formed, whose first company consisted almost entirely of RCMP volunteers (113 of 115 were RCMP personnel). Traffic was a principal concern. One writer states: "The task of the provost section was to ensure, as far as possible, that designated routes and timings were followed, congestion avoided and accidents prevented."[11] In 1942 they also assumed responsibility from the RCMP for apprehending absentees and deserters.

By 1944 8,000 members of the Canadian Provost Corps were serving overseas and another 3,500 in Canada. There were also large numbers of police for the navy and airforce. The latter had about 5,000 military police by the end of the war, concerned mainly with protecting the security of air bases. The numbers naturally declined after the war but grew again with the Cold War and Canada's involvement with NATO, Korea, and West Germany.

The three services continued to have their own military police and intelligence services. In August 1964, however, the first step toward unification of police and intelligence services was made by integrating the intelligence functions of all three services into the Director General of Intelligence under the Vice Chairman of Defence Staff.[12] This followed the report of the Royal Commission on Government Organization (the Glassco commission) in early 1963 and Paul Hellyer's White Paper on Defence, tabled in March 1964. At the same time, all police and security functions at Canadian Forces Headquarters in Ottawa were to be organized into a single directorate, later called the Directorate of Security, which assumed responsibility for functions previously performed by the security units of the three services.

Unification of security and intelligence functions occurred in 1968. The many twists and turns leading to unification in 1968 and the *Canadian Forces Reorganization Act*[13] are documented in an article in *On Guard For Thee*, published in 1993 on the 25th anniversary of the founding of the Security Branch. One significant change occurred in 1982 when a separate Intelligence Branch was formed. Counter-intelligence, however, remained with the Security and Military Police.[14]

MILITARY POLICE POWERS

This is not the occasion for a full discussion of the powers and jurisdiction of the military police. Two official military volumes discuss this in detail: volume 4 of the Security Orders for the Department of National Defence and the Canadian Forces, *Military Police Procedures* (1991);[15] and a volume of Police Policy Bulletins. A very much revised version of *Military Police Procedures*[16] appeared in late 1995, incorporating many of the bulletins. The earlier versions are referred to in this study because they were the documents in use at the time Canadian Forces were in Somalia. Moreover, the process of incorporating the bulletins is not yet complete.

In brief, military police are "specially appointed persons" under section 156 of the *National Defence Act*[17] and have the power to arrest,[18] investigate,[19] and use force in certain circumstances.[20] Military police do not, however, have the authority to initiate the laying of a charge (including a charge for a criminal offence) under the Code of Service Discipline. That authority resides in the commanding officer of the unit or his or her delegate (see discussion of MP independence, later in this chapter). Specially appointed persons are also peace officers[21] within the meaning of section 2 of the *Criminal Code*, which states that a peace officer includes

officers and non-commissioned members of the Canadian Forces who are (i) appointed for the purposes of section 156 of the *National Defence Act*, or (ii) employed on duties that the Governor in Council, in regulations made under the *National Defence Act* for the purposes of this paragraph, has prescribed to be of such a kind as to necessitate that the officers and non-commissioned members performing them have the powers of peace officers.

The Queen's Regulations and Orders provide that for purposes of subsection (ii) of section 2 of the Code,

it is hereby prescribed that any lawful duties performed as a result of a specific order or established military custom or practice, that are related to any of the following matters are of such a kind as to necessitate that the officers and non-commissioned members performing them have the powers of police officers: (a) the maintenance or restoration of law and order; (b) the protection of property; (c) the protection of persons; (d) the arrest or custody of persons; or (e) the apprehension of persons who have escaped from lawful custody or confinement.[22]

As civilian peace officers[23] they can arrest for *Criminal Code* offences under section 495 of the Code and can lay charges in civil courts without the concurrence of the commanding officer.

Military Police Procedures describes the jurisdiction of the military police as follows:

7. MP are the primary police force of jurisdiction and exercise police authority with respect to:
a. persons subject to the Code of Service Discipline, without regard to their rank, status or location; and
b. any other person, including civilian employees, dependants, visitors or trespassers, in regard to an event, incident or offence, real or alleged, which occurs or may occur on or in respect to defence establishments, defence works, defence materiel or authorized Canadian Forces programmes, activities or operations.

8. Prior to exercising police authority off a defence establishment, MP must first satisfy themselves that some other police agency does not have a right of primary jurisdiction. A connection, or nexus, to the Service is an essential prerequisite. In the absence of such a nexus, police authority should only be exercised

by MP with the concurrence of the appropriate civil authority. Police authority is clearly distinct from the implicit duties and responsibilities of any good citizen.

9. Where an offence has been committed in Canada by a person subject to the Code of Service Discipline outside of a defence establishment, the matter should be dealt with by the appropriate civilian authorities, unless a Service connection, or nexus, is apparent. In these latter cases, the matter may be considered a Service offence and dealt with accordingly.

10. NDA, Section 70, provides that certain offences shall not be tried by a Service tribunal in Canada. When an offence which should be dealt with by civil authorities is reported to MP, it shall be the responsibility of the appropriate MP or of a security adviser to ensure that the incident is expeditiously reported to the appropriate crown prosecutor or civil police. Subsequent MP enquiries will normally be conducted parallel to or in concert with any civil police investigation. Such incidents will, in any event, be documented by means of an MP report. Should the civil authority fail to act in such an instance, then an MP enquiry will be completed and recorded to the extent deemed necessary by the appropriate security adviser. Should the circumstances so warrant, local authorities will be advised of the outcome of MP inquiries conducted separately from those of the civil authority. Where appropriate, an information may be sworn. Outside of Canada, MP will investigate and report in accordance with international agreements and practices. (Chapter 2-1, paragraph 7 and following)

This describes the commonly understood working relationship between the police and civil authorities for an offence committed in Canada. If there is a clash between civil and military authorities over who has primary jurisdiction to try a person, they would, of course, attempt to resolve it. This writer's view is that if it cannot be resolved, the civil authorities have primary jurisdiction.[24] If primary jurisdiction is to belong to the military as a matter of law, it should be clearly spelled out in the *National Defence Act*. There is a long history of civil authorities having ultimate power to control the army in England and Canada. The matter might, however, be different for the Navy and for offences committed abroad.[25]

Persons subject to the Code of Service Discipline are set out in section 60 of the *National Defence Act*, which states:

60.(1) The following persons are subject to the Code of Service Discipline:
(a) an officer or non-commissioned member of the regular force;
(b) an officer or non-commissioned member of the special force;

(c) an officer or non-commissioned member of the reserve force when the officer or non-commissioned member is

     (i)   undergoing drill or training, whether in uniform or not,

     (ii)   in uniform,

     (iii)   on duty,...

(f) a person, not otherwise subject to the Code of Service Discipline, who accompanies any unit or other element of the Canadian Forces that is on service or active service in any place;

(g) subject to such exceptions, adaptations and modifications as the Governor in Council may by regulations prescribe, a person attending an institution established under section 47;

(h) an alleged spy for the enemy;...

(2) Every person subject to the Code of Service Discipline under subsection (1) at the time of the alleged commission by the person of a service offence continues to be liable to be charged, dealt with and tried in respect of that offence under the Code of Service Discipline notwithstanding that the person may have, since the commission of that offence, ceased to be a person described in subsection (1).

The military use the military justice system whenever possible. As a military police warrant officer told the Somalia Inquiry in October 1995, "If it can be handled within the military, it is handled within the military."[26] This view is set out in various official publications. Police Policy Bulletin 3.0/94 provides that for persons subject to the Code of Service Discipline the military police should use "the military disciplinary system whenever legally possible", whether the conduct occurred on or off DND property. Similarly, paragraph 13 of chapter 2-1 of *Military Police Procedures* states:

13. MP shall not resort to the indiscriminate use of the civilian courts in dealing with persons subject to the Code of Service Discipline, when it would be more appropriate to permit a commanding officer to deal with such persons in a Service proceeding. Notwithstanding the foregoing, prosecutions for drinking and driving offences on a defence establishment in Canada, involving privately owned vehicles, shall be processed through the appropriate civilian courts.

The civilian courts are used for drinking and driving offences because military tribunals do not have the authority to prohibit a convicted person from driving.[27]

MILITARY POLICE IN SOMALIA

One of the issues the Inquiry will want to examine carefully is why only two military police went to Somalia with the Canadian contingent. With a total Canadian force of more than 1,000, two military police amount to less than one-fifth of one per cent of the force. By comparison, military police accounted for about seven or eight per cent of the U.S. force in the Gulf in 1990-91.[28]

One reason that so few Canadian military police went to Somalia was that cabinet had set an upper limit on the number of troops that could be deployed.[29] DG Secur had recommended that a much larger number of military police be sent,[30] but those deciding who was to go had to choose between military police and other important personnel such as soldiers and cooks. Although it would have been possible to go back to cabinet for permission to increase the number, this might have caused the military embarrassment for not getting the number right in the first place. It is clearly desirable for the government to determine the degree of commitment to an operation, but there should perhaps be some flexibility. Legislation could provide, for example, that a percentage — say 10 per cent — above the established number could be permitted with the approval of the Minister of National Defence.[31]

Another reason why so few military police were sent to Somalia is that when the force was first organized, it was to be deployed in the context of a Chapter VI United Nations peacekeeping operation.[32] In such operations, the United Nations usually provides most of the military police, made up of police from other forces. Individual forces may have their own police — the United States always does — but in such cases there is obviously less need for a large number of police. There was also the feeling that U.S. military investigators could be used, an idea that was looked upon with disfavour by DG Secur.[33]

In December 1992 the operation turned from a peacekeeping to a peacemaking operation under Chapter VII of the United Nations Charter.[34] In this type of operation, the individual forces usually bring their own military police (although in Bosnia, also a Chapter VII operation, there were both United Nations and Canadian military police). It seems, then, that cabinet established the troop numbers when Somalia was a Chapter VI operation and did not change them when it became a Chapter VII operation.[35] With the change in the mission, the U.S. military police could not provide effective back-up for Canadian forces, because they were deployed hundreds of miles (and perhaps 10 or 12 hours) away.

It seems reasonably clear from the documents I have seen that DG Secur wanted substantially more military police than the two who were sent. The Provost Marshall for the mission, Major J.M. Wilson, argued throughout December 1992 for more police.[36] "Two MP are not sufficient," he wrote on 18 December 1992, "to provide the required MP support. There should be capability to conduct the following functions concurrently: (1) investigation, (2) service detention, (3) handling detainees, (4) security duties, and (5) police patrol."[37] He had wanted a staff officer assigned to Canadian headquarters in Somalia and, in addition to military police attached directly to the Airborne Regiment, there should have been a second line MP unit, which "could vary from a section of 12 commanded by a Sergeant up to a small platoon, depending upon anticipated employment."[38] Major Wilson anticipated problems with respect to persons detained for criminal acts, which of course is one of the problems that did occur in Somalia.

In May 1993, five more military police personnel went to Somalia, including Major Wilson.[39] In an after-action report in May 1994, Wilson again emphasized the need for first-line military police and a platoon "to properly support an operation the scope of OP DELIVERANCE."[40] It is difficult to disagree with Colonel A.R. Wells, DG Secur, who wrote to the Board of Inquiry:

If there had been a military police presence in theatre both of the Somalia incidents [March 4th and 16th, 1993] which brought such discredit on the Canadian Forces in general and the Airborne Regiment in particular may have been avoided.[41]

Colonel Wells went on to state that one of the reasons for having military police take the responsibility for prisoners — and this would apply to detainees — is that it "gets the captured combatants away from the front line troops where the heat of emotions is high."[42] These are issues that the Somalia Inquiry will undoubtedly explore in depth.

SPECIAL INVESTIGATION UNIT

One issue that has persisted in the police and security area is the extent to which the security function should be separate from the police function. After unification, the special investigation elements of the forces were combined into the Special Investigation Unit (SIU). One of its principal tasks is to handle security clearances. It also handles security investigations and, until recently, conducted serious criminal and service discipline investigations. In 1990, however, a report by the Honourable René Marin recommended that the SIU's criminal and service discipline function be removed.[43] Part of the motivation for this separation was the same as the one that had influenced the separation of the security service (now CSIS, the Canadian Security Intelligence Service) from the RCMP, following the McDonald Royal Commission.[44] Marin referred to the "very different investigative skills" required for security and criminal investigations.[45]

As a result of Marin's report, security investigations and criminal investigations were separated. The SIU, which had consisted of about 200 persons spread out in various detachments, continued. Marin did not recommend that a specialized criminal investigation unit be set up. "It would be preferable," he wrote, "to explore ways of ensuring that MP detachments, and their Commanders, find ways of sharing resources and cooperating in cross-jurisdictional investigations."[46]

The co-operative approach did not work out, however. In his 1994 follow-up report, Marin stated: "I now understand that experience has shown that resource sharing between Commands has not worked well and, as a consequence, a National Investigation Section (NIS) has been established within the Directorate of Police Operations."[47] He was not impressed with this solution, however, stating that he remained "somewhat sceptical of the wisdom of placing a police operational unit under the direct command and control of a headquarters policy unit."[48] Marin had also wanted the link between the military police and the SIU to be broken in another respect, stating that "selection criteria for SIU duties should be broadened to facilitate entry from other occupations within the CF."[49] But the link has remained, and personnel move back and forth between the police and the SIU.[50]

The National Investigation Service was apparently set up shortly after the Somalia events in March 1993, when police personnel from headquarters were sent to investigate the situation. It was clear that a criminal investigation unit was needed, and seven persons were subsequently transferred into the new NIS. The NIS has not as yet been referred to officially in a CFAO; rather, its existence is recognized by a memorandum of understanding. A recent document prepared by the military police states that the role of the NIS is to "conduct nationally mandated criminal investigation beyond the scope of base/command resources or those of an extremely sensitive nature."[51]

The situation still seems to be in flux. The SIU is still called the Special Investigation Unit, even though Marin had recommended that it be renamed the Security Investigation Unit.[52] Moreover, the CFAO dealing with the SIU has not been changed since the 1990 Marin Report, a fact he comments on in his 1994 report.[53] Further, there seems to be a strong desire by the military to link security and military police by adopting the acronym SAMP — Security and Military Police — when they discuss their operations. The term SAMP is now used in *Police Policy Bulletins*[54] and in current writings.[55]

I am not in a good position to analyze what is happening behind the scenes. I suspect that most personnel in DG Secur do not agree with Marin's 1990 report. I personally find it unpersuasive. Separating the security service from policing by setting up CSIS made considerable sense on the national scene. In that area, the skills and techniques required by the two services are indeed quite different. CSIS is protecting the security of the country and may well be more interested, for example, in "turning" a "spy" to act as a double agent than in prosecuting the individual. I cannot see the security side of the military engaging in such activities; indeed, I would not want them to do so, but would prefer that CSIS be called in to handle the situation. There seems to me to be a fairly clear link between security and policing in the military, although the emphasis for each aspect may be somewhat different. Arson, theft, sabotage, and mutiny, for example, are both security and criminal matters. A clear separation may not be possible. But what the organizational structure should be I leave to others to work out.

One major difference between SIU personnel and military police is that the latter are part of the chain of command of the base or unit where they serve, and their career prospects are determined within that structure. The SIU, on the other hand, is centrally organized under NDHQ command, with four detachments across the country. There is therefore greater autonomy for its operations. The military police now operate under the chain of command of the base or unit, with the possibility of intervention by the NIS. One of the questions the Somalia Inquiry will want to examine is whether police investigations should have the same independence from the base or unit chain of command as the SIU. We examine this issue in the next section.

MILITARY POLICE INDEPENDENCE

As a result of the 1990 Marin Report, police investigations were removed from the semi-autonomous SIU. In a 1994 follow-up report, however, Marin expressed concern about the independence of military police:

...I remain unconvinced that a serious problem of accountability will not develop in the future. Military Police personnel are, after all, soldiers by trade and police officers by selection. The existence of a rigid military culture which demands, first and foremost, total loyalty to its own beliefs and institutions may not always be compatible with the dynamics of the law in its reflection of public values and attitudes. For example, while the civil police are held accountable to the public they serve, not only by the Courts, but by various external oversight committees, boards and commissions, the Military Police respond primarily to their own internal command structure...

I should add that there is some question in my mind as to the Military Police officer's individuality, or independence of action and ability to exercise the discretionary powers of a peace officer in view of the 'tasking' philosophy prevalent in organizations which place great emphasis on 'chain of command'. The fact that a Commanding Officer, who may have little knowledge of the law or criminal procedures, is in a position to influence the course of a police investigation certainly bears further scrutiny.[56]

There is no question that the military police are part of the chain of command within their units. Various official orders make this clear. The *Military Police Procedures* volume of the Security Orders for the Department of National Defence of the Canadian Forces, for example, states under the heading "Chain of Command":

MP form an integral part of CF organizations and are operationally responsible to their commanders and commanding officers (COs) for the provision of effective police and security services. Specialist advice and technical direction, on these services, is provided by security advisers within their respective organizations.[57]

A recently promulgated Police Policy Bulletin reinforces this position. The military police, the document states, "are subject to orders and instructions issued by or on behalf of Commanders." "Police and investigative functions," the document goes on to state, "must be conducted in such a manner to, within the law, support the Commander's legitimate operational mission." Another section states: "Specially Appointed Persons [i.e., the military police] and Commanders share a common interest of maintaining discipline and reducing the incidence of crime and criminal opportunities. Specially appointed persons must therefore be the agent of their Commander and his community in the attainment of this goal."[58]

There are, however, some significant links to National Defence Headquarters. Chapter 1-1, paragraph 12 of the volume on *Military Police
Procedures* states that the military police are "technically responsible" to
Headquarters: "MP assigned to bases, stations and CF units are under the
command and control of the appropriate commanders or commanding
officers (CO). However, when performing a specific policing function
related to the enforcement of laws, regulations and orders, they are also
technically responsive to NDHQ/DG Secur and D Police Ops."[59] The Director General of Security, according to CFAO 22-4, paragraph 5, "is the
Department's senior security and police advisor, and is responsible for
the technical direction, coordination and supervision of all security and
police matters in the CF and DND." DG Secur in turn is responsible to the
Deputy Chief of Defence Staff.

It is not clear to me when National Defence Headquarters should be
called in. Perhaps it is simply when the military police on a base consider
they are in over their heads or when National Defence Headquarters indicates they would like to be involved. The senior military police personnel
in Somalia, for example, called in NDHQ as a first step. As stated earlier,
there were only two Canadian military police in Somalia. The evidence
of Sergeant Robert Martin during the court martial of Private Kyle Brown
in relation to the death of Shidane Arone on 16 March 1993 illustrates the
involvement with Headquarters:

Q. Sergeant Martin, good afternoon. Could you please identify yourself for the
court by the use of your full name, your rank, service number, and would you
spell your last name, please?
A. Sir, I am R59 092 863 Sergeant Martin, M-A-R-T-I-N, given names Robert,
Alan, I'm an MP 811. I'm currently employed at the Canadian Forces School of
Intelligence and Security in Borden.
Q. And that would indicate that you are a military policeman by trade, Sergeant
Martin?
A. Yes, sir.
Q. How many years have you been in the Canadian Forces?
A. I'll have 20 years in May, sir.
Q. What is your present position at Canadian Forces School of Intelligence and
Security?
A. I'm the Platoon 2IC for the basic training platoon.
Q. Could you please indicate to the court to what unit you were posted in March
of 1993?
A. In March '93, I was with the Canadian Airborne Regiment on duty in Somalia.

Q. And with the Airborne Regiment, what was the position that you held?

A. I was the Regimental MP Sergeant.

Q. Sergeant Martin, it's my understanding that you became involved in an investigation related to the death of a Somali prisoner on or about the 18th of March 1993, is that correct?

A. Yes, sir, it's correct.

Q. How did you become involved in that investigation?

A. On the 18th of March '93, I returned from two weeks leave in Nairobi, Kenya. On arrival back into the country of Somalia, I was advised by my 2IC that there had been an incident on the evening of the 16th, the morning of the 17th, in which a person, a local Somali had died under unusual circumstances while in custody of 2 Commando.

Q. What did you do as a result of that information being conveyed to you?

A. After initially talking with my 2IC, I went and I had a conversation with the Deputy Commanding Officer, Major MacKay, and he gave me information to the fact that a serious incident did occur, a Somali did die, and they were, the Regiment itself, had begun an investigation into the matter itself.

Q. And what did you do as a result of that information?

A. For the rest of the night, I went back. I discussed things over with my 2IC to find out exactly what we should do as military police, and...

Q. What did you decide?

A. We decided that there should be a military police investigation conducted immediately into the circumstances surrounding the incident.

Q. What did you do to effect that?

A. The next morning, the morning of the 19th, I went and talked again to Major MacKay. I told him of my decision I had made, and I requested to him that he ceases any investigation that the Regiment was doing itself as I was going to assume responsibility for a military police investigation into the matter.

Q. And what were your steps of investigation. How did you commence?

A. Well, my first step was to request through my Headquarters a special investigation team from Ottawa to come over and take over the investigation from me, because I have limited experience in this type of investigation. I felt that much more was required in order to achieve the results.[60]

Various official orders attempt to tie the military police into National Defence Headquarters. CFAO 22-4 provides in paragraph 5 that "The Director General Security (DG Secur) is the Department's senior security and police advisor, and is responsible for the technical direction, coordination and supervision of all security and police matters in the CF and DND." The same CFAO also provides that "significant or unusual incidents" be reported to headquarters. Paragraph 14 states: "Significant or unusual incidents having criminal, service or security implications and involving the CF or DND will be reported forthwith by the military police via a Military Police Unusual Incident Report (MPUIR)...directly to DG Secur." The submission of such a report "does not absolve commanders of the requirement to submit a Significant Incident Report (SIR) in accordance with CFAO 4-13, Unusual Incidents."[61]

A new police policy, published in 1994, deals with the reporting requirements of Canadian military police deployed as part of a multi-national force. No doubt the experience in Somalia caused a tightening up of military police procedures. Police Policy Bulletin 14.0/94 now provides (paragraph 6) that "the senior Canadian Military Police member appointed as a SAMP Advisor of a Canadian Contingent deployed overseas shall be at least a Warrant Officer notwithstanding the size of the Canadian Contingent." If the policy had been in place in 1993 a sergeant would not have been the most senior Canadian military police person in Somalia. The SAMP Advisor is to "ensure that all investigations involving members of the Canadian Contingent are conducted in accordance with DND Police Standards and Policies." (paragraph 8) The policy makes it clear that "all incidents involving Canadian Contingent members which would be reportable if they had occurred in Canada, must be reported to D Police Ops" (paragraph 9) and that a copy of all reportable incidents that have been investigated be sent to D Police Ops (paragraph 10). This was probably already the requirement,[62] but the new policy now makes it very clear.

Another section encourages widespread communication outside the chain of command, by providing: "To facilitate the resolution of matters related to police and security inquiries, lateral and vertical channels of communication are authorized between military police at all levels.[63] In addition, Military Police Investigation Reports of more than "local significance" are sent to NDHQ.[64]

Another important control technique to prevent the chain of command improperly influencing military police decisions is to require Headquarters approval to stop an investigation. Paragraph 20 of CFAO 22-4 states that military police "shall consult NDHQ/Director Police Operations (D Police Ops), through the appropriate chain of command, PRIOR TO discontinuing or cancelling military police investigations."[65]

A further section is relevant. Police Policy Bulletin 3.2/95 provides that a military police person must notify the senior local military police person if "aware of an attempt, by any person, to influence illicitly the investigation of a service or criminal offence" (paragraph 25). Further, paragraph 27 states that "if the allegation of illicit influence involves a Superior Specially Appointed Person, the member shall submit their complaint to the next senior Specially Appointed Person in the military police technical net/channel." Police Policy Bulletin 3.11/94 (paragraph 14-10) provides that a military police appointment may be suspended for "submission to improper or illicit influences with respect to the performance of their duties." These provisions recognize the danger of influence being exerted by persons within the chain of command, particularly by those higher up the chain.[66] Thus there are important specific linkages and techniques designed to give the police a measure of autonomy from command influence within the unit or the base.

How can the military police be accountable to the commanding officer and yet still be able to act independently? The techniques described above help achieve both objectives. Should further changes be made? Should the military police be entirely outside the chain of command, just as the Judge Advocate General's branch is? This would not seem to be a practical solution because of the great importance of the military police in battle situations — for example, in directing military traffic. There is certainly much to be said in favour of having the military police attached to a unit integrated with the chain of command for purposes of cohesion and internal discipline. But there should be some independent military police unit for serious misconduct. A solution adopted by the U.S. Army is an independent military body, the U.S. Army Criminal Investigation Command, to conduct and control all Army investigations of serious crimes as well as certain other categories of offences. In addition, the body provides criminal investigative support to all U.S. Army elements and conducts sensitive or special investigations as directed by certain senior bodies.[67] The command was apparently set up during the Vietnam War because of black market operations by the military police within the units.[68] Serious crime is defined in another regulation[69] to include all felonies and a limited number of misdemeanours (s. 3-3(3)), except as prescribed by regulation. Another Army regulation provides that "military police/security police will refer all crimes, offences or incidents falling within CID investigative responsibility to the appropriate CID element for investigation... Investigation of other crimes, incidents, or criminal activities will be conducted by military police, unless responsibility is assumed by USACIDC in accordance with established procedures."[70] Routine criminal cases therefore remain within the chain of command. The U.S. Army procedure is one that the Somalia Inquiry may want to examine.

A different approach is taken in England, where in addition to military police for each service[71] there is a unified Ministry of Defence Police force made up of civilian police officers. The force consists of 5,000 police officers, the fifth largest civil police force in Britain. The force has responsibility for crime prevention and detection, physical protection of defence establishments, and the security of Crown property. Offences committed by civilians relating to the military are dealt with by Ministry of Defence police forces. Offences by military personnel are generally dealt with by the service police, although in certain garrison towns ministry police operate like a general police force with respect to civilians and military personnel.[72] Such a civilian force might be considered by the Somalia Inquiry for policing in Canada. The RCMP could be an appropriate body to take on this task.

If the U.S. Army approach is thought to go too far — and I do not believe it does — it might be possible to achieve greater independence by ensuring that performance evaluation and career decisions, at least for the very senior military police, are not made by the regiment or unit chain of command but by NDHQ. Such assessments are now done within a base or unit chain of command, usually by the base administrative officer. Senior military police, in turn, evaluate those who report to them. This would give Headquarters more clout in controlling the military police in the regiments and would remove from the military police the fear that there might be consequences of opposing those higher up the chain of command.

Another change that might be considered is to give the military police the power to charge persons with military offences,[73] without obtaining the permission of the commanding officer or his or her delegate. Military police can now charge persons with offences in civilian courts without such authorization. If they have this power, why not the normally less serious power of charging persons with military offences? National Defence Headquarters should, however, have the power of staying a military charge, just as the attorney general can now enter a *nolle prosequi* or a stay in civilian proceedings.

The military police have the authority to commence investigations. Commanding officers, as we have seen, cannot in theory block the start of an investigation or stop one that has started (see CFAO 22-4, paragraph 20), although they can dismiss a charge "where, after investigation, a commanding officer considers that a charge should not be proceeded with."[74] The authority to commence an investigation in spite of a summary investigation or a board of inquiry should also be made clear.[75] One problem faced by the military police in Somalia was initial resistance to DG Secur's desire to send a team to Somalia to investigate the 4 March 1993 incident. Although DG Secur could investigate, understandably they required permission from CDs to go to Somalia.[76]

RESTRUCTURING THE SECURITY AND MILITARY POLICE

The security and military police, like other parts of the Canadian Forces, are going through a restructuring. They anticipate a substantial reduction in their numbers. One knowledgeable insider anticipates that numbers may be reduced from the present 1,300 to 1,000.[77] Some fundamental questions are being asked. Can they continue to do all the things they do now? How can they avoid inappropriate command influence? How can they effectively task and control major military police investigations? Are they too top heavy with command and control structures? What training should they receive? What oversight of the military police should there be? Should they rely more on the civilian police? How can they ensure that enough military police are available for combat operations? These are the questions a task force, known as Operation Thunderbird, is exploring.[78] Draft proposals from Operation Thunderbird will likely be available in the fall of 1996.[79]

I do not have sufficient knowledge or experience in military matters to offer strong views on these important issues. The Somalia Inquiry may wish to explore some of these matters. The following observations are based on reading some of the literature and discussing the issues with military personnel and others.

A large number of military police are obviously required for conventional wars. They control battlefield traffic, provide area security, deal with prisoners of war, and maintain law and order among the troops. As we saw at the beginning of this section, the U.S. military has been able to sustain almost double the proportion of military police that Canada has, and the Canadian proportion may well decline further. One difference between the U.S. and Canadian military in relation to military police is that U.S. military police, starting with the Vietnam War, have been given greater tactical battle responsibility.[80] They were involved in jungle patrols, locating and destroying Viet Cong tunnels, and in active strike operations.[81] Like the Canadian military police, the Americans are rethinking the role of the military police in the light of the fact that non-war operations will continue to constitute a major part of military activities.[82] One solution that will likely be explored in both countries is to use the reserves more in such operations.[83] It is arguable that a member of the reserve will be as effective in routine policing operations as a member of the regular force. Indeed, greater objectivity in policing could be provided by persons for whom the military is not the sole means of livelihood.

There may also be some operations where the military police will serve a mission better than regular combat forces. The United States, for example, deployed military police, rather than combat arms, to Cuba in 1991-92 in support of the Haitian relief operation at Guantanamo Bay. This was done because of their training in riot control and their ability to handle civilians with restraint.[84]

Military police will be understandably reluctant to rely on civilian police for extensive policing of the military within Canada. Civilian police are also pressed for resources and may not willingly take on the task. Moreover, a civilian police force may not be sensitive to the needs of the military. They might not treat a matter (e.g., striking a military officer or theft in the barracks) with sufficient seriousness, or might treat a matter more seriously than is warranted from a military perspective. Still, greater co-operation between the military and civilian police may provide a measure of security for emergency situations and avoid some duplication of resources. And, as we saw earlier, the U.K. special civilian force for patrols within England is worth careful consideration for Canada.

In any event, there could, for example, be even greater co-operation between the military and the RCMP. This is already fairly extensive.[85] The RCMP and the military share a number of activities, generally under the auspices of memoranda of understanding, for example, in drug enforcement, counter-terrorism, and aid to the civil power. The Oka situation in 1990 was a recent example of military aid to the civil power.[86] Co-operation is also found in external missions. The military gave logistical support, for example, to the RCMP mission to Namibia in 1989. (The RCMP went to Namibia to support the United Nations Transition Assistance Group and help monitor the country's elections and move to independence.)[87] Co-operation might also work the other way; the RCMP could accompany military missions such as the one to Somalia. The RCMP are now playing a role in the mission to Haiti, and it will be recalled that the first military police at the start of the Second World War were RCMP officers.

Operation Thunderbird will probably also consider the issue of recruitment. The vast majority of military police join by direct entry, while a minority transfer from other trades and classifications within the military. In 1991, 72 per cent of MPs had joined by direct entry and the remainder by transfer.[88] René Marin suggested that military police not be recruited directly, so that more mature personnel could be recruited.[89] Commander Paul Jenkins, deputy head of Operation Thunderbird, has written that consideration should be given to at least equalizing the numbers recruited through the two types of entry, "thereby improving maturity at the working level and probably resolving other problems such as the large number of transfers to civil policing."[90] Young recruits appear to be more likely to consider policing an occupation (rather than being attracted to the military as an institution) and are therefore more likely to be lost to civilian forces, where the pay is better.[91] Recent documents suggest that transfers now require higher educational qualifications than direct entry to the military. A high school diploma is mandatory, and post-secondary certificates, diplomas or degrees are preferred.[92] This is in line with civilian policing standards across the country.

CONCLUSION

The military police provide an obviously important means of controlling improper conduct in the military in addition to their importance in battle-field operations and in security. It would probably be unwise to reduce their numbers significantly. Ways should be found to increase numbers for specific operations by using reserves or civilian police such as the RCMP in addition to the regular military police. Certainly, a future Somalia-type operation should not be forced to operate in the absence of sufficient numbers of military police. A larger number of military police than were sent to Somalia have recently been sent to Bosnia as part of the 1,000-person contribution to the NATO force.[93]

In this chapter we have considered how to achieve greater independence from command influence for the military police. One change suggested is to have the career prospects of military police determined outside the regimental chain of command. Another is to permit the military police to bring charges for military offences without the consent of the commanding officer. Still another is to consider adopting something similar to the U.S. Criminal Investigation Division, a military body that investigates all serious offences but whose command structure is independent of the units to which accused persons belong.

CHAPTER SIX

Military Justice

The military justice system is the core technique for controlling misconduct in the military. When less harsh controls — leadership, loyalty to
one's unit or comrades, administrative sanctions, rewards — fail, it is the
military justice system that is expected to deter improper conduct on and
off the battlefield. In his excellent study, *Combat Motivation*, Anthony
Kellett states that the "first and, perhaps, primary purpose of military
discipline is to ensure that the soldier does not give way in times of great
danger to his natural instinct for self preservation but carries out his orders, even though they may lead to his death." A further purpose, he writes,
"is to maintain order within an army so that it may be easily moved and
controlled so that it does not abuse its power. If an army is to fulfil its
mission on the battlefield, it must be trained in aggression; however, its
aggressive tendencies have to be damped down in peacetime, and the
medium for this process is discipline." Kellett adds a third purpose: "the
assimilation of the recruit and the differentiation of his new environment
from his former one." The military requires almost instinctive obedience
to lawful military orders. Drill is used to instill instinctive obedience,
Kellett writes.[1] The military justice system also serves this purpose.[2]

During the second half of the nineteenth century, discipline was widely
used in the British Army. Flogging was used until abolished in 1881.
Courts martial involved between 10,000 and 20,000 men each year. During the First World War, discipline was particularly harsh; there were
more than 300,000 courts martial, more than 3,000 men were sentenced
to death, and almost 350 of them were actually executed. Twenty-five
Canadians were shot for disciplinary offences during the war.[3] By contrast, only one American was executed for desertion (11 were executed
for murder or rape), and no Australians were executed for desertion. Instead, the Australians' sentences were commuted to imprisonment and
their names sent to their home towns. During the Second World War, the
desertion rate for British troops was lower than in the First, even though

the death penalty had been removed.[4] A great number of German troops on the Eastern Front were executed for desertion, however. On the Western Front, the cohesiveness of small units and the relationship between officers and men created high morale, but this broke down on the Eastern Front after very heavy losses and, as recent evidence shows, more than 15,000 men were executed by their own officers for desertion and similar offences.[5]

Let us first examine the issue of a separate system of military justice.

SEPARATE SYSTEM

In the 1992 case *Généreux*, the Supreme Court of Canada upheld the concept of a separate military system of criminal justice.[6] Chief Justice Lamer asked: "is a parallel system of military tribunals, staffed by members of the military who are aware of and sensitive to military concerns, *by its very nature* inconsistent with s. 11(d) of the Charter [trial by an independent and impartial tribunal]?"[7] Chief Justice Lamer, writing for the Court, answered in the negative — indeed, it was conceded by all parties that there is a need for separate tribunals:

The purpose of a separate system of military tribunals is to allow the armed forces to deal with matters that pertain directly to the discipline, efficiency and morale of the military. The safety and well-being of Canadians depends considerably on the willingness and readiness of a force of men and women to defend against threats to the nation's security. To maintain the armed forces in a state of readiness, the military must be in a position to enforce internal discipline effectively and efficiently. Breaches of military discipline must be dealt with speedily and, frequently, punished more severely than would be the case if a civilian engaged in such conduct. As a result, the military has its own Code of Service Discipline to allow it to meet its particular disciplinary needs. In addition, special service tribunals, rather than the ordinary courts, have been given jurisdiction to punish breaches of the Code of Service Discipline. Recourse to the ordinary criminal courts would, as a general rule, be inadequate to serve the particular disciplinary needs of the military. There is thus a need for separate tribunals to enforce special disciplinary standards in the military.[8]

The Court held, however, that the tribunals as constituted at the time were not "independent".

In an earlier case, *MacKay*, decided in 1980, the Supreme Court had held that military tribunals did not violate the Bill of Rights.[9] Justice Ritchie stated for the Court: "The power to allow prosecutions by military authorities is a necessary aspect of dealing with service offences, which have always been considered part of military law."[10] As Chief Justice Lamer had done in *Généreux*, Justice Ritchie referred to theft from a comrade and striking a superior officer as examples of conduct that would warrant more severe punishment by a military than a civilian tribunal.[11]

Chief Justice Laskin (with whom Justice Estey concurred) dissented, holding that ordinary criminal law offences (both MacKay and Généreux had been convicted of offences against the *Narcotic Control Act*) should be tried by the regular courts:

In my opinion, it is fundamental that when a person, any person, whatever his or her status or occupation, is charged with an offence under the ordinary criminal law and is to be tried under that law and in accordance with its prescriptions, he or she is entitled to be tried before a Court of justice, separate from the prosecution and free from any suspicion of influence of or dependency on others. There is nothing in such a case, where the person charged is in the armed forces, that calls for any special knowledge or special skill of a superior officer, as would be the case if a strictly service or discipline offence, relating to military activity, was involved.[12]

A number of other countries — West Germany, Sweden, Austria and Denmark — abolished their court martial systems after the Second World War. "The need for reexamination," one author states, "was most critical in Germany whose World War II court-martial system reflected both Prussian severity and Nazi arbitrariness."[13] Commanders may, however, still give minor penalties for minor offences.

Canada has maintained a separate system, but has brought the standards of military justice applied by military tribunals closer to those of the civilian criminal justice system. In my view, this is a better solution than abolishing military tribunals. As Joseph Bishop has written, "Military discipline cannot be maintained by the civilian criminal process, which is neither swift nor certain... An army without discipline is in fact more dangerous to the civil population (including that of its own country) than to the enemy."[14]

We turn now to a brief look at the present system.

THE PRESENT SYSTEM

Conduct subject to military justice is set out in Part V of the *National Defence Act*. It ranges from serious offences such as behaving "before the enemy in such a manner as to show cowardice", which is subject to the death penalty if the "person acted traitorously", to drunkenness by a member not on duty, which is subject to up to 90 days' detention (sections 74(1), 97). Military offences — referred to in the *National Defence Act* and QR&Os as service offences — include some offences with an exact counterpart in civilian law, such as stealing and receiving property obtained by crime (sections 114-115).

Others offences have no civilian counterpart. Section 129 of the *National Defence Act*, for example, involving conduct to the prejudice of good order and discipline, is widely used. Section 129(1) states: "Any act, conduct, disorder or neglect to the prejudice of good order and discipline is an offence and every person convicted thereof is liable to dismissal with disgrace" and may be sentenced to imprisonment for less than two years. Subsection (2) states that an act or omission constituting a contravention of the *National Defence Act*, "any regulations, orders or instructions published for the general information and guidance of the Canadian Forces or any part thereof, or...any general, garrison, unit, station, standing, local or other orders, is an act, conduct, disorder or neglect to the prejudice of good order and discipline."[15] The section has been upheld constitutionally as not being too vague.[16] One knowledgeable military observer recently observed, "its use is seen as the most expedient and efficient way to deal with many cases, and reflects an attitude that serious criminal charges should be reserved for the true criminals who are to be weeded out of the military community while disciplinary charges should be used in the case of misconduct that is correctable."[17]

In addition, section 130 of the *National Defence Act* provides that a breach of the *Criminal Code* or any other act of Parliament, whether the conduct takes place in Canada or abroad, is a service offence and is punishable by the same penalties as prescribed in the *Criminal Code* or other federal statute. Service tribunals cannot, however, try certain offences committed in Canada. Section 70 of the *National Defence Act* states that a service tribunal shall not try a person charged with committing the offence of murder, manslaughter, sexual assault, or abduction of a young person if committed in Canada. Murder charges arising out of incidents in Somalia were possible because the offences were not committed in Canada.

Further, section 132 of the *National Defence Act* makes it an offence to commit an act outside Canada that "would, under the law applicable in the place where the act or omission occurred, be an offence if committed by a person subject to that law." Penalties are to be "in the scale of punishments that [the tribunal] considers appropriate, having regard to the punishment prescribed by the law applicable in the place where the act or omission occurred and the punishment prescribed for the same" conduct in Canada. None of the offences tried by courts martial arising from the incidents in Somalia was the subject of a charge under section 132 of the *National Defence Act* as offences under Somali law. Most charges were for the military offence of negligent performance of a military duty under section 124 of the *National Defence Act*. Some charges were laid under section 130 of the act, however. Private E.K. Brown, for example, was charged, under section 130, with murder and torture in contravention of the *Criminal Code*[18] and was found guilty of manslaughter and torture.

Section 139 of the *National Defence Act* sets out the punishments that can be imposed in respect of service offences: death, imprisonment for two years or more, dismissal with disgrace from Her Majesty's Service, imprisonment for less than two years, dismissal from Her Majesty's Service, detention, reduction in rank, forfeiture of seniority, severe reprimand, reprimand, fine, and minor punishments. The military's brief to the Somalia Inquiry on military justice noted that "instruction has been given to take steps to remove" the punishment of death from the *National Defence Act*.[19] Minor punishments are set out in QR&O 104.13: "(a) confinement to ship or barracks; (b) extra work and drill; (c) stoppage of leave; (d) extra work and drill not exceeding two hours a day; and (e) caution."[20] Any term of imprisonment imposed on an officer is deemed to include dismissal from service, but dismissal is discretionary for non-commissioned members.[21]

Who is subject to military discipline? Section 60 of the *National Defence Act* states that all full-time military personnel are subject to the Code of Service Discipline. The same is true of members of the reserve force in certain limited circumstances, such as when they are in uniform or on duty. Further, the Code covers certain civilians such as a person "who accompanies any unit or other element of the Canadian Forces that is on service or active service in any place." Persons who have left the military are still technically subject to military justice for offences committed while they were in the military. There is, however, a three-year limitation period for all military offences except mutiny, desertion, absence without permission, offences for which the maximum penalty is death, and certain breaches of the Geneva Convention.[22] With this background, let us look at the various types of military tribunals.

There are two main types of military justice proceedings in Canada: summary proceedings and courts martial. Summary proceedings are by far the most prevalent. There are usually up to 4,000 summary trials each year, but fewer than 100 courts martial.[23] Summary trials therefore account for about 98 per cent of all military trials.

The chain of command is central to the military justice system. It is the commanding officer of the offender's unit who decides how a matter will proceed. Some incidents are so serious or are so much in the public eye that courts martial are convened. As explained below, courts martial can impose greater sentences than summary trials. The summary trial, on the other hand, is generally used more as a means of instilling military values and reintegrating the member into the military culture.[24] "The summary trial", the brief on military justice states, "is meant to be corrective with the goal of socializing members to the habit of discipline, while at the same time fostering morale, esprit de corps, group cohesion, good order, and operational effectiveness and capability."[25] The brief states that the summary trial system "provides speedy, uncomplicated proceedings and is administered by officers holding positions in the chain of command who are not only directly responsible for the maintenance of discipline in the Canadian Forces, but who also must lead in armed conflict."[26]

There are four different forms of courts martial and three types of summary proceedings. The highest form of court martial, the general court martial, consisting of five officers,[27] has jurisdiction to try any military offence against any person who is subject to military discipline.[28] All the courts martial arising out of the Somalia affair were general courts martial. A general court martial can award any punishment,[29] including death.[30] Legal aspects of the proceedings (for example, rulings on evidence and the charge to the members of the tribunal) are handled by a judge advocate,[31] appointed by the chief military trial judge.[32] The accused is entitled to be defended by a military legal officer, provided by the military at public expense, or by his or her own legal counsel[33] at his or her own expense.[34]

The procedure followed at general and other courts martial resembles that in the civilian criminal courts.[35] There is an exhaustive code of rules of evidence[36] but no preliminary inquiry. Instead, the accused is given a synopsis setting out the evidence and witnesses to be called by the prosecution.[37] Guilt or innocence, as well as the appropriate sentence,[38] are decided by majority vote (in the absence of the judge advocate).[39]

A disciplinary court martial, consisting of three officers,[40] is for the most part similar to a general court martial. It cannot, however, award a punishment of imprisonment of two years or more[41] and cannot try officers above the rank of major.[42]

The little-used special general court martial can try (as can a general court martial) civilians subject to military jurisdiction. The trial is conducted by a judge who is a judge of a superior court in Canada or is a barrister or advocate of at least 10 years' standing.[43]

Finally, in a standing court martial,[44] the accused is tried by a military judge alone; as in a disciplinary court martial, the judge cannot sentence an accused to two years or more.[45] Standing courts martial are by far the most commonly used form of courts martial, as the following statistics show:

Year	Total	GCsM	SCsM	DCsM	SGCsM
1988	95	4	67	10	14
1989	96	2	65	17	12
1990	72	4	35	23	10
1991	72	4	38	19	10
1992	59	6	43	10	0
Total	**394**	**20**	**248**	**79**	**46**[46]

Summary proceedings are of three types: those conducted by the commanding officer, by a superior commander, and by a delegated officer. In brief, a commanding officer can try persons below the rank of warrant officer as well as officer cadets.[47] Warrant officers and officers (below the rank of lieutenant-colonel) can be tried summarily only by an officer referred to as a "superior commander".[48] More senior officers (lieutenant-colonel and above) cannot be tried summarily and must be proceeded against by court martial.[49] Civilians cannot be tried by a summary trial.[50]

A superior commander can issue a reprimand and a fine equal to 60 per cent of the officer's monthly basic pay.[51] A commanding officer has wider powers of punishment. Among other punishments, for example, sergeants down to privates can be sentenced to 90 days' detention, be given a fine equal to 60 per cent of the member's monthly basic pay, and be reduced in rank. In addition, privates can be given 14 days' extra work and drill and 21 days' confinement to ship or barracks.[52] If more than 30 days' detention is given to a private or any detention to a person above the rank of private, approval of the sentence by a higher authority is required.[53]

The accused tried by a commanding officer or superior commander[54] has the right to elect a court martial in certain circumstances. In the case of trial by a commanding officer, the accused has the right of election when tried for a listed offence or when "the commanding officer concludes that if the accused were found guilty a punishment of detention, reduction in rank or a fine in excess of $200 would be appropriate."[55] The list includes a number of serious military offences, as well as civil offences that can be tried by service tribunals under section 130 of the *National Defence Act*.[56] The accused is then given not less than 24 hours to decide whether to elect to be tried by court martial.[57] The accused is entitled to the assistance of a non-legal assisting officer[58] appointed under the authority of the commanding officer[59] and may, at the discretion of the commanding officer, have legal counsel.[60] The assisting officer explains to the accused the following differences between a summary trial and a court martial: a court martial has greater powers of punishment; the accused has the right to legal counsel at a court martial; the military rules of evidence apply at a court martial; and, unlike a summary trial, there is a right of appeal from a court martial.[61] The commanding officer must, as in a court martial, find that the charge "has been proven beyond a reasonable doubt" before convicting.[62] If the CO finds that the powers of punishment are inadequate, the case can be stopped and sent to court martial.[63]

The third type of summary trial is by a "delegated officer,"[64] that is, an officer to whom a commanding officer has delegated some powers of punishment within the limits prescribed in the *National Defence Act* and the QR&Os. A delegated officer (who must hold the rank of captain or above) can try summarily members below the rank of warrant officer.[65] Punishments that can be imposed are limited to a reprimand, a fine of up to $200, stoppage of leave for 30 days, and, for privates, confinement to ship or barracks for 14 days and extra work and drill not exceeding 2 hours a day for 7 days. The accused is not entitled to elect another method of trial[66] but is entitled to an assisting officer.[67] The delegated officer is precluded from hearing the case if the delegated officer considers his or her "powers of punishment to be inadequate having regard to the gravity of the alleged offence";[68] nor can a delegated officer try an accused for any offence for which an election would have been required if tried by a commanding officer.[69]

U.S. MILITARY JUSTICE

The U.S. military justice system is fairly similar to the Canadian one. Although the terminology differs, there are three types of courts martial.[70] The general court martial, like the Canadian general court martial, can be used to try anyone subject to military discipline and impose a penalty of death. It is composed of at least five members but at the request of the accused can be composed of a military judge alone.[71] A special court martial is like the Canadian disciplinary court martial in that it is composed of at least three members (but like the general court martial the court can consist of a military judge alone at the request of the accused) and has a limited jurisdiction to punish. The U.S. special court martial can impose confinement at hard labour for six months.[72] Finally, the summary court martial is like the Canadian summary trial by a commanding officer. The accused is tried by a commissioned officer, who may be (but need not be) a lawyer, and is not assigned a military lawyer, although he may have a civilian one at his or her own expense. The maximum punishment that can be imposed includes confinement at hard labour for one month and forfeiture of two thirds of one month's pay. Despite the limited power to punish, a summary court martial can theoretically be used to try any offence except one punishable by death.[73]

Another type of summary disciplinary proceedings in the U.S. system is the Article 15 proceeding, referred to as non-judicial punishment, which is conducted by the commanding officer or his or her delegate. The possible punishments vary with the status of the officer trying the case and the accused. A major, for example, can impose correctional custody of 30 days on persons who are not officers, whereas an officer below the rank of major has a limit of 14 days.[74] There are no specific limits on the offences that can be tried under an Article 15 proceeding, but a trial for what the statute refers to as a "serious crime" does not preclude a subsequent court martial, although any sentence imposed will be taken into account in later proceedings.[75] Legal counsel do not take part in Article 15 proceedings, although the accused may consult with a military lawyer to decide whether to elect trial by court martial.[76] There is no judicial appeal from an Article 15 proceeding, but as in Canada there is a review by a judge advocate,[77] and the accused is entitled to make a redress of grievance application to a higher authority in the chain of command.[78]

The U.S. Army has divided Article 15 proceedings into two types: those referred to as "summarized proceedings", where there can be no imprisonment (though there may be certain restrictions for 14 days), and "formal" proceedings where more severe punishments can be imposed.[79] Other differences between the two procedures include giving an accused in a "formal" proceeding 48 hours to decide whether to elect a court martial and the right to have a spokesperson, whereas only 24 hours is given in the case of summarized proceedings, and there is no right to a spokesperson at trial.[80] As in Canada, the vast majority of proceedings are under Article 15. Major Kenneth Watkin cites statistics showing that in 1989, 83,413 proceedings (more than 95 per cent of all disciplinary proceedings) were held under Article 15; of the 3,985 courts martial, 1,365 were summary courts martial.[81]

A BRIEF HISTORY OF MILITARY JUSTICE

How did we end up with the current system of military justice? Only a very brief summary will be attempted here. Much of the material that follows is drawn from Lieutenant-Colonel R.A. McDonald's very helpful 1985 article, "The Trail of Discipline: The Historical Roots of Canadian Military Law."[82]

Until the *National Defence Act* was enacted in 1950, the Canadian army and air force were governed by British military law. Parliament had enacted the *Naval Service Act* in 1944,[83] which included provisions on naval discipline, but as McDonald observed, "almost all of the provisions relating to discipline were merely the British provisions with a coating of Canadian terminology."[84] Each of the three Canadian services therefore had its own separate system of discipline before 1950, each adopting the British military law of that service.

The British army in Canada in the last century and earlier had, of course, followed British military law, and the Canadian militia, under the *Canadian Militia Act* of 1868, did the same. Like the present reserves, members of the militia were, in general, subject to military discipline while on duty or in uniform.[85] When a Canadian "permanent force"[86] replaced British troops in Canada, it was natural to continue using British military law. During the First World War, Canadian air force personnel flew with the British air force or navy. The British air force had adopted the army system of discipline with certain changes in terminology.[87] The RCAF was established in 1924 (although it was not given statutory status until 1940).[88] Like the Canadian army, it used British military law until the *National Defence Act* of 1950. The Canadian navy, established in 1910,[89] also adopted British naval law.[90]

The British navy — and therefore the Canadian navy — was governed by the British *Naval Discipline Act* of 1866.[91] It punished certain specified acts and "any other Criminal Offence punishable by the Laws of England."[92] A legislative code of discipline for the navy had been enacted much earlier, in 1661.[93] It applied initially to those on board ships but was later extended to crews on shore.[94] The 1661 act provided for courts martial involving five captains when death was a possible punishment, but a ship's captain also had considerable authority over "All other Faults, Misdemeanours and Disorders committed at Sea, not mentioned in this Act."[95]

Unlike the case of the navy, there was always considerable fear of having a standing army in England. In the seventeenth century, the civil war had established that there could be no standing army without the consent of Parliament.[96] The first *Mutiny Act*, passed in 1689,[97] provided for disciplining troops stationed in England; before this, troops could be punished only by the civilian courts. The act was made necessary by the mutiny of troops loyal to the deposed James II rather than to the new King, William of Orange.[98] Re-enacted every year until 1879, the law provided that "Soldiers who shall Mutiny or Stirr up Sedition, or shall desert Their Majesty's Service be brought to a more exemplary and speedy Punishment than the usual Forms of Law will allow."

After 1689, therefore, the ordinary criminal law was supplemented by military law, but only for mutiny, sedition, and desertion.[99] Troops abroad continued to be governed by Articles of War. In Canada, therefore, British troops and, later, the Canadian Militia were governed by a combination of Articles of War, the British *Mutiny Act*, and the British Queen's Regulations and Orders. Over the centuries, the jurisdiction of British courts martial kept expanding to cover all but a small number of very serious offences committed in England.[100]

Canada's *National Defence Act* of 1950 was designed, in part, to unify as much as possible the procedures for disciplining members of all three services.[101] Brigadier W. J. Lawson, then Judge Advocate General of the Canadian Forces, stated in an article in 1951: "The *National Defence Act* is an attempt to amalgamate in one statute all legislation relating to the Canadian Forces and to unify in so far as possible, having regard to differing conditions of service, the fundamental organization, discipline and administration of the three armed services."[102] In addition, it was part of a move, also undertaken in countries like the United States, to improve the system of military justice. As one commentator recently stated with respect to the United States:

Approximately two million courts-martial were convened during World War II — about one for every eight service members. Nearly everyone who served in World War II was exposed to the military justice system. This exposure resulted in a call for reform of the military justice system, which culminated in the enactment of the Uniform Code of Military Justice in 1950.[103]

The original drafts of the *National Defence Act* maintained many of the differences between the services, but the political process produced virtually one code of service discipline,[104] even though administration of the code was still handled by the individual service in which the member was enrolled.

One major change brought about by the 1950 act was to increase the authority of commanding officers to award more serious penalties to persons tried summarily. Before the 1950 act, a commanding officer in the army or air force could sentence a person to only 28 days' imprisonment.[105] A naval commanding officer, by contrast, could sentence a person to imprisonment for three calendar months. The new act adopted the naval approach, allowing the imposition of 90 days' detention by commanding officers in all three services. There was apparently a desire to increase the potential penalties because of the number of courts martial that had been required during the war.[106] The act said nothing, however, about giving the accused the right to elect trial by court martial, even though Britain's *Army Act* gave the member this right when a minor punishment was awarded.[107]

The Canadian act also provided, as the British law did, for a summary trial by a delegated officer, but this was only for punishments of a fine not exceeding $10, a reprimand, or minor punishment.[108] In 1952, the power of the delegated officer was increased to provide for up to 14 days' detention and a severe reprimand.[109] The 1950 Act also provided, for the first time, for a right of appeal by the accused to the civilian Court Martial Appeal Board, as it was then called.[110] "It was then thought," states Janet Walker, "that civilian appellate review was the key to ensuring standards of fairness in military courts commensurate with those of civilian tribunals."[111]

THE *CANADIAN CHARTER OF RIGHTS AND FREEDOMS*

The *Canadian Charter of Rights and Freedoms* has had a very significant impact on Canadian military justice — for the most part by forcing anticipatory changes by the military.

The 1960 Bill of Rights, by contrast, had virtually no impact on the military. The courts martial system in place at that time was upheld by the Supreme Court of Canada in *MacKay* in 1980 — the only military case involving the Bill of Rights to reach the Supreme Court.[112] Three other cases involving the Bill of Rights were dealt with by the Court Martial Appeal Court,[113] but, as with *MacKay*, none resulted in a change of law or practice.

Military justice is dealt with in only one section of the Charter.[114] Section 11(f), which provides for trial by jury when there is a possibility of imprisonment for five years or more, is preceded by the words "except in the case of an offence under military law tried before a military tribunal." In the recent Court Martial Appeal Court case, *Brown*, it was argued that paragraph 11(f) "must be narrowly construed so as to restrict [the exception] to cases which must, of necessity, be tried by a Court Martial, i.e., cases in which no civilian court in Canada has jurisdiction and the exigencies of military service require that the trial take place outside of Canada."[115] The Court Martial Appeal Court rejected the argument, and the Supreme Court of Canada refused leave to appeal.[116]

It seems that the military had sought a general exemption from the Charter, but this was resisted by the Department of Justice.[117] The Charter applies to military discipline, although not always in the same way as it applies to civilian criminal proceedings.[118] The military set up a Charter Working Group to examine what changes would be required to pass Charter scrutiny.[119]

The Charter Working Group introduced changes in the QR&Os in late 1982 and early 1983[120] and proposed amendments to the *National Defence Act* that were enacted in 1985[121] and came into effect, along with amended QR&Os, in 1986.[122] The 1982-83 amendments to the QR&Os dealt with a number of topics. An accused who was to be tried summarily by a commandingofficer would now have the right to elect a court martial in all cases where the CO was of the opinion that detention, reduction in rank, or a fine in excess of $200 would be appropriate.[123] In the 1950 *National Defence Act*, no such election was mentioned, even though 90 days' detention was permitted. In 1959, however, the act had been amended to confer the right of election when an accused was tried for a military offence that was also a *Criminal Code* offence. Apparently this was done in anticipation of the enactment of the Bill of Rights.[124]

A further change to the QR&Os was to remove the authority of the delegated officer to award detention.[125] In 1952, it will be recalled, the delegated officer had been given the power to award 14 days' detention.[126]

There were other changes to the summary trial procedure, such as providing for an adjournment to permit the accused to prepare a defence.[127] And there were changes in the pre-trial procedures, such as giving the accused a copy of the charge report specifying the alleged offence before trial.[128]

In 1985, a federal omnibus government bill was enacted dealing with potential Charter conflicts in a large number of areas, including the military.[129] The Minister of Justice, John Crosbie, stated in the House:

It was the decision of our Liberal predecessors, with which I agree, that the statutes should be reviewed based on the assumption that it was preferable to change questionable legislation rather than leave it to individual litigants to assert their rights in court. That involves costs, delay and hardships. So where it is clear that legislation is questionable, we are now changing it so it does not have to be challenged in court.[130]

Changes were made in many areas to bring the military justice process closer to the ordinary criminal process. Amendments to the *National Defence Act* required that a warrant to search be based on reasonable, rather than suspicious grounds.[131] There were new provisions relating to arrest,[132] bail pending trial,[133] and appeal.[134] A section was introduced stating that "All rules and principles from time to time followed in the civil courts that would render any circumstance a justification or excuse for any act or omission or a defence to any charge are applicable in any proceedings under the Code of Service Discipline."[135] Further, a section of the *National Defence Act* permitting differential punishments for women was repealed.[136]

The QR&Os and CFAOs were changed to reflect the changes in the act, and at the same time some additional rights were given to the accused. For example, chapter 108 of the QR&Os relating to summary trials was amended to give the accused "the right to be represented at a summary trial by an assisting officer"[137] as well as the possibility, if the officer conducting the hearing so decided, to be represented by legal counsel.[138] "I am satisfied," wrote General P.D. Manson, Chief of Defence Staff, in 1986 in a Notice of Amendments to the QR&Os, "that the amendments...represent the best balance that could be achieved between the Charter rights of individuals and the need to maintain operational effectiveness of the CF."[139]

Double Jeopardy

Another important change in the 1985 amendments to the *National Defence Act* related to double jeopardy. This was brought about by section 11(h) of the Charter: "Any person charged with an offence has the right...if finally acquitted and punished for the offence, not to be tried or punished for it again." Whereas the previous double jeopardy provisions in the *National Defence Act* applied only to a subsequent trial by a service tribunal,[140] the new section provides that a person who has been found guilty "and has been punished" or found not guilty or who has had the charge dismissed by a service tribunal "may not be tried or tried again in respect of that offence or any other substantially similar offence arising out of the facts that give rise to the offence."[141]

The double jeopardy section is therefore very wide. Service tribunals include summary trials before a commanding officer or delegated officer,[142] and the double jeopardy bar operates after a dismissal by a commanding officer before a trial "where, after investigation, a commanding officer considers that a charge should not be proceeded with."[143] Unlike courts martial, there is no appeal by the prosecutor from a decision in a summary proceeding.[144] The section therefore goes further — too far, in my opinion — than the U.S. army's Article 15, which does not bar a further military proceeding for a "serious crime" (see discussion earlier in the chapter), although in other respects it is in line with the U.S. common law rule, enunciated by the U.S. Supreme Court in 1907 in *Grafton*,[145] that a military trial would bar a later prosecution at least in the federal courts.[146] It is arguable that a similar common law double jeopardy rule applied in Canada, even without the new legislation.[147]

Military personnel in Canada are still subject to civilian law. The *National Defence Act* has always stated that "nothing in the Code of Service Discipline affects the jurisdiction of any civil court to try a person for any offence triable by that court."[148] There is usually consultation between military and civilian police or prosecutors to determine who should try the accused. Kenneth Watkin writes:

While theoretically such overlapping has the potential to create a problem, in practice, conflict is avoided by liaison between the civilian and military authorities. In addition, policies are in place that require certain offences, such as impaired driving, to be dealt with by the civilian criminal justice system... Similarly, jurisdiction is often waived by civilian authorities in order to allow the military to commence disciplinary action.[149]

The interesting question is what happens when military and civil authorities both insist on trying the accused. Who should have primary jurisdiction? Should the race be to the swift? As stated in a recent Australian case, "a competition to be first to exercise jurisdiction would be unseemly, to say the least."[150] If there is a true conflict in the sense that both military and civilian authorities wish to try the accused, the civil authorities should have the power to proceed, whatever the military chooses to do. Civilian courts should have primary jurisdiction, if civilian authorities choose to exercise it, over criminal law offences committed in Canada, although not those committed abroad. A necessary result of asserting that the civilian authority is paramount is to disregard a prior military judgement if, but only if, military jurisdiction was assumed without the express or implied consent of civilian authorities.[151] A civilian tribunal in such a case would, of course, take into account any punishment already imposed. It is possible that civilian courts would construe the new section 66 in this manner and prevent the application of a double jeopardy bar where civilian authorities expressed a desire to try the accused for a criminal offence committed in Canada. In my opinion, the *National Defence Act* should be amended to state this clearly.

Independent Tribunals

As we saw earlier, the Supreme Court of Canada upheld the concept of a separate system of military justice in the 1992 case, *Généreux*. Although the Court allowed Généreux's appeal on the basis that the general court martial that had tried him was not an independent tribunal within the meaning of section 11(d) of the Charter, as interpreted in *Valente*,[152] the Court indicated that steps taken subsequently to make the tribunal more independent had "gone a considerable way towards addressing the concerns"[153] expressed by the Court.

The QR&Os had been changed after the 1990 Court Martial Appeal Court case, *Ingebrigtson*, in which the court held that the single-judge standing court martial was not an independent tribunal. The court stated that the QR&Os in effect at the time did not "expressly insulate presidents of Standing Courts Martial from the incidence of command influence or direction incompatible with their judicial independence."[154] The court pointed to defects in security of tenure and financial security and went on to say:

Given the present statutory framework which...could accommodate a truly independent Judge Advocate General, it may be that appropriate amendment of the QR&Os could achieve the measure of judicial independence constitutionally required to preserve a desirable judicial institution.[155]

The military decided to accept the *Ingebrigtson* decision, and the suggested changes to the QR&Os were made by the cabinet and the minister. This was done not only so that standing courts martial could continue to operate, but also because the *Généreux* case was about to be heard by the Supreme Court of Canada, and such changes would indicate to the Supreme Court that the military was willing to make adjustments to preserve a separate system of military justice.[156] The changes were also made, writes Janet Walker, because "the Legal Branch of the Canadian Forces wished to improve the procedural fairness of courts martial so they could be compared favourably with the ordinary courts."[157]

The general court martial's finding of guilt in *Généreux* had, in fact, been upheld by the Court Martial Appeal Court[158] before its decision in *Ingebrigtson*. The *Ingebrigtson* decision noted that general and disciplinary courts martial "are the traditional types of courts martial which evolved in the British Army over centuries", whereas standing courts martial were not introduced until 1944 and at first had very limited jurisdiction. The standing courts martial were thus accorded far less deference by the appeal court than general courts martial. Chief Justice Mahoney went so far as to state: "Whether they can, as a matter of fact, be characterized as integral to the otherwise 'long established tradition' of a separate system of military law and tribunals is, in my respectful opinion, most dubious."[159]

Amendments to the QR&Os following *Ingebrigtson* applied to all types of courts martial, not just standing courts martial.[160] The QR&OS, for example, provided for a fixed term for military trial judges of normally four but not less than two years. They also required that military judges not perform any other duties during that term, placed restrictions on terminating a judge's appointment, and provided that the chief military trial judge, not the judge advocate general, has formal authority to appoint a judge advocate at a court martial.[161] In relation to financial security, the QR&Os provided for the elimination of the consideration of judicial performance in deciding an advancement or pay.[162]

The Supreme Court held in *Généreux* that the regulations existing at the time of the court martial violated all three requirements of judicial independence set out in *Valente*. The Court noted that the amendments to the QR&Os had corrected the deficiencies with respect to security of tenure and financial security, but further changes were required in relation to "institutional independence", the third requirement set out in *Valente*. Chief Justice Lamer pointed to one specific area of concern:

The convening authority appoints the president and other members of the General Court Martial and decides how many members there shall be in a particular case. The convening authority, or an officer designated by the convening authority, also appoints, with the concurrence of the Judge Advocate General, the prosecutor (s. 111.23, Q.R. & O.). This fact further undermines the institutional independence of the General Court Martial. It is not acceptable, in my opinion, that the convening authority, *i.e.*, the executive, who is responsible for appointing the prosecutor, also have the authority to appoint members of the court martial, who serve as the triers of fact. At a minimum, I consider that where the same representative of the executive, the 'convening authority', appoints both the prosecutor and the triers of fact, the requirements of s. 11(*d*) will not be met.[163]

Following the *Généreux* decision, further changes were therefore made to the *National Defence Act* and the QR&Os. There was some urgency. On second reading of the act in May 1992, the government spokesperson stated: "Since the decision of the Supreme Court in mid-February it has been impossible to hold trials either by general or disciplinary court martial. The Canadian forces have therefore been deprived of the use of these essential tools in our disciplinary system, and not surprisingly a backlog of cases has built up and continues to build."[164] The Somalia Inquiry may wish to explore whether this gap in discipline six months before troops left for Somalia may have contributed in some small way to problems encountered later.

The amendments make it clear, as the Supreme Court required, that the person who convenes a court martial must not be the person who appoints its president and members.[165] QR&O 111.051 expands on the procedures by providing that it is the chief military trial judge who appoints the president and members of the court martial and does so "using random methodology."[166] Further, a CFAO now states that "The Chief Military Trial Judge is, by law, independent in the performance of his/her duty" and that legal officers who are "posted to military trial judge positions" are not "directly responsible to the JAG for the performance of their duties."[167] The amendments to the *National Defence Act*, the QR&Os and the CFAOs have produced a much improved system of military justice.

The United Kingdom appears to have gone further in some respects and not as far in other respects in ensuring independence. The judge advocates at courts martial are appointed by a completely independent civilian judge advocate general, who is in turn appointed by the Lord Chancellor and holds office until age 70. As with other civilian judges, the judge advocate general is removable for only inability and misbehaviour. The various judge advocates are also civilian barristers or advocates and also hold office during good behaviour.[168]

On the other hand, the U.K. does not provide a random method of selection of members of courts martial, and it is the convening officer who selects the president and members of the tribunal.[169] Although there are restrictions on who can be a member of a court martial — for example, a person who investigated the charge or held an inquiry into the subject matter of the charge cannot sit[170] — the convening officer still has considerable influence in shaping the tribunal. One civilian lawyer with experience in courts martial work recently denounced the U.K. system in an article:

The most glaring of this myriad of breaches [of human rights] is the failure to separate the prosecuting arm from the court itself so that the prosecution and the defence are on equal footing in compliance with the doctrine of 'equality of arms'. An army court martial is set up by the 'convening officer'. The convening officer is also the prosecuting authority. The convening officer selects the members of the court, commands them during the existence of the court, is even responsible for appointing part or all of the defence team.[171]

He referred to a 1992 Divisional Court case, *Ex parte Findlay*, in which "the five officers appointed by the convening officer to the board trying the case had been drawn from units within the convening officer's own command and were therefore the direct subordinates of the prosecuting authority." The appeal by the accused to the Divisional Court was dismissed, but the case was taken to the European Court of Human Rights.

In December 1995 the European Commission of Human Rights found that the U.K. procedures breached article 6(1) of the European Convention of Human Rights, which guarantees a "fair and public hearing before an independent and impartial tribunal."[172] The matter now goes before the full European Court of Human Rights, which is likely to hear the case in the fall of 1996. The British government is expected to make a vigorous defence of the present system.[173] Previous decisions have held that the European Convention applies to military disciplinary tribunals,[174] and it appears likely that the court will agree with the unanimous 17-person view of the commission that the present U.K. procedures breach the convention. In the meantime, a number of changes are being proposed to the U.K. Armed Forces law as part of the regular five-year review of the act. Whether these changes will meet the requirements of the convention remains to be seen.

Command influence, as it is usually called in the United States, continues to be a major concern for the U.S. military. The U.S. Court of Military Appeals has referred to unlawful command influence as "the mortal enemy of military justice."[175] A leading writer on military justice states that "despite prohibitions in the Uniform Code of Military Justice and strong admonitions in case law, unlawful command influence has remained a perpetual problem." The author goes on to state:

While most commanders are sensitive enough to the problem to avoid open attempts to influence a court-martial, it is more common for well-intended commanders, or members of their staff, to make passing comments on the merits of past or pending cases. Pragmatically, no matter how well intentioned or careful the commander or staff officers might be, such comments can be interpreted by subordinates as a 'command' or 'desire' for a particular result.[176]

As in the U.K., the convening officer selects the members of the court martial. Although there are some restrictions — for example, an investigating officer cannot be selected — the statute gives the convening officer the authority to select "such members of the armed forces as, in his opinion, are best qualified for the duty by reason of age, education, training, experience, length of service, and judicial temperament."[177] There is no random selection of members, as is now required in Canada. There are, however, a number of appeal cases stating that selection of court members to secure a more favourable result to the prosecution amounts to unlawful and punishable command influence.[178] Article 37(a) of the Uniform Code of Military Justice states that no person "may attempt to coerce or, by any unauthorized means, influence the action of a court-martial or any other military tribunal or any member thereof."[179]

Another issue that has been widely debated in the United States is whether there should be fixed terms for military judges. Military judges are officers who are members of a bar who have been certified by the judge advocate general of their branch to conduct courts martial and are assigned by the judge advocate general to specific hearings. There are about 75 judges certified for general courts martial. While serving as judges they may, with the permission of the judge advocate general, engage in other tasks unrelated to their judicial duties.[180] The U.S. Supreme Court recently rejected the fixed term as a constitutional requirement under the Fifth Amendment's due process clause. Chief Justice Rehnquist, giving the judgement for the Court in *Weiss*,[181] referred to the great judicial deference traditionally accorded by the courts to Congress with respect to military matters,[182] the fact that courts martial "have been conducted [in the United States] for over 200 years without the presence of a tenured judge, and for over 150 years without the presence of any judge at all,"[183] and the fact that "the applicable provisions of the UCMJ, and corresponding regulations, by insulating military judges from the effects of command influence, sufficiently preserve judicial impartiality so as to satisfy the Due Process Clause."[184] The Court referred, *inter alia*, to Article 37, quoted above; Article 26, which places military judges under the authority of the appropriate judge advocate general, rather than under the authority of the convening officer,[185] and allows the accused to challenge both a court martial member and a court martial judge for cause; and the fact that the entire system "is overseen by the Court of Military Appeals, which is composed entirely of civilian judges who serve for fixed terms of 15 years."[186]

David Schlueter, author of *Military Criminal Justice*, believes that fixed terms for judges would be "both difficult to implement and largely unnecessary" and suggests that "perhaps the best answer rests not in drastically reforming the structure of the system, but in enforcing those rules and laws which currently proscribe command influence and in ensuring careful appellate review."[187]

F.A. Gilligan and F.I. Lederer, authors of another leading text, *Court-Martial Procedure*, take the position that "the sole solution is the creation of an independent full-time judiciary whose future is not subject to evaluation on traditional military lines." The "real problem," they state, "is command control of the judiciary. So long as the judge knows that his or her future is in the hands of those who have non-judicial interests, both the perception and the reality of possible tampering will exist."[188] They do not expand on the concept, but presumably the judges would be selected from military trial lawyers toward the end of their military careers.

The term "command influence" in Canada is usually reserved for pre-trial proceedings.[189] The military brief to the Somalia Inquiry on military justice states (p. 3): "Custom and practice, amplified by appellate court decisions, provide that in disciplinary matters the decision of a commanding officer to proceed or not to proceed with charges must be taken without interference or influence from any superior." Major G. Herfst expanded on the concept in the oral presentation, stating:

While it would not be necessarily command influence, if a commanding officer were to seek advice from his superiors on how to deal with certain types of cases providing that he or she preserves to him or herself the prerogative of making the ultimate decision in a particular case, it would be command influence if the superior prevailed upon the commanding officer and the commanding officer felt compelled to act upon the wishes or instructions of that superior.

As it was put in the leading case on command influence by Noël, the Acting Chief Justice, in *Nye v. The Queen*, a 1972 case from the Court Martial Appeal Court, at page 93 — and I quote, "a commanding officer must always be able to discharge his duties in the judicial process with quiet and impartial objectivity."[190]

In summary trials in Canada it is difficult, if not impossible, to avoid at least the appearance of command influence (using the term as the Americans use it) because it is the commander (or his or her delegate) who makes the decision. An attempt was made to cut down on extreme conflicts of interest in such cases by amending the *National Defence Act* in 1985:

163(1.1) Unless it is not practical, having regard to all the circumstances, for any other commanding officer to conduct the summary trial, a commanding officer may not preside at the summary trial of any person charged with an offence where
(a) the commanding officer carried out or directly supervised the investigation of that offence; or
(b) the summary trial relates to an offence in respect of which a warrant was issued pursuant to section 273.3 by the commanding officer.[191]

The real solution here is to make sure that the accused has a genuine, fully informed election — a matter examined in more detail later.

Military Nexus

One issue of continuing interest in Canada is whether there has to be a "military nexus" between an alleged offence and the need to exercise military discipline. The requirement for a military nexus was first discussed in Canadian courts in the 1980 Supreme Court decision by Justice McIntyre (Justice Dickson concurring) in *MacKay*. Their judgement was a concurring one, not the judgement of the Court, which was delivered by Justice Ritchie (four other members of the court concurring) and did not mention the need for a service connection. Justice McIntyre stated:

Section 2 of the *National Defence Act* defines a service offence as "an offence under this Act, the *Criminal Code*, or any other Act of the Parliament of Canada, committed by a person while subject to the *Code of Service Discipline*." The Act also provides that such offences will be tryable and punishable under military law. If we are to apply the definition of service offence literally, then all prosecutions of servicemen for any offence under any penal statute of Canada could be conducted in military courts... Our problem is one of defining the limits of their jurisdiction...

The question then arises: how is a line to be drawn separating the service-related or military offence from the offence which has no necessary connection with the service? In my view, an offence which would be an offence at civil law, when committed by a civilian, is as well an offence falling within the jurisdiction of the courts martial and within the purview of military law when committed by a serviceman if such offence is so connected with the service in its nature, and in the circumstances of its commission, that it would tend to affect the general standard of discipline and efficiency of the service. I do not consider it wise or possible to catalogue the offences which could fall into this category or try to describe them in their precise nature and detail. The question of jurisdiction to deal with such offences would have to be determined on a case-by-case basis.[192]

Justice McIntyre observed that "this approach has been taken in American courts where a possible conflict of jurisdiction had arisen between the military tribunals and the civil Courts."[193]

The U.S. Supreme Court had, over the years, been limiting the jurisdiction of military tribunals, rejecting the continuing exercise of military jurisdiction over honourably discharged servicemen for offences committed while in the military,[194] over families accompanying those serving abroad,[195] and over civilians serving abroad.[196] In 1969, in *O'Callahan* v. *Parker*, the court went much further and limited jurisdiction over active service personnel by requiring that to fall under military jurisdiction, the alleged offence "must be service connected." Justice Douglas wrote on behalf of the court that "history teaches that expansion of military discipline beyond its proper domain carries with it a threat to liberty." He did not think much of military justice, stating that "courts-martial as an institution are singularly inept in dealing with the nice subtleties of constitutional law" and that "a military trial is marked by the age-old manifest destiny of retributive justice."[197] The *O'Callahan* approach required a case-by-case determination, guided by a list of 12 factors developed in a later Supreme Court case.[198]

This approach was eventually rejected, however, in the court's 1987 decision in *Solorio*, where the court held that the jurisdiction of a court martial depends solely on the accused's status as a member of the armed forces and not on the "service connection" of the offence charged. Chief Justice Rehnquist, writing for the majority of the court, referred to the "doubtful foundations" of the *O'Callahan* test, the "time and energy...expended in litigation", and "the confusion created by the complexity of the service connection requirement."[199] In addition, as we saw in the discussion of the *Weiss* case, the court is now prepared to give great judicial deference to Congress in the area of military justice.[200] One of the main reasons for this — the change in the composition of the court is, of course, another — is the improvement in military justice procedures since *O'Callahan* was decided in the late 1960s. As Janet Walker rightly observes, "When military justice was viewed as unduly harsh or objectionable, its jurisdiction was construed narrowly, and when it met current standards, civilian courts refrained from interference through a generous construction of court martial jurisdiction."[201]

The Canadian Court Martial Appeal Court has continued to follow the *O'Callahan* approach, however, which was adopted by Justice McIntyre in *MacKay*. Why the court chose Justice McIntyre's opinion, rather than Justice Ritchie's majority approach, which did not involve a service connection test, is not clear. Perhaps the compromise position between Justice Ritchie's permissive approach and the strong dissent of Chief Justice Laskin and Justice Estey, denying military jurisdiction for civilian offences, was attractive,[202] particularly considering that Justice McIntyre and Justice Dickson had both had distinguished military careers.

A number of Court Martial Appeal Court cases have required a service connection.[203] The court has not been reluctant, however, to find a service connection. In *Ionson* (1987), the accused seaman was convicted of possession of cocaine by a standing court martial, and the majority of the Court Martial Appeal Court held that there was a service connection, even though the accused was in civilian dress at the time of the offence, off duty, away from a military establishment, and not involved with any other military members.[204] Ionson's appeal to the Supreme Court of Canada was dismissed on the grounds that the majority of the Court Martial Appeal Court had not erred.[205] The most recent decision was that of the Court Martial Appeal Court in *Brown*, arising out of the Somalia affair.[206] In rejecting the appeal, however, Justice Huggesen stated for the court that "It is now well settled that the exception to the guarantee of the right to a jury trial in paragraph 11(f) is triggered by the existence of a military nexus with the crime charged."[207] There was, of course, as the appellant conceded, a clear military nexus in the case.[208] The Supreme Court of Canada refused leave to appeal.[209]

Is the military nexus requirement still part of Canadian law? The military brief to the Somalia Inquiry mentions its continuing existence, referring to the

common law rule known as the doctrine of "military nexus" [which] operates to limit jurisdiction in certain cases... The doctrine may be applied in cases of serving members where the commission of the offence bears little or no connection with military duties, such as where an accused commits a drinking and driving offence during off-duty hours without the presence of any indicia of military service.[210]

It is not clear, however, whether the brief is referring to cases where the military would not normally claim jurisdiction, or to cases where they could not constitutionally exercise jurisdiction. The oral presentation suggests the former. Major Herfst states:

Thus, except in those cases involving what might be called purely military offences such as operational offences or offences like absence without leave, a determination is made regarding who will take jurisdiction in the case. The factors affecting such a decision and the test, if I might put it that way, applied in such circumstances is whether the accused's avoidance of punishment by a service tribunal will adversely affect the general standard of discipline and efficiency of the Canadian Forces.[211]

The *National Defence Act* does not mention a service connection requirement, and section 60(2) of the act provides that a person who commits an offence while subject to service discipline shall "continue to be liable to be charged" for a three-year period after the offence, notwithstanding that the person may have ceased to be subject to military discipline.[212] A note to QR&O 102.01 states, however,

Judicial interpretation of subsection 60(2) of the *National Defence Act*, taken with subsections 69(1), restricts the exercise of jurisdiction of service tribunals over a person who was subject to the Code of Service Discipline at the time of the alleged commission of a service offence to cases where it can be demonstrated that:

(i) trial by a service tribunal is dictated by disciplinary considerations essential to the maintenance of the morale and readiness of those remaining in the Service; and

(ii) not to exercise jurisdiction will adversely affect the general standard of discipline and efficiency of the service.

The *Généreux* decision did not deal with the issue, even though the question of jurisdiction was discussed in the factums and the charge of trafficking in narcotics off the base lent itself to a discussion of the issue.[213] One is tempted to agree with Janet Walker, who claims in a 1993 article that the military nexus doctrine is now a thing of the past.[214] While this is probably so for those tried while still members of the military, the doctrine may still have relevance with respect to persons who are no longer members of the military[215] and possibly to civilians working with the military abroad and to families accompanying members of the military overseas.[216] As for serving members, the better solution would be to give the military courts concurrent jurisdiction to proceed whenever the accused is still a member of the military and to let civil and military authorities work out who should prosecute.[217] As stated earlier, if they cannot resolve the issue of who should exercise jurisdiction, primary jurisdiction should be with civil authorities. We will have to see how the courts resolve the military nexus issue.

Summary Proceedings

The major issue facing military justice in Canada is whether summary proceedings can withstand a Charter challenge. As described earlier, there are three types of summary proceedings: those conducted by a commanding officer; those by a superior commander; and those by a delegated officer.

There is no question that summary proceedings are very important to the military. The military brief to the Somalia Inquiry states that the summary trial system "provides speedy, uncomplicated proceedings."[218] Major Kenneth Watkin presents a similar view in his LL.M. thesis, "Canadian Military Justice: Summary Proceedings and the Charter," stating: "summary trials represent a part of the military justice system where particular emphasis is placed on an expeditious and uncomplicated disposal of disciplinary matters." "Summary proceedings," he notes, "are the overwhelmingly predominant and most important forum for the trial of disciplinary offences."[219] James Lockyer put the matter particularly strongly in a speech in 1993: "The summary trial process, from an operational point of view, is so fundamental to the military system that, quite possibly, a military society could not govern itself without it. It is the crucial structure upon which the discipline of military society is based."[220]

The summary procedure is so important to the military that some writers are willing to go a very long way in making changes to make it safe from a Charter challenge. James Lockyer suggests that "if the summary trial process were limited to non-criminal matters, its constitutionality and compatibility with the Charter would be confirmed."[221] He adds: "This proposed jurisdiction may be the only way to preserve the summary trial process."

Kenneth Watkin suggests a large number of changes because he believes that "challenges to the constitutionality of summary proceedings, based on the Charter, have a very good likelihood of success." His suggested changes include limiting the power of commanding officers to those civilian offences that can be dealt with summarily (including hybrid offences) under civilian law; limiting the jurisdiction of delegated officers to try service offences (they cannot now try criminal offences) to those carrying a penalty of less than two years; providing a more complete trial procedure, including rules on the admissibility of documentary evidence; giving all persons charged with a service offence, including those dealt with by a delegated officer, the right to elect court martial; making any detention ordered in a summary proceeding more remedial in nature, including "more drill and basic training associated with the development of collective discipline (recruit camp)"; and, if detention is maintained in its present form, giving persons sentenced to detention the right of appeal by way of trial *de novo* to a court martial.[222]

Steps are now being taken within the military to make changes that will help protect summary proceedings from a Charter challenge. The changes made by the military in anticipation of the Supreme Court decision in *Généreux* paid off. Similar pre-emptive action is being contemplated with respect to summary proceedings.[223]

No one can say with certainty what the Supreme Court is likely to do with respect to summary proceedings. Obviously, the more changes made in advance, the greater likelihood there is of withstanding a Charter challenge. In this writer's opinion, however, it is not advisable to go too far in making a summary proceeding into a regular trial. The Supreme Court is unlikely to demand it. It is better to provide procedures that are desirable from a military perspective and at the same time respect the rights of soldiers than to devise procedures because of fear of how the Supreme Court might rule. The Court demonstrated in *Généreux* that it is prepared to uphold a reasonable system of military justice.

The danger in making summary disciplinary proceedings too complicated is that the summary procedure may then not be used to the extent required for proper discipline or, just as undesirable, alternative illegal punishments or "barrack-room justice" will be used instead.[224] Apparently, there was an almost 50-per cent reduction in the total number of summary trials after the first changes to the QR&Os were implemented in 1983.[225] Membership in the Canadian Forces remained steady, at about 80,000, throughout the early 1980s, yet between 1982 and 1984 the number of summary trials dropped from 10,058 to 6,349. There was no increase in the number of courts martial over the period; there were 157 in 1982 and 152 in 1984.[226] There are now said to be about 4,000 summary proceedings for about 65,000 personnel, so the relative charge rate today is about half what it was in 1982. Further, between 1986 and 1991 the use of detention dropped significantly. The reduction was particularly dramatic for the three regiments contributing personnel to the Airborne Regiment. In the Princess Patricia's Canadian Light Infantry, for example, from which 2 Commando was drawn, the number of detention days per 1,000 personnel dropped from 649 in 1986 to 85 in 1991. These decreases in charges and rates of detention were occurring at the same time they were rising in the civilian population.[227]

The Somalia Inquiry may wish to explore the pattern of summary proceedings at Petawawa over the years, and in particular for the Airborne Regiment, to see whether a reduction in summary proceedings and detention might have contributed to the discipline problems in that regiment. Both the Board of Inquiry and the Hewson Report suggest that a lack of summary discipline affected performance. The Board of Inquiry, for example, noted the importance of the master corporal level in discipline enforcement and the failure of the corporals to play their proper role in discipline.[228] Again, looking at the role of the corporal, the Hewson Report pointed out that a delegated officer could not confine a corporal to barracks as a method of discipline, which the delegated officer could do for a private.[229] This writer does not have the expertise to comment on these observations, except to say that jurisdiction for summary proceedings and the rules that they must follow will have an effect on discipline and, ultimately, on success in operations. The 1985 Hewson Report recommended that "the principle of accountability be reinforced by visible disciplinary action when warranted."[230] The use of detention following the Hewson Report suggests that this view was not shared by commanding officers. The Somalia Inquiry will want to explore this issue carefully.

It is difficult to believe that the delegated officer procedure is vulnerable to Charter challenge. The delegated officer has very limited jurisdiction. As we saw earlier, the punishment that can be imposed is limited to reprimands, a fine of up to $200, stoppage of leave for 30 days, and, for privates, confinement to ship or barracks for 14 days and extra work and drill not exceeding two hours a day for 7 days. The hearing officer is precluded from hearing the case if the delegated officer considers his or her "powers of punishment to be inadequate having regard to the gravity of the alleged offence" and cannot try an accused for any of the offences for which an election would have been required if tried by a commanding officer, which includes a number of military offences and all *Criminal Code* and other civilian offences.[231]

Moreover, the procedures before a delegated officer are reasonable for the type of proceeding being conducted. The accused is entitled to the help of an assisting officer, is not obliged to make any admissions, and is to receive, 24 hours before the trial, "all documentary evidence and all statements made in relation to the incident...including any statement of the accused." Further, the case must be proved beyond a reasonable doubt and, while no appeal procedure is provided, various forms of review and redress of grievance are available.[232]

Proceedings by a delegated officer would not appear to come within section 11 of the Charter, which refers to a person charged with "an offence". It is unlikely (though always possible) that the Supreme Court will hold that a hearing by a delegated officer is either "by its very nature, criminal" or that the possible sanctions are "true penal consequences,"[233] within the meaning of the language of the two leading Supreme Court of Canada cases, *Shubley* and *Wigglesworth*.[234]

In *Wigglesworth*, an RCMP disciplinary hearing for an offence punishable by a year's imprisonment was, understandably, considered to involve "a true penal consequence", although the hearing itself was not considered "by its very nature, criminal."[235] *Shubley* involved a disciplinary hearing for an inmate in a provincial correctional institution. The Court held unanimously that the hearing was not "by its very nature, criminal", and a majority of the Court held that it did not involve "true penal consequences", even though the penalty could have been close (solitary) confinement for 30 days and forfeiture of the inmate's remission.[236] The language used by Justice McLachlin suggests that the same result would follow with respect to delegated officers:

Was the prison disciplinary proceeding to which the appellant was subject, by its very nature, criminal? I conclude it was not. The appellant was not being called to account to society for a crime violating the public interest in the preliminary proceedings. Rather, he was being called to account to the prison officials for breach of his obligation as an inmate of the prison to conduct himself in accordance with prison rules.[237]

On the second branch of the test, Justice McLachlin stated:

I conclude that the sanctions conferred on the superintendent for prison misconduct do not constitute "true penal consequences" within the *Wigglesworth* test. Confined as they are to the manner in which the inmate serves his time, and involving neither punitive fines nor a sentence of imprisonment, they appear to be entirely commensurate with the goal of fostering internal prison discipline and are not of a magnitude or consequence that would be expected for redressing wrongs done to society at large.[238]

Thus, in my opinion, proceedings conducted by a delegated officer would not come within section 11 of the Charter. Indeed, the financial jurisdiction of the delegated officer could no doubt be raised to, say, a percentage of the accused's monthly pay, so long as it was not considered a "punitive fine". (One of the consequences of this approach is that there would be no *constitutional* bar to a second proceeding in the regular courts, although as we saw earlier, there is now a statutory bar.[239]) If the proceedings did come within section 11, it should surely be relatively easy to have them fit within section 1 of the Charter, which permits such "reasonable limits prescribed by law as can be demonstrably justified in a free and democratic society."[240]

The process would also have to withstand a challenge under section 7 of the Charter (the right to "life, liberty and security of the person and the right not to be deprived thereof except in accordance with the principles of fundamental justice"). Justice McLachlin stated in *Shubley*: "I agree with [Justice Wilson's] conclusion that 'it is preferable to restrict s. 11 to the most serious offences known to our law, i.e., criminal and penal matters and to leave other 'offences' subject to the more flexible criteria of 'fundamental justice' in s. 7."[241]

Section 7 is so flexible and amorphous that it is particularly difficult to predict what a court might do under that section. In the 1976 case, *Middendorf* v. *Henry*, the U.S. Supreme Court held that the Fifth Amendment's due process clause, which is comparable to section 7 of the Charter, was not violated by the lack of counsel at a summary court martial by a commanding officer, a proceeding that is a step above Article 15 hearings and for which a penalty of confinement for one month and two thirds of one month's pay can be imposed.[242] Justice Rehnquist stated for the court that the "presence of counsel will turn a brief, informal hearing which may be quickly convened and rapidly concluded into an attenuated proceeding which consumes the resources of the military to a degree...beyond what is warranted by the relative insignificance of the offenses being tried."[243]

Thus, I believe that the military can continue with the present delegated officer procedure without giving the accused an election for trial by court martial or providing legal counsel. (The accused is, however, given the help of an assisting officer, normally one selected by the accused.[244]) If an election were given, very few would take it,[245] but it would require delaying the proceedings to give time to consider whether to exercise the option and it can be argued that, at least in battle conditions, the quick and simple imposition of these very minor penalties by a delegated officer is desirable. Nevertheless, both Britain and the United States allow for the right to elect court martial in all cases, including non-punitive Article 15 proceedings.[246]

A commanding officer's authority is much greater than that of a delegated officer. Sergeants down to privates can be sentenced to 90 days' detention.[247] In *Généreux*, Chief Justice Lamer stated that "the appellant faced the possible penalty of imprisonment in this case...therefore, section 11 of the Charter would nonetheless apply by virtue of the potential imposition of true penal consequences."[248] Such a potential penalty would surely be considered true penal consequences within the meaning of *Shubley* and *Wigglesworth*,[249] even if it were possible to categorize the proceeding as not "by its very nature, criminal."[250] Thus, section 11 of the Charter is applicable, as is section 7.

The proceedings clearly breach the section 11(d) requirement that the person be tried by "an independent and impartial tribunal." The commanding officer is the person who authorized the charge and so can hardly be considered independent. The CO does not have security of tenure, financial security, or institutional independence, all required by *Valente*.[251] It is also likely that the absence of the right to legal counsel would breach the "fair hearing" part of section 11(d).[252] This does not mean, however, that the Supreme Court will necessarily strike down the procedure as contrary to the Charter. There are two ways it can be saved.

The first is a section 1 justification of the procedure as a "reasonable limit prescribed by law" that can be "demonstrably justified in a free and democratic society." This would not be easy to do because of the possible 90-day detention period. The U.S. law upheld in *Middendorf* v. *Henry* provided for only a one-month period of confinement.[253] A commanding officer below field rank in the British army can summarily award detention for only 28 days.[254] (In the nineteenth century the British commanding officer could award only 14 days' imprisonment.[255]) Further, as stated earlier, it was the *National Defence Act* of 1950 that first introduced the 90-day detention period for summary trials.[256] Before that, an army or air force commanding officer could sentence an accused to only 28 days. The special circumstances in the navy had, however, permitted a sentence of three calendar months by a commanding officer.

Thus, it is hard to argue that a "free and democratic" society requires a 90-day detention period for summary trials. If the period were reduced to, say, 30 days, there is a reasonable possibility that the court would say that the proceedings did not even come within section 11 of the Charter or violate section 7, thus not requiring a section 1 justification.[257] In any event, such a reduction would seem to make sense in the absence of any constitutional requirement. A sentence of 90 days' detention should, in this writer's opinion, require a more formal and independent tribunal, giving the accused the right to retain legal counsel. (An exception might be warranted, however, for ships at sea on lengthy manoeuvres.) It is better to concentrate on a limit to the punishment that can be awarded by the tribunal than on the maximum penalty for the offence if tried by a court martial or a civilian court. If the jurisdiction of a summary trial were controlled by the potential penalty, then a commanding officer could not try a person for disobeying an officer, which has a potential penalty of life,[258] or a minor trafficking offence,[259] which also carries a potential life penalty. Many more charges would be brought and tried by the commanding officer as a result under the less specific label "conduct to the prejudice of good order and discipline."

Summary proceedings by a commanding officer might also be upheld, because a right to elect trial by court martial is given to the accused in all cases where there are potentially serious consequences. In the case of trial by a commanding officer, the accused has the right of election when tried for a listed offence, which includes all criminal offences brought into the Code of Service Discipline under section 130 of the *National Defence Act*, or when "the commanding officer concludes that if the accused were found guilty a punishment of detention, reduction in rank or a fine in excess of $200 would be appropriate."[260] In cases where no election need be given, the analysis in the earlier discussion of the delegated officer would lead to the conclusion that the proceedings would not come within section 11 of the Charter.

If a decision by an accused not to elect trial by court martial is a genuine waiver of trial by court martial, with full knowledge of the consequences, then there is a good chance that the summary procedure would be upheld, in the same way that a waiver of trial by a guilty plea is not a violation of the Charter. Justice Lamer (as he then was) set out a test for waivers in the 1982 Supreme Court decision in *Korponey*,[261] a test that was later adopted by Justice Wilson in the 1986 decision in *Clarkson*.[262] Justice Lamer stated in *Korponey* that any waiver "is dependent upon it being *clear and unequivocal that the person is waiving the procedural safeguard and is doing so with full knowledge of the rights the procedure was enacted to protect and of the effect the waiver will have on those rights in the process.*"[263]

The U.S. Supreme Court relied on the concept of waiver in *Middendorf*, where Justice Rehnquist wrote that if the accused "feels that in order to properly air his views and vindicate his rights, a formal, counselled proceeding is necessary he may simply refuse trial by summary court-martial and proceed to trial by special court-martial at which he may have counsel." The Court referred to the waiver of trial by a guilty plea, stating:

We have frequently approved the much more difficult decision, daily faced by civilian criminal defendants, to plead guilty to a lesser included offence... In such a case the defendant gives up not only his right to counsel but his right to any trial at all. Furthermore, if he elects to exercise his right to trial he stands to be convicted of a more serious offense which will likely bear increased penalties.[264]

But can there be a true waiver without the assistance of counsel? Possibly, but the military would be on safer ground by making objective legal advice available to the accused in such cases. Justice Lamer stated in *Korponey* that a major factor in deciding whether there was an effective waiver "will be the fact that the accused is or is not represented by

Counsel."[265] The rules now provide for a 24-hour delay before an election has to be made, so that the accused can consult with an assisting officer or, at the accused's own expense, with civilian legal counsel.[266] Military duty counsel are available only if the accused is arrested or detained.[267] Why should duty counsel not be available to any person faced with a waiver who requests legal assistance whenever it is reasonable and practicable to provide such communication? Even an accused at sea in most situations could contact counsel by phone. And why should the consequences of waiving trial by court martial not be clearly set out in a form to be signed by the accused, as is done in the United States?[268]

Reducing the period of possible detention to something like 30 days aı.d providing an effective waiver of trial by court martial would, in my view, likely lead the Supreme Court of Canada to uphold summary proceedings by commanding officers, under a doctrine of waiver, under section 1 of the Charter, or under a combination of the two. A further change that could be considered is to give a member sentenced to a period of detention above a very minor amount the right to appeal by way of trial *de novo* to a court martial. Such a procedure, which would be resorted to rarely, would further strengthen the likelihood that the Supreme Court would uphold the constitutionality of summary proceedings by commanding officers.

CONCLUSION

The military justice system is a crucial part of the range of techniques available to control improper conduct in the military. The Somalia Inquiry will wish to explore whether the decline in the use of military justice in the ten years preceding the unfortunate events in Somalia may have contributed to the lack of discipline that was evident in the Canadian Airborne Regiment.

Data provided earlier in the chapter show that after the *Canadian Charter of Rights and Freedoms* was enacted in 1982, the number of summary disciplinary proceedings dropped significantly[269] and has remained relatively low compared to previous experience, even though the number of Canadian Forces members increased slightly in that period. Further, between 1986 and 1991, use of detention declined significantly. This trend is contrary to trends in the civilian criminal justice system.[270] Courts martial of Canadian Forces members in Canada and abroad were also low in 1993 compared to ten years earlier — 68 in 1993,[271] compared with 169 in 1983.[272]

It may well be that apprehension about the constitutionality of the military justice system after introduction of the Charter, together with new and more onerous regulations and statutory changes, were partly responsible for this decline in the use of the military justice system. As we saw in the discussion of the history of military justice, changes were made to the QR&Os in 1982 and 1983, extensive changes were made to the *National Defence Act* and the QR&OS in 1986, and further changes were made in 1991 and 1992, in anticipation and as a result of the *Généreux* decision. The court martial system is now reasonably secure constitutionally, following *Généreux*.

There is still considerable uncertainty, however, about the constitutional legitimacy of the summary justice system, and we are likely to see further amendments in anticipation of a possible challenge. It will certainly be good for the proper application of summary military justice to have the Supreme Court's stamp of approval on its procedures, whether in their present form or in a modified form.

The summary justice system is of great importance to the Canadian military, just as it is to all military forces. It provides a relatively quick, easily understood, non-legalistic, and reasonably fair system of imposing minor penalties on military personnel. Two changes in the system were recommended; if these were introduced, in this writer's opinion, the system would likely be upheld by the Supreme Court of Canada. Indeed, even without the changes, there is some reasonable chance that it would be found not to violate the Charter or would be upheld under section 1. The changes recommended are, first, that persons being tried summarily who must be asked whether they wish to elect trial by court martial be given the opportunity to consult with a military lawyer (or with a civilian lawyer at their own expense) before making the choice, and, second, that the authority of a commanding officer to award 90 days' detention be reduced to about 30 days. A person arrested or detained before trial now has the right to consult with military duty counsel, but a person subject to a summary trial that might result in a period of detention does not. This does not mean that counsel should take part in a summary proceeding, but rather that the accused be able to consult with counsel before the proceeding. A third change that could be considered is to permit a member sentenced to detention above a certain level by a commanding officer to have a new trial by court martial as of right. If these changes were made, it is very likely that the Supreme Court of Canada would uphold the procedures on the basis of waiver of rights, or because summary proceedings did not come within section 11, or, if they did violate the Charter, that they are a reasonable limit on rights under section 1.

The chapter also discussed command influence, the "mortal enemy of military justice." Canada has brought in some significant improvements in this area. Members serving on courts martial are chosen randomly, and the judge advocate conducting the proceedings has a fixed term of office of from two to four years. One further possible change that the Somalia Inquiry may wish to explore is the U.K. system of using independent civilian judges or military judges recently retired or at the end of their careers to conduct the proceedings.

CHAPTER SEVEN

Civil Control, Integration, and Oversight

CIVIL CONTROL

Civil control of the military is a fundamental principle of Canadian society. It does not by itself ensure that the military — individually or collectively — will not go astray, but it helps keep it on track.

United Kingdom

Civil control of the military in the United Kingdom can be traced to fear of a standing army arising from Cromwell's adventure in the seventeenth century.[1] Today, Parliament through the cabinet has the ultimate control of the military. During the Second World War, Winston Churchill and the war cabinet were in charge of military strategy.[2] Churchill was the minister of defence as well as the prime minister.[3] Direction of the military during peacetime is vested in the chief of defence staff, but *control* is the province of the secretary of state for defence.[4] Unlike the case in many other countries, the military has not interfered in British politics for the most part.[5] One recent commentator observed:

British civil-military relations are rather boring... While the military has played a central role in British history, in the past 100 years, the British military, unlike other European nations, has not interfered in politics... In Modern British history, British officers have never challenged the primacy of politics. In fact, they have tended to remain rather distanced from debate and aloof from controversy.[6]

Canada

Canada has more or less followed England's lead. The military has not and cannot be involved in party politics.[7] What would have happened to the military if the sovereignists had won the November 1995 referendum in Quebec, in view of the Bloc québécois letter to the Canadian Forces in Quebec to switch their allegiance to Quebec, is not known.[8] It had the potential to bring the military more directly into politics than they have ever been.

The *National Defence Act* makes it clear that the minister of national defence "has the management and direction of the Canadian Forces and of all matters relating to national defence."[9] The minister is, of course, subject to the control of the cabinet and, beyond that, Parliament. The chief of defence staff, on the other hand, is charged under the act with "the control and administration of the Canadian Forces", and all orders or instructions to the Canadian Forces "shall be issued by or through the Chief of the Defence Staff." But this is "subject to the regulations and under the direction of the Minister."[10]

The *National Defence Act* of 1951 was designed, in the words of Brooke Claxton, the defence minister of the day, to make clear "in plain words" that the military's authority was "subject to the Governor-in-Council and the direction of the minister."[11]

Douglas Bland has commented that the *National Defence Act* "is written with the clear intention of separating the authority of the minister over defence policy generally and the chief of the defence staff's responsibility to command the Canadian Forces." Cabinet has ultimate control over the chief of defence staff, however, because the chief is appointed by cabinet and serves at pleasure. Moreover, the minister has a veto over appointments to the rank of brigadier general or higher. The recommendation for appointment comes from the chief of defence staff, however, not the minister, thus helping to eliminate party politics from appointments.[12]

Cabinet can declare war without parliamentary approval, although, as in the Gulf War, it will if possible obtain the approval of Parliament as a matter of practice.[13] A cabinet declaration of an international or war emergency is covered by the 1988 *Emergencies Act*.[14] An "international emergency" is defined as "an emergency involving Canada and one or more other countries that arises from acts of intimidation or coercion or the real or imminent use of serious force or violence that is so serious as to be a national emergency" (section 27). Such a cabinet declaration is good for 60 days unless revoked or continued by Parliament (sections 59-60, 28-29). Parliament is to meet within seven sitting days after the declaration is issued (section 58). A "war emergency" is defined to mean "war or other armed conflict, real or imminent, involving Canada or any of its allies that is so serious as to be a national emergency" (section 37). If the cabinet "believes, on reasonable grounds, that a war emergency exists" it may by declaration so declare (section 38). In such a case the proclamation is good for 120 days, unless it is revoked or continued by Parliament (sections 39, 59-60).

United States

Civilians also have direction of the military in the United States. The president is the commander in-chief of military forces.[15] The secretaries of defence and of the various services must be civilians.[16] As Kemp and Hudlin comment in a recent article, "the ends of government policy are to be set by civilians; the military is limited to decisions about means." The commentators conclude: "The principle of civil supremacy over the military, and the subsidiary principle of civilian control, are important features of the American system of government."[17] General MacArthur, it will be recalled, was relieved of his command in the Korean War when he resisted President Truman's order that the war not be allowed to escalate.

Although civil control in the United States is clear, it is not entirely clear what the respective roles of Congress and the president are.[18] Under the constitution, Congress enjoys the exclusive authority to initiate an offensive war.[19] As Jean Smith has written, "The framers of the Constitution were realists. They divided the war powers along functional lines. The president, as commander-in-chief, possessed the necessary authority to repel sudden attacks, but the power to initiate war rested with Congress."[20] The line between the functions is not easy to draw. President Kennedy became involved in the Cuban Missile Crisis and Vietnam without congressional consent. In 1973, Congress passed a joint resolution, the War Powers Resolution — over President Nixon's opposition — requiring the president to "consult with Congress before introducing United States Armed Forces into hostilities", to submit a report in writing to Congress within 48 hours on action taken, and to terminate use of U.S. forces within 60 days without congressional approval.[21] The constitutionality of the resolution is doubtful, and all presidents since its passage have adhered to the position that the decision remains the responsibility of the president as commander in chief.[22] "Congress' ultimate military check on the president," Smith points out, "lies in the appropriations process."[23]

INTEGRATION AT NDHQ

In Canada, integration of the headquarters personnel of the military and the deputy minister took place in 1972 when the present National Defence Headquarters (NDHQ) was established. Harriet Critchley describes the background as follows:[24]

In spite of consolidation into one department in 1946, creation of a chairman, Chiefs of Staff Committee, in 1953, integration of the armed services under the command of a chief of defence staff and reorganization of headquarters along functional lines in 1964, and reorganization of the armed forces into a single service in 1968, "there were still problems in the Department of National Defence management."[25] Those problems continued to be the need for better coordination of planning and budgeting, better accountability and control of capital acquisitions, elimination of costly duplication of effort and expense, and more effective relationships with other government departments that had an input into defence decision making. The persistence of these basic problems led to the appointment of the Management Review Group (MRG) — known as the Pennyfather Commission — in 1971.[26]

Among other concerns, the Pennyfather Commission wrote about the "lack of unity of purpose due to a high degree of parallelism and duplication of management responsibility among its three major divisions — the deputy minister's staff, the Canadian Armed Forces, and the Defence Research Board — and instead, the development of adversary relationships and undue compartmentalization."[27] There are now about 8,000 persons at NDHQ.

Scholars have taken different positions on the effectiveness of integration. Douglas Bland, for example, has a generally negative view:

The integration of the NDHQ civilian and military staff has heightened, not lessened, the conflict between the two elements in headquarters and it has created institutional ambiguity where none need exist...people from "two distinctly different cultures and with different sets of values are required to work side by side."[28] The result of this dysfunctional dynamic is that the defence policy process can become seriously unbalanced.[29]

Harriet Critchley, on the other hand, sees integration as generally successful:

This integration did not result in an influx of civil servants into the organization. It merely brought together the two sets of people — in two hierarchies, working largely separately from one another. The aim of that integration and the organization of headquarters along functional lines was to provide for better coordination and management of defence in Canada. In the process, rather than allowing for increased civilianization, the military has — by virtue of its increased membership in each of the senior committees — *more influence*, over a broader range and at a higher level, on defence decision making than in the past. This is a fact that current commentators, particularly military personnel critical of the current organization of headquarters, would be wise to consider very carefully when entertaining ideas of returning to the Canadian headquarters system of 1963 or the adoption of the organizational systems of foreign headquarters.[30]

The issue was discussed by the Special Joint Committee on Canada's Defence Policy, which reported in 1994, but the committee could not reach a conclusion:

Since 1972, the military headquarters of the Canadian Forces has been integrated with the Department of National Defence in an effort to provide more efficient management of both resources and operations. The Committee heard conflicting testimony on whether this arrangement is appropriate for the needs of the Canadian Forces today. Some witnesses were strongly supportive; others favoured a return to an independent military headquarters.

The Committee was not able to reach a conclusion on this matter and *recommends instead that the issue be pursued by the new Standing Joint Committee.*[31]

This writer is not in a position to assess accurately the effect of integration on the effective functioning and oversight of the military. Having civilians integrated into military headquarters at a very senior level may act as a check on improper conduct — the focus of this paper. On the other hand, there is a danger that integration will cause co-option of the civilians into military values, rather than the other way around. Further, there is a concern that the military may pay too much heed to party political considerations. Having a more arm's-length relationship along with other forms of oversight may be more effective in helping assure civil control over the military. But this is not an area I have studied carefully. The question of integration of senior military and civil service personnel is an important one and one the Somalia Inquiry may wish to consider.

PARLIAMENTARY OVERSIGHT

A brief prepared by the Department of National Defence for the 1994 Joint Parliamentary Committee on Canada's Defence Policy briefly outlined the existing parliamentary oversight process:

Some observers appear to believe that there is insufficient parliamentary oversight of the military. Clearly, control over the military is the prerogative of the Executive. It is just as clear, however, that the Minister — indeed, the Prime Minister and Cabinet — are accountable to Parliament for the directions they give the armed forces.

Parliament has other oversight powers. It, or its committees, can call upon members of the government — or government officials — to provide a full explanation of government decisions. The Standing Committee on National Defence and Veterans Affairs (SCONDVA) already has the power to call witnesses and demand details on any matter dealing with the development or use of Canada's armed forces. In the past, SCONDVA and its Senate equivalent have used their access to government to produce thoughtful studies of specific military issues. Indeed, an important way in which both committees fulfil their oversight mandate is through keeping defence issues in the public eye. In recognition of this role, the Government asked that a Special Joint Committee of the House and Senate be the principal venue for public consultation during the defence policy review. Beyond this, the Government has deliberately taken other initiatives to involve Parliament in defence issues — as can be seen in the recent House of Commons debates on peacekeeping and cruise missile testing.[32]

There was unanimity among members of the Joint Committee that the parliamentary role should be strengthened. The committee stated: "whatever our individual views on particular issues of defence policy or operations, there was one matter on which we agreed almost from the beginning — that there is a need to strengthen the role of Parliament in the scrutiny and development of defence policy."[33]

Douglas Bland supports the committee's view and would go further: "An active parliamentary defence committee provided with adequate research support, could not only oversee defence policy, but it could also provide the counter-expert body ministers have sought for years."[34] "In Canada," he points out, "there have been remarkably few occasions since 1945 when Parliament has truly directed defence policy outcomes."[35]

It is difficult for Parliament to play much of a role in the actual operation of the military as distinct from overall defence policy. Much of military information in the Anglo-Canadian system is classified, so there is a paucity of information available.[36] It is unlikely that more information will be made available while a significant proportion of Parliament is made up of members of a political party promoting the break-up of the country.[37]

As is well known, the U.S. Congress plays a more active role in relation to the military. "In no other country," one observer states,

is parliamentary involvement in national security affairs as great as in the United States. In the Congress there are four major committees (the Appropriations and Armed Services Committees in each house) that review virtually the whole of the defence budget in a detailed manner, as well as a number of other committees (such as Government Operations) that wield significant power over parts of the Defense Department.[38]

The writer goes on to observe, however, that political considerations often come to the fore:

The principal defect of the heightened congressional role is that it encourages the intrusion of narrow political considerations into the determination of matters that ought ideally to be resolved by professional experts.[39]

He cites as an example the endorsement of Senator Edward Kennedy and others from Massachusetts of the F-18, the engine of which is produced in that state. (Of course, similar political considerations may exist when the decision is made by cabinet.)

In Britain, MPs appear to play a less active role than in Canada in overseeing military activity. One study expresses a very pessimistic outlook on the British MP's role:

MPs have many roles to fulfil and of these sitting on select committees is for many the least desirable aspect of their job. Furthermore, there is little compelling reason in an unreformed parliament for MPs to involve themselves in the detailed scrutiny of the minutiae of government business — especially when their actions rarely influence government policy directly. MPs prefer, therefore, to play the role of the political magpie and pursue issues which provide them with the opportunity to make a media or debating impact in the hope of preferment by their political leaders.[40]

There is considerable truth in this observation for Canada as well.

Parliament can, however, play a role in receiving reports from bodies that report to Parliament. The Auditor General, who has responsibility for examining the financial affairs of the Department of National Defence, reports direct to Parliament.[41] Similarly, as we will see, the various inspectors general in the U.S. report to Congress. There are now no annual reports to Parliament by the military or the Department of National Defence, although there are annual budget estimates. Nor is there an annual report to Parliament by a review group such as the Security Intelligence Review Committee in connection with the security service. Parliament has also given up an important area of review by not reviewing orders in council and other statutory instruments relating to the military.[42] Let us now examine some possible review mechanisms.

OTHER REVIEW BODIES

Summary Investigations and Boards of Inquiry

A "summary investigation" can be ordered by the chief of defence staff where "he requires to be informed on any matter connected with the control and administration of the Canadian Forces." It can also be ordered by a commanding officer where "he requires to be informed on any matter connected with his command...or affecting any officer or non-commissioned member under his command." The procedure for conducting such an investigation is not spelled out in the regulations. The investigation, the QR&O simply states, is to be conducted "in such manner as he sees fit."[43] There is no provision for anyone other than a member of the military to be involved in the investigation.

A more formal procedure is the board of inquiry, which, unlike summary investigations, is provided for in the *National Defence Act*:

45.(1) The Minister, and such other authorities as the minister may prescribe or appoint for that purpose, may, where it is expedient that the Minister or any such other authority should be informed on any matter connected with the government, discipline, administration or functions of the Canadian Forces or affecting any officer or non-commissioned member, convene a board of inquiry for the purpose of investigating and reporting on that matter.[44]

Chapter 21 of the QR&Os spells out in some detail how a board of inquiry is to be conducted.[45] In addition to those entitled to convene a summary investigation, a board of inquiry can be convened by the minister of national defence. (The board that investigated the situation in Somalia was established by the chief of defence staff.[46]) A board consists of two or more officers. "Under exceptional circumstances", the QR&O states, the convening authority may appoint civilians as additional members of the board. Indeed, where a board is convened by the minister, "the Minister may, under exceptional circumstances, appoint a civilian as president of the board."[47] Two civilians were appointed to the Somalia Board of Inquiry, but at a later stage they became special advisers.[48] Further, cabinet can appoint a civilian commission of inquiry under the *Inquiries Act*,[49] as in the case of the Commission of Inquiry into the Deployment of Canadian Forces to Somalia.

There is considerable discretion about whether a summary investigation or a board is to be ordered. Investigation of an injury or death, otherwise than in action, for example, is mandatory, but can be either a summary investigation or a board of inquiry. The same is true of "a fire, explosion or similar occurrence" that damages property. Death or serious injury in an aircraft accident, on the other hand, must be examined by a board of inquiry.[50] In Canada, therefore, there may "under exceptional circumstances" be non-military investigations of military problems, but the normal practice is for the military to conduct its own inquiries.

As in Canada, there are "investigations" and "boards of officers" for the U.S. military. Procedures for the army are set out in an Army Regulation, with — as is often the case — greater detail than is found in Canadian regulations and orders.[51] Again, civilians can join the investigating team to give credibility to the board. This was done in the Peers Inquiry, which investigated the My Lai incident in 1969. Two prominent New York lawyers joined the investigating team. "With these steps", Seymour Hersh wrote, "the military blunted the demand, from liberals and conservatives alike, that an outside panel be established to investigate the cover-up."[52]

The Auditor General of Canada examines the accounts of the Department of National Defence and also looks at specific areas from time to time. In 1992, for example, the Auditor General examined capital projects and reserves; in 1994 he looked at defence management systems, information technology, and infrastructure.[53] In the United States, as we will see, in addition to the auditor,[54] there is significantly greater civilian review of military conduct.

The U.S. Inspector General

There is nothing comparable in the Canadian or British military to the U.S. Inspector General.[55] The situation is relatively complex in the United States because there is both a civilian statutory inspector general for the department of defense (IG, DOD) and a purely military inspector general for each of the three services. The IG, DOD was established as recently as 1983, whereas the military inspector general positions are very much older.

George Washington appointed the first inspector general during the War of Independence in 1777. The inspector general was to superintend the training of the entire army in order to ensure troop proficiency in common tactics. A Prussian officer was appointed to the post. Apparently, the first inspector general in western culture was used in the French army in the seventeenth century. In 1668, an inspector general of infantry and an inspector general of calvary were appointed, with the principal duties of reviewing the troops and reporting to King Louis XIV. George Washington's inspector general, Baron von Steuben "is generally credited with developing the standardization, discipline, and concern for soldiers which allowed the moulding of militia remnants at Valley Forge into the victorious Continental Army of the American Revolution."[56] The inspector general's role has continued to evolve.[57] A recently retired army inspector general told the Senate:

Army IGs continued to be active throughout the War of 1812, the Civil War, the Indian Wars, Spanish-American War, World Wars I and II, Korea, Vietnam and, most recently, Operations DESERT SHIELD/STORM. They have maintained a focus on discipline, training, morale, efficiency, economy, and overall readiness. The Army Inspector General's role has been defined in four functions: inspection, investigation, assistance, and teaching and training. IG inspections have sought and identified the underlying cause of systemic problems and deficiencies; determined responsibility for corrective action; followed up to ensure corrections were made; and spread innovative ideas. Inspectors General have investigated alleged violations of policy, regulation or law, mismanagement, unethical behavior, and misconduct.[58]

The army inspector general is appointed by the secretary of the army and confirmed by the Senate. Reports are made to the chief of staff, to the secretary of the army,[59] and, as we will see, to the IG, DOD.[60] The military inspector general usually serves for about 3 years.[61] The former inspector general just quoted above served 4 years and then became the vice chief of staff for the army.[62]

Below the army inspector general are many other inspectors general. The system is decentralized, with policy and procedures initiated by the inspector general at the Pentagon and with field inspectors general working directly with their commanders.[63] At the end of the Second World War there were 3,000 U.S. army inspectors general.[64] Army inspectors general around the world today receive more than 40,000 complaints, allegations of impropriety, and requests for assistance each year from soldiers, family members, and civilians. Civilians account for about 15 per cent of the matters dealt with.[65] Inspectors general maintain toll-free hotlines to receive calls, which can, if the caller wishes, be dealt with anonymously. As discussed earlier, an attempt is made to protect whistleblowers.[66] The regulations include a sample notice that states: "All soldiers have the right to present complaints, grievances or requests for assistance to the inspector general. These may include what the soldiers reasonably believe evidences fraud, waste, and abuse."[67] The notice identifies the local inspector general, but then states that

if you believe your local inspector general's response to you is not fair, complete, or in accordance with law and regulations; or if you believe your interests may be jeopardized by visiting your local inspector general, you may write to [a named more senior inspector general]. You may also call the Inspector General, Department of the Army or the Inspector General, Department of Defence (IG, DOD) hotline. Their [toll-free] telephone numbers are...

Superimposed on the army inspectors general is the centralized statutory inspector general for the department of defense.[68] Statutory inspectors general were introduced into the U.S. system of government post-Watergate by the *Inspector General Act, 1978*,[69] which established them in 12 federal departments and agencies. Like the military inspector general, the idea owed its origins to George Washington's colonial army.[70] The department of defense was not one of the initial departments but was added in 1983.[71] By 1989 the inspector general concept had been expanded to include the rest of the federal government, including 34 small agencies.[72] All statutory inspectors general are required to send semi-annual reports to Congress. These reports, in the words of Bernard Rosen, an expert on accountability of American government bureaucracies,

- describe significant problems, abuses, or deficiencies in agency operations and programs and the recommendations for corrective action;
- identify important recommendations described in previous semiannual reports on which corrective action has not been completed;
- identify matters referred to prosecutive authorities and resulting convictions; and
- list each audit report completed by the inspector general during the six-month period.[73]

In addition, special reports must be prepared and sent to the appropriate congressional committees when the inspector general is informed of particularly serious problems or abuses. Bernard Rosen continues: "This is the bedrock of the inspector general's independence — that the semi-annual and special reports be sent by the agency head *without alteration* to the appropriate committees of Congress. The agency head is free to send comments along with each report."

After the 1978 law was enacted, the secretary of defense was directed to establish a task force to report to Congress on whether a department of defense statutory inspector general should be added. The task force recommended against a centralized statutory body. The military, it was argued, is not like any other department or agency of government, because the unique command and control structure suited to the conduct of war requires that decision-making authority and accountability for success or failure be delegated to commanders at every level. The task force recommended instead the establishment of an under secretary of defense for review and oversight who would report to the secretary and deputy secretary of defense.[74]

Congress did not accept the task force recommendations, however, and superimposed a department of defense inspector general on top of the military inspectors general. The new law gave the inspector general of the department of defense responsibilities that include (in the language of a former inspector general of the army),

providing advice to the Secretary of Defense in the detection and prevention of fraud, waste, abuse and mismanagement; initiating audits and investigations within the Department of Defense; providing policy direction for audits and investigations; requesting assistance as needed from other audit, inspection and investigative units in the Department of Defense; and giving particular regard to the activities of the internal audit, inspection, and investigative units of the military departments with a view toward avoiding duplication and insuring effective co-ordination and cooperation.[75]

The mission statement of the IG, DOD states that the office:

a. Conducts, supervises, monitors and initiates audits, investigations and inspections of DoD programs and operations.
b. Provides leadership and coordination and recommends policies for those activities whose mission is to promote economy, efficiency and effectiveness, and to detect and prevent fraud and abuse in the Department's programs and operations.
c. Keeps the Secretary of Defense and the Congress fully and currently informed about problems and deficiencies in the administration of such programs and operations and recommends corrective measures.[76]

The inspector general of the army is required to submit a semi-annual report to the IG, DOD, summarizing activities of army audit, inspection and investigation activities.[77] The IG, DOD in turn submits semi-annual reports to Congress through the secretary of defense.[78] The IG, DOD, the largest of the statutory IGs,[79] has offices outside the Pentagon.

The U.S. military thus has two layers of review by inspectors general, one within the command structure of the military, and the other entirely outside the military structure. Canada has neither.

The Military Ombudsman

An inspector general is more or less the equivalent of an ombudsman.[80] There are many different types of ombudsman around the world dealing with military matters. The federal government in Canada does not have an ombudsman for the military or a general federal ombudsman, although it does have a number of specialized bodies to deal with other areas of federal jurisdiction. Donald Rowat identifies five specialized complaints officers:[81] the Commissioner of Official Languages;[82] the Correctional Investigator;[83] the Privacy Commissioner;[84] the Information Commissioner;[85] and the Public Complaints Commissioner for the RCMP.[86]

A number of countries have an ombudsman with responsibility for dealing with complaints about the military. Sweden, Denmark, and Australia, for example, are in this category. From its establishment in 1809 until 1915, the Swedish ombudsman had authority over certain military matters, but from 1915 to 1968 there was a separate military ombudsman. In 1968, however, the two bodies were merged, and now there are three ombudsman positions, one of which is responsible for the military. The Danish ombudsman has had responsibility for servicemen from its inception in 1955.[87]

The Australian commonwealth ombudsman, following a change in the governing statute, now has responsibility for some aspects of the armed forces.[88] A separate section of the ombudsman's report is devoted to the report of the defence force ombudsman. The most recent report states:

The Defence Force Ombudsman (DFO) investigates complaints from current and former members of the Australian Defence Force and their dependants about the actions of Commonwealth agencies in relation to matters which arise during their service, or matters that have arisen as a consequence of their service. The most significant difference with this Ombudsman jurisdiction is that we investigate complaints about employment matters. Most DFO complaints are about members' employment in the Defence Force, particularly in relation to promotion, discharge, accommodation and other employment conditions.[89]

The jurisdiction of the Australian defence force ombudsman, while important, is thus relatively narrow in comparison with that of U.S. inspectors general. Moreover, the DFO system requires that the service person first exhaust the entire range of internal redress of grievance procedures.[90]

A number of countries, such as Norway and Germany, have a military ombudsman in addition to or in the absence of a general ombudsman. The Norwegian ombudsman for the armed forces was set up in 1952. The military was not included in the mandate of the regular ombudsman because the military ombudsman not only investigates complaints but is the head of the system of representative committees. These committees, which allow members of the armed forces to elect their own representatives to discuss issues with their superior officers, were established during the First World War.[91]

The German military ombudsman was established in 1956.[92] There is no civil ombudsman in Germany at the federal level.[93] The office was intended to assure parliamentary control over the military and safeguard the rights of the citizen-soldier in a military based officially on democratic principles but with deep authoritarian roots.[94] The aim of the 1956 legislation "was to create an army of 'citizens in uniform' with far greater rights, including the right to join a trade union, than German soldiers had ever enjoyed before."[95] The military ombudsman was to be the "eye of

Parliament."[96] The office was given the authority under the German constitution to oversee the conduct of the military generally and safeguard the rights of soldiers. The ombudsman can receive complaints direct from soldiers of the lowest ranks and has the authority to investigate them at any level of the military or department of defence, including the right of access to all relevant documents. Further, the military ombudsman makes a yearly report to parliament summarizing the complaints received and making appropriate recommendations for change.[97]

The impact of this office reached its zenith with the Heye affair. In 1964, Germany's second military ombudsman, Helmuth Heye, created controversy by publishing a series of articles in a popular magazine criticizing the German military and asking whether it might be returning to its "old authoritarian ways".[98] The fact that Heye was a vice-admiral known to be of independent mind and quite willing to speak out against his superiors — he had been a critic of the Nazi regime's buildup of the armed forces in the 1930s — lent credence to this fear and prompted a heated public debate. In the end, the government that had ignored Heye's first two reports was forced to re-examine its policy with respect to the military and appointed, in addition to a military ombudsman, an inspector general of the armed forces.[99] While the Heye affair illustrates the potential impact of a military ombudsman on government policy, it also reveals the potential for the office to become overtly political.[100]

CONCLUSION

Canada does not have a military ombudsman or a general ombudsman with jurisdiction over the military. Nor does it have an inspector general system, as in the United States, or a civilian complaints tribunal like the one for the RCMP.[101] The Somalia Inquiry may wish to explore whether some such body would be an important additional technique for controlling improper conduct in the military.

It is not realistic to expect Parliament to play a major supervisory role with regard to military conduct. It can do more than it has been doing, but it works most effectively when reports are prepared by independent nonpolitical bodies such as the Auditor General or the Security Intelligence Review Committee. The deputy minister and others at National Defence Headquarters provide considerable control over military activities, but they are the "eye of the *executive*" on military matters, not the "eye of parliament". The press will undoubtedly continue to play an important investigatory role with respect to the military, using the *Access to*

Information Act and other sources of information.[102] In my opinion, more should be done.

What type of governmental structure could provide effective review? There is tension between two models: the internal military model, within the chain of command (this was the U.S. model before 1983); and the "eye of parliament" model, outside the chain of command, as in Germany and the U.S. inspector general of the department of defense. Both models have merit. The military will no doubt prefer the internal model. Such a model was advocated by Lieutenant Commander G.M. Aikins in a 1993 staff college paper, "An Ombudsman for the Canadian Forces":

The CF Ombudsman would be a civilian familiar with the military, who would receive complaints from individuals and ensure they were investigated and rectified. He would act not as a champion for complainants, but as an impartial facilitator to assist the chain of command in resolving problems. Service members or DND civilians would have a toll-free line to provide anonymous (but detailed) information to commence investigations into allegations of any nature against military personnel, or request the advice or assistance of the Ombudsman in resolving personal harassment problems. All investigations would be turned over to the appropriate level within the chain of command for necessary action. The ombudsman also would make recommendations as appropriate to alter procedures or regulations.[103]

In my opinion, a better solution would be to have both an internal ombudsman or inspector general[104] and an independent body external to the military that can review the reports of the internal body and report to Parliament. The United States and Germany have both an internal and an external body. In the security field, Canada has both an internal inspector general (reporting to the solicitor general) and an external Security Intelligence Review Committee that prepares an annual report for Parliament and reviews the activities of the Canadian Security Intelligence Service and the inspector general.[105]

Both the internal and external bodies should, as in the United States, receive complaints from civilians as well as the military, provide anonymity to persons reporting, and have a toll-free hotline to make it easier for individuals to lodge complaints. There should be no requirement for military personnel to exhaust internal redress of grievance procedures before having their concerns dealt with.[106] The exhaustion of internal remedies may be desirable in many situations, but it should not be a bar to action.

CHAPTER EIGHT

Conclusion

This study has examined a wide range of techniques available for controlling misconduct in the military. Such control is imperative. Military personnel are, by the nature of their activity, aggressive. Although the present system contains many valuable features, it can be improved. What are some of the techniques used, and what changes should be made?

In Chapter 1 we described a number of techniques. Proper selection is an obvious first step in controlling subsequent behaviour, including using adequate background checks and possibly psychological fitness testing. Training was also discussed, including sensitivity training, which is obviously desirable for humanitarian missions such as the one to Somalia. The importance of effective leadership was also briefly discussed in the introductory chapter.

The experience of the United States contingent in Somalia and in other missions suggests that some problems can be avoided by banning alcohol on such missions, a step that Canada should consider taking. Alcohol continues to be a problem in the Canadian military. Further, about 12 per cent of the U.S. force in Somalia consisted of women, and a recent study indicates that this probably had a beneficial effect on the behaviour of U.S. forces there. Women are less likely to have negative stereotypes of the local inhabitants, for example. This also raises the question of whether aggressive combat forces such as the Airborne Regiment (now disbanded) are the right forces to send on peacekeeping or peacemaking missions. It is always better to find ways of preventing undesirable conduct in advance than to deal with it after the event.

Further, it is essential that the rules to be followed be known by those to whom they are directed. The military does fairly well in making its personnel aware of what is expected. Unfortunately, the rules of engagement, setting out when force can be used on a particular mission, were not brought out in time to be part of the members' ingrained knowledge.

The suggestion is made in Chapter 1 that rules of engagement should be part of a member's regular training. Similarly, the rules of war should be part of the member's basic training, and something similar to the nine-item U.S. "Soldier's Rules", set out in Chapter 1, should be considered for adoption by Canadian Forces.

This raises the issue whether a code of ethics would be desirable. Such a code — several examples are given in Chapter 1 — encourages discussion of ethical values. "It may not help," one writer states, "but it can't hurt."[1] The final issue discussed in the introductory chapter is civil liability. The technique has some potential for controlling improper conduct in the military, but will not be as potent a force as other techniques. Nevertheless, some of the possible restrictions now placed on bringing civil actions should be modified, in particular the rule that the government cannot be liable unless an individual can be held liable, and the statutory provision giving the Crown immunity from suit when the military activity is "for the purpose of the defence of Canada or of training or maintaining the efficiency of, the Canadian Forces."[2]

Rewards as a technique for influencing behaviour are discussed in Chapter 2. No other major institution in society makes such a display of rewards as the military does. They permeate all aspects of military life. As one writer states, "there is an emerging consensus that the effects of punishment on performance are not as strong as the influence of rewards."[3] Their use should be encouraged, but continuing study should be made by the military to find the appropriate balance between sanctions and rewards and to ensure that promotions, medals, and other forms of rewards are administered fairly.

The following chapter looks at reporting wrongdoing, which is required in part to ensure that problems in the military are dealt with adequately and in part to enable the military and the government to keep on top of issues that may become public. Just as it is important for regulations and information to flow down the chain of command, it is equally important for information to flow upward. Techniques should be developed to permit anonymous and easy reporting of incidents and to protect whistleblowers.

Chapter 4 examines administrative and informal sanctions. These are very important in shaping behaviour in the military. A great range of administrative sanctions can be applied. A noncommissioned member, for example, is subject to the following administrative sanctions: verbal warning, recorded warning, counselling and probation, suspension from duty, and compulsory release. These can be applied instead of or in addition to disciplinary measures. Unlike the administrative sanctions, informal sanctions are not set out in rules or regulations. Yet, as discussed in the chapter, every member of the military knows that minor punishments, such as extra work or drill, are imposed, albeit within reasonably well understood limitations and boundaries. Their use should be regularized in the QR&Os.

The military police play a very important role in controlling misconduct in the military. Their function is similar to that performed by the civilian police: deterring wrongdoing, stopping improper conduct, and investigating and prosecuting wrongdoers. In addition, military police have other functions such as the movement of traffic in a battlefield and receiving prisoners of war. There are now about 1,300 security and military police out of a total regular force of about 65,000 members, that is, about one police member for every 50 members of the military. Yet only two military police went to Somalia with the 1,000 or so Canadian troops, an obviously inadequate number. One senior Canadian military official has written:

if there had been a military police presence in theatre both of the Somalia incidents [4 and 16 March 1993] which brought such discredit on the Canadian forces in general and the Airborne Regiment in particular may have been avoided.[4]

The military police in fact wanted to have more members in Somalia, but the overall number of troops that could go to Somalia was set by cabinet. The suggestion is made in Chapter 5 that some flexibility should be built into the figures set by cabinet for future such missions.

It is clearly desirable to have an adequate number of military police in the armed services generally and on specific missions. It would probably be unwise to reduce their numbers significantly in the downsizing of the military that is now taking place. It should be noted that military police make up about three to four per cent of the U.S. army, whereas the military police account for only two per cent of Canadian military personnel. About seven to eight per cent of the U.S. force in the Gulf in 1990-91 consisted of military police, and it is likely that there was a similar percentage in Somalia. One reason for the higher U.S. numbers is that U.S military police have greater tactical responsibilities than the Canadian military police, a function that should be considered for Canadian MP to justify greater numbers. The numbers could also be increased by using reserves or civilian police such as the RCMP for special missions, in addition to the regular military police.

The chapter also looked at ways of obtaining greater independence from command influence for the military police. One change suggested is to have the career prospects of military police determined outside the regimental chain of command. Another is to permit the military police to bring charges for military offences without the consent of the commanding officer. Still another is to consider adopting something similar to the U.S. criminal investigation division, whereby all serious offences are investigated by a body outside the units to which accused persons belong. All three suggested changes are desirable.

Military justice is explored in detail in Chapter 6. The 1992 Supreme Court of Canada decision in *Généreux* settled the question of the constitutional legitimacy of a separate system of military justice. The relatively complex system of courts martial and summary proceedings is described in the chapter. The key constitutional question remaining is the validity of the system of summary proceedings before commanding officers and delegated officers. Summary proceedings are the most widely used form of proceedings, accounting for 98 per cent of military trials. There are about 4,000 summary trials each year and only about 100 courts martial. Summary trials are extremely important in shaping the conduct of military personnel, constituting a form of "reintegrative shaming". As John Braithwaite writes in *Crime, Shame and Reintegration*:

Reintegrative shaming is superior to stigmatization because it minimizes risks of pushing those shamed into criminal subcultures, and because social disapproval is more effective when embedded in relationships overwhelmingly characterized by social approval.[5]

The suggestion is made in Chapter 6 that the substantial decline in the use of summary justice and military detention in the ten years preceding the events in Somalia may well have contributed to the events by not properly controlling disciplinary problems.

Summary proceedings before a commanding officer are vulnerable to constitutional challenge under the Charter because, among other things, it is difficult to argue that the proceeding is before an "independent and impartial" tribunal, as required by section 11(d) of the Charter. Moreover, the absence of a right to counsel would likely breach the "fair hearing" part of section 11(d). Two changes should be made and a third considered. The 90-day period of detention that can now be imposed by a commanding officer conducting a summary proceeding almost certainly brings such proceedings within section 11 ("charged with an offence").

The 90-day period is much longer than commanding officers could impose before the *National Defence Act* was enacted in the early 1950s and much longer than can be imposed by commanding officers in the U.S. or British military. It is therefore recommended that the period of detention be reduced substantially, to about a month, which may remove such proceedings from the purview of section 11 and leave it within the more flexible standards of section 7 of the Charter.

A further important recommended change is to ensure a genuine waiver of the right to a court martial, with full knowledge of the consequences of the waiver. As Justice Lamer stated in a pre-Charter case, waiver "is dependent upon it being *clear and unequivocal that the person is waiving the procedural safeguard and is doing so with full knowledge of the rights the procedure was enacted to protect and of the effect the waiver will have on those rights in the process.*"[6] It is suggested that when it is reasonable, communication with military duty counsel — at least by telephone — should always be permitted without cost to the member. The member should be told of this right. Moreover, the right to consult a lawyer and the consequences of waiving trial by court martial should be set out clearly in a form signed by the accused, as is done in the U.S. military.

A further change that could be considered is to give a member sentenced to a period of detention over a determined amount the right to appeal as of right by way of trial *de novo* to a court martial. Such a procedure, which would likely be resorted to only rarely, would further strengthen the likelihood of the Supreme Court upholding the constitutionality of summary proceedings by commanding officers.

A number of other matters are discussed in the chapter, including the military nexus doctrine, which is probably no longer part of Canadian military law. A better solution than using the military nexus concept would be to give military and civilian courts concurrent jurisdiction over serving members of the military and to let civil and military authorities work out who should try the accused.

This leads to the issue of double jeopardy, also discussed in Chapter 6. A 1985 amendment to the *National Defence Act* goes too far. It provides that *any* military proceeding is a bar to a civilian proceeding.[7] This applies to summary trials for criminal offences before a commanding officer or delegated officer. It even applies "where, after investigation, a commanding officer considers that a charge should not be proceeded with."[8] Primary jurisdiction to try an accused for a criminal charge committed in Canada, if there is a desire to prosecute by both military and civil authorities, should be in the civil authority. A necessary result of asserting that the civilian authority is paramount is to disregard a prior military judgement for an offence committed in Canada if, but only if, military jurisdiction was assumed without the express or implied consent of the civilian authorities. The civil authority would, however, take any punishment into account. It is possible that civilian courts would so construe the present legislation, but it would be better if it were clarified by a further amendment to the *National Defence Act*.

The chapter also discusses command influence, "the mortal enemy of military justice."[9] Canada has brought in some significant improvements in this area. Members serving on courts martial are chosen randomly, and the judge advocate conducting the proceedings has a fixed term of office of from 2 to 4 years. One further possible change that the Somalia Inquiry may wish to explore is the U.K. system of using independent civilian judges, with no career ambitions in the military, or military judges at the end of their careers, with no further career ambitions, to conduct proceedings.

Finally, Chapter 7 examines external systems of control. Civilian control of the military is a fundamental principle of Canadian, British, and U.S. society. Parliament, cabinet and the appropriate minister have ultimate control of military operations. One method of control used in Canada is to integrate in the same headquarters the top department of national defence civil servants and the most senior military personnel. The success of the integration is explored, but a firm conclusion on its desirability is not put forward by this writer.

The role of Parliament in overseeing military activities is then examined. The 1994 report of the Joint Committee on Canada's Defence Policy concluded unanimously that Parliament's role should be strengthened, stating:

whatever our individual views on particular issues of defence policy or operations, there was one matter on which we agreed almost from the beginning — that there is a need to strengthen the role of Parliament in the scrutiny and development of defence policy.[10]

This is easier said than done, however. Nevertheless, Parliament should receive more reports on military matters. There are now no annual reports to Parliament by the military or the department. Nor is there an annual report to Parliament by a review group such as the Security Intelligence Review Committee in connection with the security service.

Parliament has also given up an important area of review by not examining orders in council and other statutory instruments relating to the military.

What type of governmental structure could provide effective review? The conclusion is reached that two types of review are desirable. One is a body internal to the military, comparable to the U.S. inspector general of the army. This is an important office within the military, with inspectors general of lesser rank throughout the army. They receive complaints, allegations of impropriety, and requests for assistance. The other type of review should be by a civilian body outside the military that reports to Parliament. This could be an office like the Security Intelligence Review Committee, an external military ombudsman, or a statutory civilian inspector general such as the position introduced in the United States in 1983. Both the internal and the external body should, as in the United States, receive complaints from civilians as well as the military, provide anonymity to persons reporting, and have toll-free lines to make it easier for persons to call. There should be no requirement for military personnel to exhaust internal redress of grievance procedures before their concerns are dealt with.

In the opening section of this study, I quoted senior U.S. army officials who told researchers for the Somalia Inquiry that as a result of changes introduced after My Lai, "they are sure that a situation such as the conduct of 2 Commando at Belet Uen could not occur in the U.S. army."[11] I commented that the task of the Somalia Inquiry is to set the stage so that the Canadian military will be able to say the same. It is my hope that this study will help the Somalia Inquiry with this important task.

Notes

CHAPTER ONE — INTRODUCTION

1 See Seymour Hersh, *Cover-Up* (New York: Random House, 1972); J.F. Addicott and W.A. Hudson, "The Twenty-Fifth Anniversary of My Lai: A Time to Inculcate the Lessons" (1993) 139 *Military Law Review* 153; Clifton D. Bryant, *Khaki-Collar Crime* (New York: Free Press, 1979), pp. 217-218.

2 For background on why Canadian troops were in Somalia, see the United Nations Reference Paper, *The United Nations and the Situation in Somalia*, April 1995, p. 6. On 3 December 1992, the Security Council unanimously adopted resolution 794 authorizing the use of "all necessary means to establish as soon as possible a secure environment for humanitarian relief operations in Somalia" and, acting under Chapter VII of the Charter (it was to have been a traditional peacekeeping operation under Chapter VI), the council authorized the secretary general and participating member states to make arrangements for "the unified command and control" of the military forces that would be involved. Canada contributed to that force. See also the military brief to the Somalia Inquiry, "Legal Basis for Chapter VI and Chapter VII UN Sanctioned Operations". See generally Chester A. Crocker, "The Lessons of Somalia, Not Everything Went Wrong" (1995) 74 *Foreign Affairs* 1; and Richard B. Lillich, "The Role of the UN Security Council in Protecting Human Rights in Crisis Situations: UN Humanitarian Intervention in the Post-Cold War World" (1994) 3 *Tulane J. of Int. & Comp. Law* 1.

3 Commission of Inquiry into the Deployment of Canadian Forces to Somalia, Gilles Létourneau, chair, established by Order in Council, P.C. 1995-44, 20 March 1995.

4 See Appendix H to the internal document by Jim Simpson and François Lareau, "Report of Visit to U.S. Army Headquarters — Washington, D.C.", 18 September 1995, p. 1.

5 I was not asked to set out what should be treated as misconduct and who should define misconduct, both important questions. Further, I did not limit my analysis to peacekeeping and peacemaking activities, even though these will continue to be the predominant use of the Canadian military in the future. See Allen G. Sens' study for the Somalia Inquiry, "A Mandate Too Far: The Changing Nature of Peacekeeping and the Limits of Force: The Implications for Canada" (Ottawa, 1995).

6 See M.L. Friedland, *Securing Compliance: Seven Case Studies* (University of Toronto Press, 1990); M.L. Friedland, Michael Trebilcock, and Kent Roach, *Regulating Traffic Safety* (University of Toronto Press, 1990); Friedland, *A Place Apart: Judicial Independence and Accountability in Canada* (Ottawa: Canadian Judicial Council, 1995); Friedland, *National Security: The Legal Dimensions* (Ottawa, 1980); and Friedland, *Presidential Commission on Conflicts of Interest* (University of Toronto, 1991) *The Bulletin*, 13 January 1992.

7 See Friedland, Trebilcock, and Roach, *Regulating Traffic Safety*, p. 76ff; Robert Howse, "Retrenchment, Reform or Revolution? The Shift to Incentives and the Future of the Regulatory State" (1993) 31 *Alberta L. Rev.* 455; and Friedland, "Rewards in the Legal System: Tenure, Airbags, and Safety Bingo" (1993) 31 *Alberta L. Rev.* 493.

8 There are on average only about 135 prosecutions a year. See *Report of the Auditor General of Canada* (1994), volume 16, chapter 31-17. See generally Neil Brooks and Anthony Doob, "Tax Evasion: Searching for a Theory of Compliant Behaviour", in Friedland, *Securing Compliance*, p. 120ff.

9 Lawrence B. Radine, *The Taming of the Troops: Social Control in the United States Army* (Westport, Conn.: Greenwood Press, 1977), p. 156.

10 John Braithwaite, *Crime, Shame and Reintegration* (Cambridge University Press, 1989), pp. 68, 58. See also *Report of the Commission on Systemic Racism in the Ontario Criminal Justice System* (Government of Ontario, 1995), pp. 186-187, 419.

11 See, for example, Martin Edmonds, *Armed Services and Society* (Leicester University Press, 1988), p. 30.

12 Transcript of Policy Hearings, 21 June 1995, p. 442.

13 Queen's Regulations and Orders (QR&O) 19.10(a), (b), (c); and 19.38.

14 See generally Charles C. Moskos and Frank R. Wood, eds., *The Military: More Than Just a Job?* (Washington: Pergamon-Brassey's, 1988); and

Henning Sørensen, "New Perspectives on the Military Profession: The I/ O Model and Esprit de Corps Reevaluated" (1994) 20 *Armed Forces and Society* 599.

15 Erving Goffman, *Asylums: Essays on the Social Situation of Mental Patients and Other Inmates* (Chicago: Aldine Publishing, 1962), p. xiii.

16 For example, voting is now permitted in Canadian institutions (see *Sauvé* v. *Canada (Attorney General)*; *Belczowski* v. *Canada* [1993] 2 S.C.R. 438), and persons found not guilty by reason of insanity can refuse treatment (*Criminal Code*, s. 672.55(1)).

17 See Edmonds, *Armed Services and Society*, p. 34; and Deborah Harrison and Lucie Laliberté, *No Life Like It: Military Wives in Canada* (Toronto: Lorimer, 1994).

18 See Bernard Fleckenstein, "Federal Republic of Germany", in Moskos and Wood, *The Military: More Than Just a Job?*, p. 177ff; and Jurgen Oelrich, "The German Concept of the `Citizen in Uniform'", in Daniella Ashkenazy, *The Military in the Service of Society and Democracy* (Westport, Conn.: Greenwood, 1994), p. 136ff.

19 Reuven Gal, "Israel", in Moskos and Wood, *The Military: More Than Just a Job?*, p. 274; and Gal, *A Portrait of the Israeli Soldier* (New York: Greenwood Press, 1986).

20 R. Owen Parker, a Canadian sociologist with extensive military experience, recently studied the organizational culture of the Canadian military and concluded that it has "shifted from the institutional ideal to an occupational reality." See "The Influences of Organizational Culture on the Personnel Selection Process", Ph.D. thesis, York University, 1995, p. 186. See p. 86ff for a discussion of the institution/organization debate.

21 Moskos and Wood, "Introduction", in *The Military: More Than Just a Job?*, pp. 4-5 and p. 6, summarizing Moskos, "Institutional and Occupational Trends in Armed Forces", p. 15.

22 *Solorio* v. *U.S.* 483 U.S. 435 (1987).

23 *O'Callahan* v. *Parker* 395 U.S. 258 (1969).

24 Charles Cotton, "The Institutional Organization Model and the Military", in Moskos and Wood, *The Military: More than Just a Job?*, pp. 48, 47.

25 (1992) 70 C.C.C. (3d) 1; [1992] 1 S.C.R. 259.

26 (1980) 54 C.C.C. (2d) 129; [1980] 2 S.C.R. 370.

27 *Parker* v. *Levy* 417 U.S. 733 (1974).

28 See Anthony Kellett, *Combat Motivation: The Behavior of Soldiers in Battle* (Boston: Kluwer Nijhoff, 1982), p. 10.

29 Mobile Command Study, *A Report on Disciplinary Infractions and Antisocial Behaviour Within FMC with Particular Reference to the*

Special Service Force and the Canadian Airborne Regiment (DND, 1985), p. 26 [hereafter, the Hewson Report]; and technical report by Major K.W.J. Wenek, p. 178ff.

30 Hewson Report, pp. 17-18, 186-188. In 1979-1982, sexual offences were 54 per 100,000 population in the general population and 85 per 100,000 on DND establishments. On the other hand, robbery was 102 per 100,000 in the general population and 15 per 100,000 on DND establishments. No figures are given on theft, though the extent of theft in the military may be high, because "the abundance of materiel in the military means that its control and maintenance of security is difficult to effect" (Clifton D. Bryant, *Khaki-Collar Crime: Deviant Behavior in the Military Context* (New York: The Free Press, 1979), p. 47).

31 Hewson Report, pp. 187-188.

32 Kellett, *Combat Motivation*, p. 89.

33 See Harrison and Laliberté, *No Life Like It*, p. 44 and endnote 43, p. 247.

34 See subsequently issued CFAO 19-39 (1988) regarding personal harassment and CFAO 19-36 (1992) regarding sexual misconduct.

35 Bryant, *Khaki-Collar Crime*, p. 201.

36 Hewson Report, p. 19.

37 Hewson Report, pp. 18, 30. Assaults were also high for the Royal Canadian Regiment, a fact the authors of the report were at a loss to explain (p. 33).

38 See M.R Schwabe and F.W. Kaslow, "Violence in the Military Family", in *The Military Family: Dynamics and Treatment* (New York: Guilford Press, 1984), p. 129.

39 Harrison and Laliberté, *No Life Like It*, pp. 43-44.

40 *Board of Inquiry re Canadian Airborne Regiment Battle Group* (1993), pp. 3327, 3350ff (hereafter, *Board of Inquiry*).

41 Kellett, *Combat Motivation*, p. 75, citing W. Cockerham, "Selective Socialization: Airborne Training as Status Passage" (1973) 1 *J. of Political and Military Sociology* 215.

42 See the article by Major J.K. McCollum in *Military Review*, November 1976, quoted in Hewson Report, p. 159; see also p. 45.

43 M. Weiss, "Rebirth in the Airborne" (1967) 4 *Transaction* 23, cited in Bryant, *Khaki-Collar Crime*, p. 56.

44 Hewson Report, pp. 45-47.

45 Bryant, *Khaki-Collar Crime*, p. 235.

46 Henry Stanhope, *The Soldiers: An Anatomy of the British Army* (London: Hamish Hamilton, 1979), p. 201.

47 *Board of Inquiry*, pp. 3352, 3336.

48 Hewson Report, p. 20. See also Schwabe and Kaslow, "Violence in the Military Family", p. 133.

49 Hewson Report, p. 20.

50 Harrison and Laliberté, *No Life Like It*, p. 43.

51 Hewson Report, p. 20.

52 *Board of Inquiry*, pp. 3308, 3315.

53 *Board of Inquiry*, p. 3308. See the Standing Operating Procedures for the Canadian Joint Forces Somalia, dated 1 February 1993 (DND 004027):
1. **Alcohol**. Alcohol will only be consumed in the designated area within the HQ lines out of sight of the local population if and when it is authorized.
2. A member who appears to be under the influence of alcohol will not be permitted to leave the HQ premises. Alcohol shall not be served to those nations who are prohibited alcohol (U.S. Forces).
3. The consumption of alcohol by HQ personnel in transit is prohibited.
4. In the unit canteen, rationing and control systems will be established to preclude quantities of alcohol being sold to individuals which exceed their entitlements. Special requests may be made to Sig Ops for a particular social function. The basic ration will be no more than two beer a day.
5. **Drugs**. Under no circumstances will the use of any drug be tolerated. Possession for sale, use or smuggling will be seriously dealt with. This includes the drug known as "KHAT".
6. The chewing of "KHAT" is considered poor conduct by many Somalis, particularly by clan elders. As there is a risk of confusing Canadians use of chewing tobacco with the use of "KHAT", personnel should only chew tobacco out of sight of the local population.

54 See Simpson and Lareau, "Report of Visit to U.S. Army Headquarters", Appendix H. The soundness of the decision was no doubt confirmed in the eyes of the U.S. military after the extreme embarrassment caused by the events at Tailhook later that year in which alcohol was a major contributing factor. See the report by the Office of the Inspector General, Department of Defense, *The Tailhook Report: The Official Inquiry into the Events of Tailhook '91* (New York: St. Martin's, 1993). See also Laura Miller and Charles Moskos, "Humanitarians or Warriors?: Race, Gender, and Combat Status in Operation Restore Hope" (1995) 21 *Armed Forces and Society* 615, p. 620.

55 See QR&O 19.04 (no alcohol except as permitted); QR&O chapter 20 (various forms of drug testing): random testing, 20.08; re safety sensitive positions, 20.09; testing for cause, 20.11; CFAO 19-21 (1992) (drug

control program, including paragraph 17, mandatory urine testing); CFAO 34-36 (1990) (medical examination re drunkenness); CFAO 19-31 (1988) (helping persons overcome dependence); CFAO 56-36 (1977) (drug and alcohol program).

56 *Toronto Star*, 28 January 1996. See the court martial of Major Ross Wickware for allowing drinking while on duty in Bosnia (*Calgary Herald*, 12 April 1995). The Canadian rules prohibited drinking on duty and limited off-duty soldiers to two drinks.

57 Richard Holmes, *Firing Line* (London: Jonathan Cape, 1985), pp. 244, 246, 249. See also Robert Graves, *Goodbye to All That* (Hammondsworth: Penguin, 1973): "Our men looked forward to their tot of rum at dawn stand-to as the brightest moment of their twenty-four hours; when this was denied them, their resistance weakened", quoted in Holmes, p. 249. See also Bryant, *Khaki-Collar Crime*, p. 177.

58 Harrison and Laliberté, *No Life Like It*, p. 43. It may help horizontal bonding with one's buddies, but may detract from vertical bonding with one's superiors; see F.J. Manning "Morale, Cohesion, and Esprit de Corps", in Reuven Gal and A.D. Mangelsdorff, *Handbook of Military Psychology* (New York: John Wiley, 1991), p. 463.

59 Bryant, *Khaki-Collar Crime*, p. 175. See also p. 176: "Alcohol serves the function of relieving the tension of or blunting sexual drives, acting as a kind of sexual anesthetic."

60 Byrant *Khaki-Collar Crime*, pp. 181-182; Holmes, *Firing Line*, p. 251; and Richard A. Gabriel, *To Serve With Honor* (New York: Praeger, 1982), p. 1.

61 Gabriel, *To Serve With Honor*, p. 1. It should be noted, however, that many of these persons ceased to be addicted when they returned to the United States. See L.N. Robbins et al., "Vietnam Vets 3 Years After Vietnam", in L. Britt and C. Winnick, eds., *Yearbook of Substance Use and Abuse*, volume 2 (New York: Humanities Science Press, 1980).

62 T.G. Williams, "Substance Misuse and Alcoholism in the Military Family", in *The Military Family*, pp. 75-76. Alcohol and drug use have subsequently declined, although heavy drinking, which affected one in seven active-duty personnel in 1992, is still a serious problem. See R.M. Bray et al., "Trends in Alcohol, Illicit Drug, and Cigarette Use among U.S. Military Personnel: 1980-1992" (1995) 21 *Armed Forces and Society* 271. For a discussion of treatment programs, see Paul Harig, "Substance Abuse Programs in Military Settings", in Gal and Mangelsdorff, *Handbook of Military Psychology*, p. 635ff. The U.S.

Army is, in theory, dry. The Navy stopped giving rum on ships in 1913; see Holmes, *Firing Line*, pp. 245, 251.

63 See Harrison and Laliberté, *No Life Like It*, p. 43, citing a study by P.M. Hrabok, "The Pre-Adolescent in the Military Family", in *Proceedings of the Regional Social Work Conference on the Child in the Canadian Military Family* (CFB Trenton, 1978).

64 This paragraph is drawn from a study for the Somalia Inquiry by Eugene Oscapella, "Alcohol and Drug Policies Affecting the Canadian Forces" (February 1996). The 1989 study was prepared by the Directorate of Preventive Medicine, Surgeon General Branch (A-MD-007-162/JD-Z06). The 1994 study was done by the Directorate of Health Protection and Promotion, Surgeon General Branch (May 1995). A survey by the military shows a lower rate of drug use than for the civilian population. See "Operation Cascade II, An Anonymous Urinalysis Drug Survey Conducted Across the Canadian Forces, 8 December 1992" (39065D-100-041 (DG PCOR), 25 February 1993).

65 As cited in Oscapella, "Alcohol and Drug Policies", p. 5.

66 Hrabok, "The Pre-Adolescent in the Military Family", cited in Harrison and Laliberté, *No Life Like It*, p. 18.

67 Harrison and Laliberté, *No Life Like It*, p. 18.

68 Bryant, *Khaki-Collar Crime*, p. 352.

69 Gabriel, *To Serve With Honor*, "Foreword", p. xv.

70 Gabriel, *To Serve With Honor*, p. 6.

71 See Anthony Kellett, "Combat Motivation", paper presented to a conference on Psychological War, University of North Carolina, 21 April 1995, p. 3.

72 See also Parker, "The Influences of Organizational Culture".

73 Hewson Report, p. 37.

74 See F.H. Rath and J.E. McCarroll, "Clinical Psychological Assessment", in Gal and Mangelsdorff, *Handbook of Military Psychology*, p. 579ff.

75 Hewson Report, pp. 38, 192. There were 122 cases of schizophrenia per 100,000 in the general population in 1978 and 42 in the military in about the same period; but there were 116 cases per 100,000 of personality disorders in the military and 57 in the general population. See also Harrison and Laliberté, *No Life Like It*, p. 47.

76 See Sharon Smith and Linda Siegel, "War and Peace: The Socialization of Children", in R.A. Hinde and H.E. Watson, *War: A Cruel Necessity?* (London: Tauris, 1995), p. 107.

77 Bryant, *Khaki-Collar Crime*, p. 354.

78 The author's personal observation in a continuing study of the administration of criminal justice in Niagara, Ontario and Niagara, New York.

79 Miller and Moskos, "Humanitarians or Warriors?, pp. 637, 627, 625. The authors also found (p. 627) that blacks, who constituted one third of the U.S. force, had attitudes similar to women's with regard to the local population.

80 Holmes, *Firing Line*, p. 38; Kellett, *Combat Motivation*, p. 80.

81 See U.S. Army Regulation 350-41, *Training in Units* (Department of the Army, 1993), p. 14-3.

82 Addicott and Hudson, "The Twenty-Fifth Anniversary of My Lai", 164.

83 Bryant, *Khaki-Collar Crime*, p. 355.

84 *Board of Inquiry*, p. 3345.

85 CFAO 19-43, in particular paragraphs 25 and 26. See generally the military brief to the Somalia Inquiry, "Anti-Racism Policy of the Canadian Forces". The U.S. Secretary of the Army ordered an investigation in December 1995 into the "climate" throughout the army following the killing of two blacks by white soldiers of the 82nd Airborne Division (*Globe and Mail*, 13 December 1995).

86 Military brief to the Somalia Inquiry, "Leadership Development in the Canadian Forces", pp. 2, 14.

87 Kellett, *Combat Motivation*, pp. 158-159.

88 *International Military and Defense Encyclopedia*, volume 3 (Washington: Brassey's, 1993), p. 1460.

89 Military Training Manual, *Leadership in Land Combat* (DND, 1988) B-GL-318-015/PT-001, p. 1-3.

90 Kellett, *Combat Motivation*, p. 150.

91 See R.A. Gabriel and P.L. Savage, *Crisis in Command: Mismanagement in the Army* (New York: Hill and Wang, 1978), p. 56, cited in Kellett, *Combat Motivation*, p. 162.

92 S. Rolbant, *The Israeli Soldier: Profile of an Army* (Cranbury, N.J.: Yoseloff, 1970), p. 166, as cited by Kellett, *Combat Motivation*, p. 163. There is controversy over how many American officers were killed in Vietnam in relation to the total force. Compare Kellett, *Combat Motivation*, p. 159ff, with Gabriel and Savage, *Crisis in Command*. The latter think the numbers were low; the former argues that they were high for junior officers. As we will see later, a large number of these officers were killed by their own men.

93 Hewson Report, pp. 50, 20.

94 *Board of Inquiry*, p. 3306.

95 Kellett, *Combat Motivation*, p. 169.
96 Graves, *Goodbye to All That*, cited in Kellett, *Combat Motivation*, p. 169ff.
97 Kellett, *Combat Motivation*, pp. 23, 46-47, 112ff; Kellett, *Unit Autonomy*, DSEA Staff Note No. 5/85 (June 1985); Kellett, "The Influence of the Regimental System on Group and Unit Cohesion" (preliminary draft, 1991).
98 Kellett, "Combat Motivation", p. 7.
99 Kellett, *Combat Motivation*, p. 100; see also p. 97ff. See the reference to "buddies" in the Military Training Manual, *Leadership in Land Combat*, pp. 5-6.
100 S.L.A. Marshall, *Men Against Fire* (New York: Morrow, 1947), p. 42, cited in Kellett, *Combat Motivation*, p. 98.
101 Barry Broadfoot, *Six War Years, 1939-1945: Memories of Canadians at Home and Abroad* (Toronto: Doubleday, 1974), cited in Kellett, *Combat Motivation*, p. 99.
102 See P.T. Bartone and F.R. Kirland, "Optimal Leadership in Small Army Units", in Gal and Mangelsdorff, *Handbook of Military Psychology*, p. 396, where this is referred to as horizontal bonding and bonding between leaders and subordinates is referred to as vertical bonding.
103 See Holmes, *Firing Line*, p. 329, who cites Richard Gabriel's suggestion that as many as 20 per cent of U.S. officers killed in the war may have died at the hands of their own men.
104 Kellett, "Combat Motivation", p. 6.
105 See Morris Janowitz and Roger Little, *Sociology and the Military Establishment*, revised edition (New York: Russell Sage, 1965), p. 41.
106 Kellett, *Combat Motivation*, p. 202.
107 See QR&O 4.02(e) for the obligation of officers to report and QR&O 5.01(e) for non-commissioned members.
108 See United Nations Resolution 808 (1993); United Nations Resolution 955 (1994).
109 Ian Brownlie, *Principles of International Law*, fourth edition (Oxford: Clarendon Press, 1990), p. 562.
110 Germany had a large War Crimes Bureau throughout the war, in anticipation of a German victory. See A.M. deZayas, *The Wehrmacht War Crimes Bureau, 1939-1945*, translated from the German (University of Nebraska Press, 1989).
111 Draft Statute of the International Criminal Court, International Law Commission, 46th Session, U.N. Doc. A/CN.4/L/491/Rev. 2 (1994). See generally the fine LL.M. thesis by Bradley E. Berg, "World Criminals and

First Principles: The Jurisdiction of an International Criminal Court",
University of Toronto, 1995.

112 See Berg, "World Criminals and First Principles", chapter 2.

113 See *Criminal Code*, s. 7(3.71)ff, upheld in *Finta* [1994] 1 S.C.R. 701, pp.
805-8; 88 C.C.C. (3d) 417.

114 Friedland, Trebilcock, and Roach, *Regulating Traffic Safety*. See also the
work of William Haddon, especially "On the Escape of Tigers: An
Ecologic Note" (1970) 60 *American J. of Public Health* 2229.

115 Friedland, Trebilcock, and Roach, *Regulating Traffic Safety*, p. 17. See
generally R.V.G. Clarke and P. Mayhew, *Designing Out Crime* (London:
H.M.S.O., 1980).

116 See M.L. Friedland, *Access to the Law* (Toronto: Carswell/Methuen,
1975).

117 *National Defence Act*, R.S.C. 1985, c. N-4 (hereafter, NDA). The federal
government has exclusive legislative authority to pass legislation in
relation to the "Militia, Military and Naval Service, and Defence" under
section 91(7) of the *Constitution Act, 1867*.

118 See NDA, s. 12, authorizing regulations under the act by cabinet, the
minister of national defence, and Treasury Board; and QR&O 1.23 and
NDA, s. 18(2): "Unless the Governor in Council otherwise directs, all
orders and instructions to the Canadian Forces that are required to give
effect to the decisions and to carry out the directions of the Government
of Canada or the Minister shall be issued by or through the Chief of the
Defence Staff."

119 QR&O 1.095 states that the notes "(a) are for guidance of members, and
(b) shall not be construed as if they had the force and effect of law but
should not be deviated from without good reason."

120 CFAO 1-1. See also Canadian Forces Supplementary Orders, described in
CFAO 1-2.

121 See QR&O 4.12; QR&O 3.23 and 4.21; CFAO 4-8, paragraph 2, stating
that routine orders "are means by which COs disseminate regulations,
orders, instructions and general information to personnel under their
command. COs of each unit of the Regular Force and Primary Reserve
shall publish ROs"; and QR&O 19.015: "Every officer and non-
commissioned member shall obey lawful commands and orders of a
superior officer."

122 Pursuant to s. 18(2) of the NDA.

123 See, for example, Officer Professional Development Program, Student
Study Guide, *Military Law 1993/94* (A-PD-050-ODI/PG-004); and
Military Police Procedures (A-SJ-100-004/AG-000).

124 QR&O 4.02 and 5.01. See to the same effect QR&O 19.01.
125 QR&O 4.26(2). COs disseminate regulations, etc. through routine orders; see CFAO 4-8-2.
126 See *Rex* v. *Ross* (1944) 84 C.C.C. 107 (B.C. County Court).
127 See James B. Fay, "Canadian Military Criminal Law: An Examination of Military Justice", LL.M thesis, Dalhousie Law School, 1974. Fay argues that the words "received at the base, unit or element" in QR&O 1.21 do not by their language encompass orders that *originate* at the base, unit or element.
128 NDA, s. 83; QR&O 19.015.
129 QR&O 19.015, notes (b) and (c). See also *Finta* (1994) 1 C.C.C. (3d) 417; [1994] 1 S.C.R. 701; and M.L. Friedland, *National Security: The Legal Dimensions* (Ottawa, 1980) pp. 104-106.
130 QR&O 103.60, note (b).
131 I am indebted to Robert Brush, now completing his third year in the Faculty of Law, University of Toronto, for his thorough analysis of rules of engagement in a research paper, "Controlling the Use of Force by Canadian Soldiers: The Place of Rules of Engagement within the Military Justice System", prepared under my supervision and on file with the Somalia Inquiry.
132 See the military brief to the Somalia Inquiry, "Use of Force and Rules of Engagement", p. 8. This definition is based almost word for word on that adopted by the Joint Chiefs of Staff of the United States Armed Services. See Lieutenant Commander G.R. Philipps, "Rules of Engagement: A Primer" *The Army Lawyer*, July 1993 (Department of the Army Pamphlet 27-50-248), p. 6.
133 See Major Mark S. Martins, "Rules of Engagement for Land Forces: A Matter of Training, Not Lawyering" (1994) 143 *Military Law Review* 1, pp. 35-36.
134 See "Use of Force and Rules of Engagement."
135 Rules of Engagement, Operation Deliverance.
136 *Use of Force in CF, Joint and Combined Operations* (DND, 1995, B-GG-005-004/AF-005). For a discussion of rules of engagement in humanitarian missions, see Jonathan T. Dworken, *Rules of Engagement (ROE) for Humanitarian Intervention and Low-Intensity Conflict: Lessons from Restore Hope* (Alexandria, Va.: Center for Naval Analyses, 1993).
137 *Mathieu* [1995] C.M.A.C. file number 379, p. 13ff.
138 *Brocklebank* [1996] C.M.A.C. file number 383, pp. 20-21, 2 April 1996; (1996) 106 C.C.C. (3d) 234.

139   Martins, "Rules of Engagement for Land Forces", p. 61. See *U.S.* v. *McMonagle* 34 M.J. 825 (A.C.M.R., 1992); and *U.S.* v. *Finsel* 33 M.J. 739 (A.C.M.R., 1991). With respect to the rules of engagement (yellow cards) for British troops in Northern Ireland, see *Jones* (1975) 2 N.I.J.B. 22; and *Clegg* [1995] 1 All E.R. 334 (H.L.), p. 338 ("it is not suggested that the yellow card has any legal force").

140   Martins, "Rules of Engagement for Land Forces", p. 82.

141   *Board of Inquiry*, pp. 3322 and 3330. Note that the rules of engagement for the division that engaged in the My Lai massacre were not issued until the very day of the massacre: see Hersh, *Cover-Up*, pp. 34-35. Hersh also notes (p. 49) that training was poor with respect to the Geneva Convention and the treatment of prisoners of war.

142   See Friedland, *A Place Apart*.

143   See the extensive bibliography on military ethics prepared by C.E. Murphy for the Canadian Forces College, Toronto, 1994.

144   Gabriel, *To Serve With Honor*, pp. 9, 140. The proposed code reads as follows:

The Soldier's Code of Ethics

The nature of command and military service is a moral charge that places each soldier at the center of unavoidable ethical responsibility.

A soldier's sense of ethical integrity is at the center of his effectiveness as a soldier and a leader. Violating one's ethical sense of honor is never justified even at a cost to one's career.

Every soldier holds a special position of trust and responsibility. No soldier will ever violate that trust or avoid his responsibility by any of his actions, no matter the personal cost.

In faithfully executing the lawful orders of his superiors, a soldier's loyalty is to the welfare of his men and mission. While striving to carry out his mission, he will never allow his men to be misused in any way.

A soldier will never require his men to endure hardships or suffer dangers to which he is unwilling to expose himself. Every soldier must openly share the burden of risk and sacrifice to which his fellow soldiers are exposed.

A soldier is first and foremost a leader of men. He must lead his men by example and personal actions; he must always set the standard for personal bravery, courage, and leadership.

A soldier will never execute an order he regards to be morally wrong, and he will report all such orders, policies, or actions of which he is aware to appropriate authorities.

No soldier will ever willfully conceal any act of his superiors, subordinates, or peers that violates his sense of ethics. A soldier cannot avoid ethical judgments and must assume responsibility for them.

No soldier will punish, allow the punishment of, or in any way harm or discriminate against a subordinate or peer for telling the truth about any matter.

All soldiers are responsible for the actions of their comrades in arms. The unethical and dishonorable acts of one diminish us all. The honor of the military profession and military service is maintained by the acts of its members, and these actions must always be above reproach.

The nature of command and military service is a moral charge that places each soldier at the centre of unavoidable ethical responsibility.

145 C.A. Cotton, "A Canadian Military Ethos" (1982) 12 *Canadian Defence Quarterly* 10, p. 13. See also the proposal by General A.J.G.D. de Chastelain, "Canadian Military Ethos", in Department of National Defence, *The Canadian Forces Personnel Concept* (Ottawa, 1987). See generally Parker, "The Influences of Organizational Culture", p. 57ff.

146 "Military Ethics: A Code for the Canadian Forces" (Canadian Staff College, 1992), p. 20.

147 Hines, "Military Ethics", p. 21. The first official call for a published code or statement of the military ethos came in the "Review Group on the Unification Task Force" Ottawa, August 31, 1980 (the Vance Report). A paper, "The Ethics and Ethos of the Military Profession", prepared by SLT Craig Martin (now a law student and my research assistant) in 1988 for the Navy Commanding Officers' Conference in Halifax was subsequently distributed to all units of Maritime Command by Vice Admiral Charles Thomas to get officers thinking more about ethical issues of leadership. For a discussion of codes of ethics in other government departments and agencies, see Bernard Rosen, *Holding Government Bureaucracies Accountable*, second edition (New York: Praeger, 1989), p. 156ff.

148 I am grateful to my colleague, Kent Roach, for his help with this section.

149 *Globe and Mail*, 21 May 1996.

150 See J.R.S. Prichard, "A Systemic Approach to Comparative Law: The Effect of Cost, Fee, and Financing Rules on the Development of the Substantive Law" (1988) 17 *J. of Legal Studies* 451.

151 But see QR&O chapter 38 and CFAO 38-1 relating to the liability of a member to the Crown by an administrative deduction for loss or damage to property.

152   See the *Crown Liability and Proceedings Act*, R.S.C. 1985, c. C-50, ss. 3, 4, 10 and 11, as amended by Stat. Can. 1990, c-8. See generally *Liebmann* v. *Canada (Minister of National Defence)* (1993) 69 F.T.R. 81 (Fed. Ct. Trial Div.).

153   See, for example, *Hendry* v. *The Queen* [1965] 1 Ex. C.R. 392 (T.D.); *Antcil* v. *The Queen* [1959] Ex. C.R. 229 (T.D.); and *The King* v. *Anthony* [1946] S.C.R. 569. There is also liability for the "escape" of dangerous objects from military testing grounds; see *Canadian Encyclopedic Digest*, third edition (Toronto: Carswell, 1991), Armed Forces, #95.

154   See section 10 of the *Crown Liability and Proceedings Act*. See also the seven-day notice period in section 12 and the six-month limitation period in section 287 of the *National Defence Act*.

155   See David Cohen, "Regulating Regulators: The Legal Environment of the State" (1990) 40 *U.T.L.J.* 213, p. 221. See also Sandra McCallum, "Personal Liability of Public Servants: An Anachronism" (1984) *Canadian Public Administration* 611.

156   Section 9 of the *Crown Liability and Proceedings Act*. Section 270 of the *National Defence Act* states: "No action or other proceeding lies against any officer or non-commissioned member in respect of anything done or omitted by the officer or non-commissioned member in the execution of his duty under the Code of Service Discipline, unless the officer or non-commissioned member acted, or omitted to act, maliciously and without reasonable and probable cause." I read this section as protecting those administering justice, not as a protection of military personnel generally.

157   See generally Peter Schuck, *Suing Government: Citizen Remedies for Official Wrongs* (New Haven: Yale University Press, 1983).

158   *Liability of the Crown*, second edition (Toronto: Carswell, 1989), p. 135.

159   Hogg, *Liability of the Crown*, p. 135. There are differences that result. The U.S. Supreme Court, for example, has held that the United States is immune from tortious liability to members of the armed services ("where the injuries arise out of or are in the course of activity incident to service": *Feres* v. *U.S.* (1950) 340 U.S. 135, p. 146), whereas the Australian High Court has held there is no such immunity: see Hogg, *Liability of the Crown*, p. 137. The U.K. *Crown Proceedings Act 1947*, s. 10, had provided immunity in tort to a member of the armed forces and the Crown for acts committed by a member of the military against another member of the military while on duty. This section was repealed by the *Crown Proceedings (Armed Forces) Act 1987*, s. 1. See generally W.V.H. Rogers, *Winfield and Jolowicz on Tort*, 14th edition (London: Sweet and Maxwell, 1994), p. 700ff.

160   The Australian courts draw a distinction between acts committed in peacetime and during "active operations against the enemy." See Hogg, *Liability of the Crown*, p. 136. See also the U.S. *Federal Tort Claims Act of 1946*, 28 U.S.C.A., s. 1346(b) which permits suits against the United States for injuries caused by "the negligent or wrongful act or omission of any employee of the Government while acting within the scope of his office or employment, under circumstances where the United States, if a private person, would be liable to the claimant in accordance with the law of the place where the act or omission occurred." Section 2680(j) of 28 U.S.C.A. provides an exception for "any claim arising out of the combatant activities of the military or naval forces, or the Coast Guard, during time of war." There is also a "discretionary function exception." See generally W.L. Prosser and W.P. Keeton, *The Law of Torts*, fifth edition (St. Paul, Minn.: West, 1984), chapter 25; Barry Kellman, "Judicial Abdication of Military Tort Accountability: But Who is to Guard the Guards Themselves?" [1989] *Duke L.J.* 1597; "Law of Damages Applicable to the Military Claims Act Outside the United States" *Army Lawyer*, November 1995, p. 55; O.M. Reynolds, "The Discretionary Function Exception of the Federal Tort Claims Act: Time for Reconsideration" (1989) 42 *Oklahoma L. Rev.* 459; and D.N. Zillman, "Regulatory Discretion: The Supreme Court Reexamines the Discretionary Function Exception to the Federal Tort Claims Act" (1985) 110 *Military Law Rev.* 115.

161   *Robitaille* v. *The Queen* [1981] 1 F.C. 90 at 93 (Trial Division) per Marceau J.

162   See Hogg, *Liability of the Crown*, pp. 143-144.

CHAPTER TWO — REWARDS

1   The recent suicide of the highest ranking naval officer in the U.S. military following allegations that he was wearing undeserved decorations is some indication of how seriously awards are taken by the military. See *Globe and Mail*, 18 May 1996.

2   See Hugh Arnold, "Sanctions and Rewards: an Organizational Perspective", in M.L.Friedland, *Sanctions and Rewards in the Legal System: A Multidisciplinary Approach* (University of Toronto Press, 1989), p. 152. See generally the entire volume and M.L. Friedland, "Rewards in the Legal System: Tenure, Airbags, and Safety Bingo" (1993) 31 *Alberta L. Rev.* 493.

3   Arnold, "Sanctions and Rewards", p. 142.

4 See Robert Howse, "Retrenchment, Reform or Revolution? The Shift to Incentives and the Future of the Regulatory State" (1993) 31 *Alberta L. Rev.* 455.

5 S.L.A. Marshall, *Men Against Fire* (New York: William Morrow, 1947), p. 22, as cited in Morris Janowitz and Roger Little, *Sociology and the Military Establishment*, revised edition (New York: Russell Sage, 1965), p. 41. For a description of important decision making by lower-level personnel on nuclear-powered aircraft carriers, see K.H. Roberts et al., "Decision Dynamics in Two High Reliability Military Organizations" (1994) 40 *Management Science* 614.

6 Janowitz and Little, *Sociology and the Military*, pp. 41-3. Military traditionalists, they point out (p. 47), are not entirely comfortable with "the use of group consensus procedures by lower commanders."

7 Richard Holmes, *Firing Line* (London: Jonathan Cape, 1985), p. 353. The author points out (pp. 354-355) that "looting was widespread in both World Wars, whatever military law-books may have to say about it" and that after the Falklands War "Argentinian binoculars and bayonets appeared with remarkable rapidity amongst the militaria dealers of [a large military base in England]."

8 See the excellent study by Anthony Kellett, *Combat Motivation: The Behavior of Soldiers in Battle* (The Hague: Kluwer Nijhoff, 1982), p. 203, which I have relied on for much of what follows.

9 Kellett, *Combat Motivation*, p. 204.

10 Kellett, *Combat Motivation*, pp. 204-205.

11 Kellett, *Combat Motivation*, p. 206.

12 See Holmes, *Firing Line*, pp. 356-357, and the studies cited in Kellett, *Combat Motivation*, p. 209.

13 Kellett, *Combat Motivation*, p. 207.

14 Holmes, *Firing Line*, pp. 357-358, 355.

15 See CFAO 49-4 (Career Policy Non-Commissioned Members Regular Force) and CFAO 11-6 (Commissioning and Promotion Policy — Officers — Regular Force). A long-serving member of the Canadian military is quoted as follows in Deborah Harrison and Lucie Laliberté, *No Life Like it: Military Wives in Canada* (Toronto: Lorimer, 1994), pp. 32-33: "The whole system has got clear steps and stages... We've got it laid out better than the civil service, and the kid sees this. We make a fuss about your promotion, okay? The responsibility we give you — we make a big deal out of it. And it works."

16 CFAO 61-8 (Military Honours and Gun Salutes).

17 Volume III (Financial) of QR&O, art. 204.015 (Pay of Officers and Non-Commissioned Members — Incentive Pay).

18 Art. 204.21.

19 CFAO 26-6 (Personnel Evaluation Reports — Officers); and CFAO 26-15 (Performance Evaluation Reports — Other Ranks...).

20 CFAO 26-6, sections 9, 25, and 13.

21 CFAO 26-15.

22 CFAO 26-15, s. 14.

23 See also CFAO 9-51 describing the issuing of a Certificate of Achievement for completing a course.

24 CFAO 26-16 (Conduct Sheets).

25 CFAO 26-16, s. 11.

26 See QR&O 114.55.

27 See Reuven Gal, "Israel", in C.C. Moskos and F.R. Wood, eds. *The Military: More Than Just a Job?* (Washington: Pergamon-Brassey's, 1988), p. 273: "Military service has become an entrance ticket to Israeli society in general and to the job market in particular. The first thing required of any young person who looks for a job is a certificate of discharge from the military."

28 For example, a person who is released (or who resigns) receives only a return of contributions if service has been less than ten years. See *Canadian Forces Superannuation Act*, R.S.C. 1985, c. C-17, s. 18(3).

29 In addition, the Treasury Board's Incentive Award Plan is applicable to the military; see CFAO 99-2 (Incentive Award Plan).

30 See CFAO 18-15 (Canadian Bravery Decorations — Cross of Valour, Star of Courage, and Medal of Bravery).

31 CFAO 18-22.

32 CFAO 18-17.

33 See *In the Line of Duty: Canadian Joint Forces in Somalia 1992-93* (DND, 1994), pp. 290-291, entered as an exhibit at the Somalia Inquiry hearings, 4 April 1996.

34 CFAO 18-11 (United Nations Medals).

35 CFAO 18-13.

36 See CFAO 18-9, (The Canadian Forces' Decoration). See generally F.J. Blatherwick, *Canadian Orders, Decorations, and Medals*, fourth edition (Toronto: Unitrade Press, 1994). For a comprehensive list of orders, decorations, and medals and the order of precedence in which they are worn, see CFAO 18-12.

37 CFAO 18-7 (Unit Awards).

38 See the discussion of peer pressure in Friedland, "Rewards in the Legal System".

39 See Kellett, *Combat Motivation*, pp. 211-213.

40 See Regulations for Service Prisons and Detention Barracks, QR&O, volume IV, Appendix 1.4. The following description is drawn from chapters 5.05 through 5.08, 6.11 and 6.13.

41 Supply and Services Canada, 1989, pp. ii, 14.

42 Kellett, *Combat Motivation*, pp. 202, 328.

CHAPTER THREE — REPORTING WRONGDOING

1 Canada eliminated felonies in 1892, so misprision of felony ceased to be part of Canadian law, assuming that it existed before then. It is no longer part of English or U.S. law. See J.C. Smith and Brian Hogan, *Criminal Law*, sixth edition (London: Butterworths, 1988), p. 763ff; and W.R. LaFave and A.W. Scott, *Criminal Law* (St. Paul, Minn.: West, 1986), pp. 600-601. Section 50(1)(b) of the *Criminal Code*, however, makes it an offence to omit to prevent treason.

2 See, for example, section 215 of the *Criminal Code*, "Duty of Persons to Provide Necessaries", which would include a duty to inform others of the situation, and section 252 with respect to the duty to stop at the scene of an accident.

3 Seymour M. Hersh, *Cover-Up* (New York: Random House, 1972), p. 37. See also L.C.West, *They Call It Justice: Command Influence and the Court Martial System* (New York: Viking, 1977), p. ix, in which a former member of the U.S. Judge Advocate General's Corps stated: "If the offense might prove embarrassing to the military or to the individual commander, it might never come to trial at all. The Green Beret assassination and the My Lai cover-up for over a year are examples of this type of case."

4 The act is replete with duties to act: section 74(c), for example, states that every person who "when ordered to carry out an operation of war, fails to use his utmost exertion to carry the orders into effect...is guilty of an offence and on conviction, if the person acted traitorously, shall suffer death."

5 See to the same effect, section 46 of RCMP Regulations 1988, SOR/88-361.

6 The following description draws on CFAO 4-13, paragraphs 2, 3, 5, 9 and 4.

7　CFAO 24-2, paragraph 2.

8　CFAO 114-3. This therefore expands on the QR&O requirement mentioned earlier that requires a report where a person above the rank of sergeant is "arrested". See also CFAO 114-2, requiring reporting to COs of summary proceedings.

9　CFAO 55-2, paragraph 1.

10　CFAO 71-9, paragraph 1.

11　CFAO 71-13, paragraph 1.

12　CFAO 71-4, paragraph 4.

13　CFAO 30-2, paragraph 4.

14　See the internal memo by Jim Simpson and François Lareau, "Notes on Sources of Military Law and Reporting Requirements", 27 September 1995, p. 11. The order signed by Colonel Labbé is found in exhibit E, vol. 6, pp. 1056-1096, of the Court Martial of Lt. Col. Mathieu under the heading "Reports and Returns", p. 1059.

15　*Security Orders for DND & CF Military Police Procedures*, A-SJ-100-004/AG-000, 1 April 1991. A revised volume, *Military Police Policies*, produced in late 1995, incorporated many of the Police Policy Bulletins. I have kept the references to the earlier documents that were applicable during the time Canadian troops were in Somalia. Moreover, the process of incorporating the bulletins is not yet complete.

16　Paragraph 14. See also the discussion in Chapter 5.

17　Paragraph 4.

18　Paragraph 5.

19　This is now found in the revised Military Police Procedures, chapter 4, in *very* abbreviated form.

20　A-SJ-100-004/AG-000, chapter 48, section 1-1. This is now in chapter 4 of Military Police Procedures.

21　Military Police Procedures, chapter 48, section 3-1.

22　Military Police Procedures, chapter 48, section 3-4.

23　This bulletin has not yet been incorporated into the revised volume on Military Police Policies.

24　As noted in Chapter 5, the new policy expands on chapter 12 of Military Police Procedures, "Military Police Procedures — International Peacekeeping Operations" and refers to the memo from Major J.M. Wilson, 8 December 1992 (document #019054) stating that "All reports other than 'local distribution' must be sent to NDHQ for D Police Ops."

25 See Army Regulation 20-1, "Inspector General Activities and Proce-
    dures", March 1994, s. 1-11:
    1-11. Confidentiality
    a. Persons who ask the IG for help, make a complaint, give evidence,
    contact or assist an IG during an inspection or investigation, or otherwise
    interact with an IG, often have an expectation of confidentiality. This
    expectation encompasses safeguarding their identity and the nature of
    their contact with the IG, and protection against reprisal. The IG has a
    duty to protect confidentiality to the maximum extent possible,
    particularly when it is specifically requested. While the need for
    confidentiality and the measures necessary to protect it will vary with the
    circumstances, the IG always gives this issue priority attention.
    (1) When a person complains or provides information about impropriety
    or wrongdoing, the IG will not disclose the complainant's identity
    outside IG channels or to the directing authority without the complain-
    ant's consent, unless the IG determines such disclosure is unavoidable
    during the course of an inquiry or investigation. If the IG determines that
    disclosure is unavoidable, the IG will try to inform the person before
    disclosure. If the person objects, the IG will coordinate with the Legal
    Office, USAIGA (Defense Switched Network (DSN): 227-9734) before
    proceeding. Efforts to notify the person and the circumstances of any
    disclosure of the person's name will be made part of the record.
    (2) When a person seeks assistance from the IG, it is often necessary to
    reveal the person's identity to obtain the help needed. The IG will inform
    the person of that necessity. The IG file will reflect that the person was
    informed.
    b. When a person requests anonymity, the IG will take more extensive
    measures to protect the person's identity. The person's name will not be
    used as a file identifier or as a means to retrieve a file. The request for
    anonymity will be prominently stated and the use of the person's name
    will be minimized in any file or record created by the IG. This is most
    easily done by referring to the person as "complainant", "witness", or
    similar title, instead of by name.
    c. The intent behind this emphasis on confidentiality is to protect
    individual privacy, maintain confidence in the IG system, and minimize
    the risk of reprisal. It is a key component of the IG system because it
    encourages voluntary cooperation and willingness to ask for help or to
    present a complaint for resolution.
    d. While protecting confidentiality is a priority concern for the IG, it
    cannot be absolutely guaranteed. IGs will not unconditionally promise

confidentiality. It may be breached if required by law or regulation, or by direction of TIG. Persons who request anonymity or who express a concern about confidentiality will be told this.

e. All IGs and IG employees are obligated to protect confidentiality after their service with the IG system has ended.

See also the statement by Lieutenant-General R.H. Griffith, Inspector General, Department of the Army, before the Committee on Governmental Affairs, United States Senate, 26 February 1992, pp. 5, 10-12. With respect to the inspector general of the department of defense, see "Organization of Functions Guide", January 1994, IGDG 5106.1, s. 9.5, "DoD Hotline": "(a). Administers the DoD Hotline program in accordance with DoD Directive 7050.1, *DoD Hotline*... (d). Ensures that the confidentiality of the complainant is protected to the maximum extent possible."

26 See Bernard Rosen, *Holding Government Bureaucracies Accountable*, second edition (New York: Praeger, 1989), pp. 147-150. See *Pickering* v. *Board of Education* 88 S. Ct. 1731 (1968); cf. *Arnett* v. *Kennedy* 94 S. Ct. 3187 (1975).

27 See Ronald Daniels and Randall Morck, *Corporate Decision-Making in Canada* (University of Calgary Press, 1995).

28 Robert Howse and Ronald Daniels, "Rewarding Whistleblowers: The Costs and Benefits of Incentive-Based Compliance Strategy", in Daniels and Morck, *Corporate Decision-Making*, p. 525, citing R.J. Herrnstein and J.Q. Wilson, *Crime and Human Nature* (New York: Simon and Schuster, 1985), and p. 545. The U.S. False Claims Act, 31 USC 3730, provides for bounties for whistleblowers.

CHAPTER FOUR — ADMINISTRATIVE AND INFORMAL SANCTIONS

1 My understanding of these issues owes much to one of my research assistants, Craig Martin, a second-year student in the Faculty of Law who was a naval officer before entering law school. Craig Martin entered Collège Militaire Royal de St. Jean in August 1981, graduated from the Royal Military College of Canada in May 1986, and served as a naval officer until August 1990, having achieved the rank of naval lieutenant.

2 CFAO 19-21, paragraph 18, Canadian Forces Drug Control Program.

3 For a discussion of comparable administrative measures in the U.S. military, see David A. Schlueter, *Military Criminal Justice: Practise and Procedure*, third edition (Charlottesville, Va.: Michie, 1992), pp. 38-39.

4 CFAO 26-17, Recorded Warning and Counselling and Probation — Other Ranks. Note that this is only a general outline of the process. There are a considerable number of qualifications to the policy and procedures for the application of these mechanisms, and the process is complicated by the fact that there are specific Recorded Warnings for reasons relating to Alcohol, Drugs, Indebtedness, and Obesity, each with somewhat different procedures.

5 QR&O 19.75: "'suspend from duty' means to relieve an officer or non-commissioned member from the performance of all military duty." The person may be suspended "in any circumstances that, in the authority's opinion, render it undesirable in the interests of the service that the member remain on duty." See its use with respect to racist conduct set out in CFAO 19-43, paragraph 22.

6 CFAO 15-2 Annex A (Specific Release Policies) section 2. See also CFAO 49-10, annex E, appendix 2 — Recommendation for Compulsory Release. See also QR&O 15.01 (under item 2 or 5F).

7 It is not strictly necessary: CFAO 26-17, paragraph 7 states that "except for shortcomings related to drugs or alcohol, the following procedures apply to C&P: a. Prior to initiating C&P, the member should first be warned of the shortcomings, verbally or by means of an RW." Nonetheless, it is customary to apply a Recorded Warning first.

8 CFAO 26-17, paragraph 6 (a).

9 See CFAO 49-4 and 49-5 regarding promotion, and CFAO 204-2 regarding incentive pay.

10 CFAO 26-17, paragraph 7(b)(2).

11 QR&O 101.11, paragraph 3. Paragraph 2 states that "a reproof shall be reserved for conduct which although reprehensible is not of sufficiently serious nature, in the opinion of the officer administering the reproof, to warrant being made the subject of a charge and brought to trial." This seems clearly more disciplinary in tone than the Recorded Warning. See also CFAO 101-1 (Reproof — Officers and Warrant Officers) for amplification of QR&O 101.11.

12 While it is supposed to be destroyed, there is apparently considerable suspicion within the service that it is not, or in any event, even if the hard copy is destroyed, the memory and negative effects of it linger on. These suspicions were given some credence in the court martial of Major Seward, where a copy of his reproof was tendered as evidence long after it should have been destroyed. See *Transcripts of Court Martial of Maj. Seward, 7th Trial within a Trial.*

13 CFAO 26-21, paragraph 1(a).

14 Interestingly, in the context of the next section on organizational culture
    and tacitly understood procedures, CFAO 26-21, paragraph 8 simply
    stipulates that there must be prior counselling, stating that "the CO shall
    personally:
    a. inform the officer of the shortcomings;
    b. counsel him on ways and means to overcome the shortcomings;
    c. stipulate a specific period in which the officer must improve;
    d. advise him that failure to correct his shortcomings in the stipulated
       period will result in his being the subject of a Report of Shortcomings;
       and
    e. note appropriate details on the officer's file."

15 DPCO procedures for dealing with all of these administrative mecha-
    nisms can be found in CPCD-OPM/110-4, p. 110-46.

16 See documents 000197 and 000199 of the Board of Inquiry, Phase I.

17 *Transcripts of Court Martial of Maj. Seward.*

18 CFAO 26-21, paragraph 3.

19 CFAO 19-38, paragraph 17 (emphasis added).

20 While this is not the place to explore the issue, the procedures do raise
    some interesting issues in administrative law. The role of the command-
    ing officer in both counselling and making the decision to take further
    action, including the final decision to recommend release, could arguably
    be sufficient to raise the question of there being a reasonable apprehen-
    sion of bias. Furthermore, given the importance of the interest at stake (a
    continued career), the absence of a more formal hearing, together with
    there being no requirement to provide evidence, the lack of any formal
    requirement of disclosure, and the lack of any real opportunity to cross-
    examine or present a counter-argument, the process leading up to
    compulsory release could cumulatively amount to the denial of the
    party's right to the protection of procedural fairness. Would the redress
    of grievance procedure cure any defects? See generally on procedural
    fairness with respect to administrative action, *Nicholson v. Haldimand-
    Norfolk Regional Board of Commissioners of Police* [1979] 1 S.C.R. 311;
    D. Mullan, "Fairness: The New Natural Justice?" (1975) 25 *U.T.L.J.* 28;
    Martin Loughlin, "Procedural Fairness: A Study of the Crisis in
    Administrative Law Theory" (1978) 28 *U.T.L.J.* 215; and Evans, Janisch,
    Mullan, and Risk, *Administrative Law: Cases, Text, and Materials*, fourth
    edition (Toronto: Emond Montgomery, 1995), p. 45ff. For Federal Court
    of Canada trial division cases imposing a duty of fairness in dismissal

from employment and similar cases, see *Miller* v. *Canada* [1994] F.C.J. No. 330; *Lecoupe* v. *Canada* [1994] F.C.J. No. 1967; and *Lee* v. *Canada* [1992] F.C.J. No. 145. Note that the U.S. Army has more written procedural safeguards. See "Procedure for Investigating Officers and Boards of Officers", Army Regulation 15-6.

21 QR&O 19.26 and 19.27; CFAO 19-32.

22 *National Defence Act*, R.S.C. 1985, c. N-4, s. 139(1).

23 See the oral presentation of the military brief to the Somalia Inquiry, 21 June 1995, pp. 10-11: "Informal sanctions may range from verbal reprimands to remedial additional training."

24 The testimony of Major Seward provided an example of informal sanctions having been applied on a large scale and also gave some insight into the implicit and tacit understanding within the military of where the appropriate limits to such sanctions lie (Transcript of Evidentiary Hearings, Somalia Inquiry, 20 December 1995, vol. 31, pp. 5891-93):

Q. Now, I want to turn to regimental Sergeant-Major Jardine. I understand, sir, it is uncomfortable for you to comment in public about someone else, although some other people haven't hesitated to do that about you.

But I understand Sergeant-Major Mills once told you about unjust punishment that was ordered?

A. Yes. Again, it was in regards to the October 3rd incidents. It was subsequent to our week of being in the field and there were a list of people who had possible involvements in that, including the regimental orderly corporal who some people thought had not come forward, readily forward with the identification of the person running from the Kyrenia Club.

The regimental sergeant-major ordered that they be employed at weekend general duty type of task. He gave that instruction to the commando sergeant-major, Sergeant-Major Mills. Sergeant-Major Mills explained to him that it was an unlawful punishment and that if he was to proceed he would like that order in writing.

Q. Why was it an unlawful punishment?

A. These men had not gone through the summary trial process.

Q. And those who committed offence subsequently did; is that correct?

A. That's correct.

Q. So Sergeant-Major Mills asked for confirmation of this in writing. I take it this was just a few days after these names came to light?

A. It was at the end of the week. So at the end of the week of the 5th of October and that punishment was effected on the Saturday and the Sunday of that week.

Q. I understand this order was, in fact, carried out by Sergeant-Major Mills?

A. It was, and with my knowledge.

Q. But what did this tell you about Mr. Jardine's approach to things? How did it differ from what you had experienced previously in your many years in the Forces?

A. To me it confirmed that the advice coming from the regimental sergeant-major regarding discipline was inappropriate.

The role of the regimental sergeant-major is to ensure the welfare of the men, and it's almost like a dichotomy. He is responsible for their welfare and yet he is very much responsible for good order and discipline within the battalion.

However, the two aren't incompatible as long as good order and discipline is effected through the due processes provided in military justice.

In my opinion, that due process was being violated.

25 The recent court martial of submarine commander Lieutenant Commander Dean Marshaw is perhaps an illustration of how this process would function in practice. See *Globe and Mail*, 3 November 1995.

26 Charles A. Cotton, "Military Mystique: Somalia Shows Dark Side of Elite Units", *Calgary Herald*, 3 September 1993. This is a reflection of what Cotton has called "beleaguered warrior syndrome", which is "characterized by a dominant focus on battle and a sense of alienation from a military that is perceived as having become too civilianized to perform its essential function of combat." See Cotton, "Institutional and Occupational Values in Canada's Army" (1981) 8 *Armed Forces and Society* 99, p. 108. This is of particular interest in light of the observations regarding "warrior strategies" and "humanitarian strategies" differing across gender and racial lines in the U.S. forces in Somalia. See Laura Miller and Charles Moskos, "Humanitarians or Warriors?: Race, Gender, and Combat Status in Operation Restore Hope" (1995) 21 *Armed Forces and Society* 615.

CHAPTER FIVE — MILITARY POLICE

1   Conversation with Commander Paul Jenkins, NDHQ, 14 May 1996.
    These figures do not include civilian employees or people working for
    the Communications Security Establishment.
2   Conversation with Colonel Marc Caron, Director of Force Concepts,
    NDHQ, 17 May 1996.
3   See Canadian Centre for Justice Statistics, *Juristat* 16/1 (January 1996),
    "Police Personnel and Expenditures in Canada — 1994".
4   See Appendix 1.4 of volume 4 of QR&O: "Regulations for Service
    Prisons and Detention Barracks", P.C. 1967-1703.
5   See the paper by Major M.R. McNamee prepared for the Naval War
    College, Newport, R.I., June 1992, "Military Police: A Multipurpose
    Force for Today and Tomorrow", p. 26.
6   See Canadian Forces School of Intelligence and Security, "Military
    Police: History" (1974), pp. 1, 8.
7   As quoted in Commander Paul Jenkins' paper, "Policing the Canadian
    Forces in the 21st Century", staff college paper, 1991, p. 1.
8   "Military Police", in *International Military and Defense Encyclopedia*
    (Washington: Brassey's, 1993), p. 1752.
9   McNamee, "Military Police", pp. 18-19.
10 This section is drawn from Canadian Forces School of Intelligence and
    Security, "Military Police: History"; and D.R. Johnson, ed., *On Guard
    for Thee: The Silver Anniversary of the Security Branch* (Winnipeg:
    Jostens, 1993).
11 Colonel A.R. Ritchie, "A Brief History of the Canadian Provost Corps",
    in *On Guard for Thee*, p. 11.
12 This section is drawn from Canadian Forces, "Military Police: History",
    p. 29ff; and *On Guard for Thee*, p. 43ff.
13 *Canadian Forces Reorganization Act*, Stat. Can. 1966-67, c-96.
14 See *On Guard for Thee*, p. 51, referring to the 1978 Craven Report and
    the 1981 DGIS Study. The Communications Security Establishment
    (CSE) is also outside the compass of the Security Branch.
15 A-SJ-100-004/AG-000, April 1991. Security procedures are published in
    A-SJ-100-001/AS-000, *Security Orders for DND & CF*.
16 A-SJ-100-004/AG-000, 31 October 1995, with additional changes on 28
    February 1996.
17 S. 156 of the *National Defence Act*, R.S.C. 1985, c. N-4, provides that
    156. Such officers and non-commissioned members as are appointed
    under regulations for the purposes of this section may

(a) detain or arrest without a warrant any person who is subject to the Code of Service Discipline, regardless of the rank or status of that person, who has committed, is found committing, is believed on reasonable grounds to have committed a service offence or who is charged with having committed a service offence;
(b) exercise such other powers for carrying out the Code of Service Discipline as are prescribed in regulations made by the Governor in Council.

QR&O 22.02(2) spells out who is included in section 156:
The following persons are appointed for the purposes of section 156 of the *National Defence Act*:
(a) every officer posted to an established position to be employed on military police duties, and
(b) every person posted to an established military police position and qualified in the military police trade, provided that such officer or person is in lawful possession of a Military Police Badge and an official Military Police Identification Card.
See also *Military Police Procedures*, chapter 2-2.

18 See QR&O 22.02 and Police Policy Bulletin 5.0/94. Section 3 of the bulletin contains the limitations on the power to arrest contained in s. 495 of the *Criminal Code*.

19 See Police Policy Bulletin 5.0/94. See also QR&O 101.12 which seems somewhat more generous than civilian procedures. Paragraphs 6 and 8 state that military police cannot read a fellow accused's statement to the accused and that the accused should not be cross-examined on a statement he or she has given.

20 See Police Policy Bulletin 7.0/94.

21 See *Military Police Procedures*, chapter 2-2. See also Police Policy Bulletin 3.11/94 (Specially Appointed Persons) and 3.2/95 (Specially Appointed Persons: Status and Discretion).

22 QR&O, section 22.01(2).

23 See *Courchene* (1989) 52 C.C.C. (3d) 375 (Ont. C.A.); and *Nolan* v. *The Queen* (1987) 34 C.C.C. (3d) 289, [1987] 1 S.C.R. 1212.

24 See M.L. Friedland, *Double Jeopardy* (Oxford: Clarendon Press, 1969), p. 335ff: "the true rule [is] simply that the civilian courts have primary jurisdiction over civilian offences committed in England. A necessary result of asserting that the civilian authority is paramount is to disregard a prior military judgment if, but only if, military jurisdiction was assumed without the express or implied consent of the civilian

authorities" (p. 336). See also the discussion of double jeopardy in Chapter 6.

25 See Friedland, *Double Jeopardy*, pp. 351-353.

26 See Transcript of Evidentiary Hearings, 11 October 1995, volume 5, p. 974. See also Clifton D. Bryant, *Khaki-Collar Crime: Deviant Behavior in the Military Context* (New York: The Free Press, 1979), pp. 198-200: "the military usually attempts to assume jurisdiction over the serviceman who commits a civilian crime, rather than allow the civilian authorities to hold sway and provide the unfavorable publicity of a civilian trial... The military attempts to preserve the image of a system beyond the influence and control of a civilian society."

27 Conversation with Commander Paul Jenkins, NDHQ, 20 September 1995.

28 See McNamee, "Military Police", p. 10.

29 The cap was apparently set when cabinet passed an order in council on 7 December 1992, placing members of the Canadian Forces on active service in Somalia. See Order No. 2 Placing Members of the Canadian Forces on Active Service (Somalia), P.C. 1992-2519, *Canada Gazette* Part II, vol. 126, no. 27, p. 5378. The published document does not mention the cap. Caps are specifically provided for under section 16(2) of the *National Defence Act* for the creation of a special force, but apparently the Somalia force was created under section 31(1)(b) of the act, not under section 16.

30 Conversation with Lieutenant Colonel P. Cloutier, 10 August 1995.

31 See the recommendations of the *Board of Inquiry Canadian Airborne Regiment Battle Group*, Phase I, vol. XI, Annex H (1993), p. 3340: "The Board recommends that flexibility be provided to the Commander of any future Canadian contingent to adjust initial staff figures and structures of his force according to his detailed operational estimate." See also the military brief to the Somalia Inquiry on the Canadian Forces in Somalia, Operation Deliverance, p. 5: "It would have been better to have given only general guidelines for manning and allow the final numbers to be developed by the HQ tasked with the mission."

32 Canada Treaty Series, 1945, No. 7, Charter of the United Nations, Chapter VI, Pacific Settlement of Disputes.

33 See letter from Colonel A.R. Wells to Board of Inquiry, 12 October 1994, document #001871. See also memorandum from Major J.M. Wilson, 18 December 1992, document #019056.

34 Security Council Resolution 794, 3 December 1992, U.N. Doc. No.S/RES/794 (1992).

35 *Board of Inquiry*, p. 3337.

36 See the following documents from Major Wilson in Tab L of François Lareau's memo of 12 October 1995: documents dated 7, 11, 15 and 18 December 1992 (#019055, 006444, 019052, 019056). These four documents are also found in the Somalia Inquiry's document books on pre-deployment: book 20, tab 20, exhibit P-64; book 21, tab 11, exhibit P-70; book 21, tab 23, exhibit P-70; book 22, tab 11, exhibit P-71.

37 Memorandum of Major J.M. Wilson, 18 December 1992 (#019056).

38 Document #019055, 7 December 1992.

39 See Major Wilson's Operation Deliverance After Action Report — Military Police Operations, 17 May 1994 (Tab L of François Lareau's memo of 12 October 1995), pp. 2 and 6 (DND #130769 and 130773).

40 Wilson, p. 17 (DND #130784).

41 12 October 1994, #001871, p. 3.

42 12 October 1994, #001871, p. 3.

43 See René J. Marin, "Report of the External Review of the Canadian Forces Special Investigation Unit" (1990). See also the follow-up report, René J. Marin, "Audit of External Review of the Canadian Forces Special Investigation Unit" (1994).

44 Mr. Justice D.C. McDonald, chair, *Commission of Inquiry Concerning Certain Activities of the Royal Canadian Mounted Police* (Ottawa, 1981).

45 Marin, 1990 Report, p. 41.

46 Marin, 1990 Report, p. 56.

47 Marin, 1994 Report, p. 17.

48 Marin, 1994 Report, p. 17.

49 Marin, 1990 Report, p. 89.

50 Conversations with Commander Jenkins, 13 October 1995 and 14 May 1996. See Marin, 1994 Report, p. 6.

51 See Memorandum by Captain R.A. Beekhuizen, 25 August 1995, "National Investigation Service", Tab B of memo by François Lareau, 12 October 1995. This is more or less the language used in chapter 18, section 2 of the revised *Military Police Policies*, effective October 1995.

52 See Marin, 1994 Report, p. 14.

53 Marin, 1994 Report, p. 13. I understand that CFAO 22-3 dealing with the SIU and CFAO 22-4 dealing with the military police are in the process of being amalgamated: conversation with Commander Jenkins, 13 October 1995.

54 See Bulletin 3.2/95.

55 See Major Tony Battista, "The Credibility of the Security and Military Police (SAMP) Branch" (1995) 1 *Thunderbird* 6.

56 Marin, 1994 Report, p. 7.

57 Chapter 11-1, paragraph 1-10. Paragraph 11 provides that the appropriate commanders and COs should be informed of military police investigations "at the earliest practical moment". See also chapter 1-1, paragraph 10.

58 Bulletin 3.2/95: Special Appointed Persons: Status and Discretion, ss. 7, 8 and 18.

59 CFAO 22-4, paragraph 4, states that "Technical direction means the specific instruction on the performance of security and military police functions provided by security advisors (with the advice and direction of military and/or civil legal authorities as the circumstances warrant)." See also Joint Doctrine for Canadian Forces: Joint and Combined Operations (1995) B-GG-005-004/AF-000) paragraph 3(d).

60 Examination in chief of Sergeant Robert Martin in second court martial of Private K. Brown, exhibit P-22.4 (transcript of Court Martial of Private Brown, volume 4), pp. 644-645.

61 CFAO 22-4 reaffirms chapter 48 of volume 4 of *Military Police Procedures*, "Military Police Unusual Incident Report", described in Chapter 3.

62 The policy expands on chapter 12 of *Military Police Procedures*, "Military Police Procedures — International Peacekeeping Operations". See also the memo from Major J.M. Wilson, 8 December 1992 (document #019054, document book 20 — pre-deployment, tab 25, exhibit P-69), stating that "All reports other than 'local distribution' must be sent to NDHQ for D Police Ops".

63 CFAO 22-4, paragraph 13.

64 See paragraph 3 of Annex B, chapter 47 of vol. 4, *Military Police Procedures*: "MPIR are distributed...on a need-to-know basis within DND." See also s. 5: "Distribution/circulation of MPIR of local significance only are usually limited to the base/station."

65 Emphasis in original. See also chapter 15-1, paragraph 8 of vol. 4, *Military Police Procedures*: "MP police and security related investigations shall only be discontinued or cancelled with the concurrence of NDHQ/Director Police Operations."

66 *Military Police Procedures*, chapter 56-1, paragraph 1, deals with complaints against military police: "Complaints made by anyone concerning the acts, inaction or behaviour of MP, in respect of their MP duties and responsibilities, shall be fully and impartially investigated." See also Marin, 1994 Report, p. 8, which complains that the activities of the military police "are not subject to the same scrutiny as are the activities of civil police officers."

67 See Army Regulation 10-87, Major Army Commands in the Continental United States, 30 October 1992, chapter 4, s. 4-1. See also s. 4-2.

68 See document #022688, July 1994, p. 2 (DND #091070).

69 Army Regulations 195-2, Criminal Investigation Activities, 30 October 1985, paragraph 1-5 and Appendix B.

70 Army Regulation 190-30, Military Police Investigations, 1 August 1978, paragraph 1-5a.

71 See U.K. QR&O (Army), chapter 4, annex c, s. 25.

72 See Les Johnston, "An Unseen Force: The Ministry of Defence Police in the UK" (1992) 3 *Policing and Society* 23. See also F.E.C. Gregory, "The Concept of 'Police Primacy' and its Application in the Policing of the Protests Against Cruise Missiles in Great Britain" (1986) 9 *Police Studies* 59.

73 For a discussion of the independence of civilian police, see *R. v. Metropolitan Police Commissioner, Ex parte Blackburn* [1968] 1 All E.R. 763 (C.A.).

74 *National Defence Act*, s. 162.

75 See the suggestion by Major J.M. Wilson in his after action report of 17 May 1994, p. 16, that the various orders and rules "should clearly state the requirement for MP investigations" in spite of a summary investigation or board of inquiry (DND #130783).

76 See letter from Colonel Wells to NDHQ, July 1994 (DND #091070).

77 Conversation with Commander Paul Jenkins, 20 September 1995.

78 Officially designated Project Charter C-18, chaired by retired Brigadier General D. McKay, with Commander Paul Jenkins as the Deputy Team Leader. See document dated 31 July 1995, "Project Charter C-18: Security and Military Police". This is part of a larger group in the DND/ CF, Management Command Control Reengineering Team (MCCRT).

   The Thunderbird is the official emblem of SAMP. "The common feature of its attributes", the main historical document on the security branch states, "concerns its role as a protecting spirit, one who gives wise counsel and guards the tribe from evil and misfortune." (See preface to Canadian Forces School of Intelligence and Security, "Military Police History" (1974).)

79 Conversation with Commander Paul Jenkins, May 1996.

80 See Lieutenant Colonel M.A. Hodge, "Training Military Police for the 21st Century" *Military Police*, August 1994. See also U.S. Army Field Manual No. 19-4, *Military Police Battlefield Circulation Control, Area Security, and Enemy Prisoner of War Operations* (Washington: Department of the Army, 1993), chapters 7 and 8.

81 *Military Police Corps Regimental History* (U.S. Army Military Police
    School, Fort McClellan, Alabama, 36205-5030, no date). U.K. military
    police are not involved directly in combat and are therefore similar to the
    Canadian military police. See Captain R.O. Gienapp, "Exchange Officer
    with the Royal Military Police" *Military Police*, Spring 1995, p. 29.
82 See Hodge, "Training Military Police", p. 29ff.
83 Hodge, "Training Military Police", p. 30. I could not see any discussion
    of the military police in the recent Report of the Special Committee on
    the Restructuring of the Reserves, Hon. Brian Dickson, chair (DND,
    1995).
84 See McNamee, "Military Police", pp. 7-8.
85 Michel Thivierge (assistant commissioner of the RCMP), "Police and
    Military Cooperation", in D.E. Code and C. Ursulak, *Leaner and
    Meaner: Armed Forces in the Post-Gulf War Era* (Ottawa: Conference of
    Defence Association Institute, 1992), p. 31ff.
86 *National Defence Act*, R.S.C. c. N-5, part XI, "Aid of the Civil Power".
87 Thivierge, "Police and Military Cooperation", p. 43.
88 Paul Jenkins, "Policing the Canadian Forces in the 21st Century"
    (unpublished, 1991), p. 22. Recruits and transfers receive four or five
    months' training at the Canadian Forces School of Intelligence and
    Security at Camp Borden, established during the Second World War. The
    schools of the three services were integrated in 1967; see Canadian
    Forces School of Intelligence and Security, "Military Police History",
    p. 29.
89 Marin, 1990 Report, p. 86.
90 Jenkins, "Policing the Canadian Forces", p. 22.
91 See the earlier discussion of the institution/occupation debate (Chapter 1).
92 Memorandum 1900-1 (D Police Services), 3 August 1995.
93 *Toronto Star*, 20 December 1995, stating that elements of 2 Military
    Police Platoon were sent.

CHAPTER SIX — MILITARY JUSTICE

1 Anthony Kellett, *Combat Motivation: The Behavior of Soldiers in Battle*
   (Boston: Kluwer Nijhoff, 1982), pp. 89, 93. See generally chapter 7, "A
   Historical Overview of Military Discipline".
2 See the evidence of Captain (N.) W.A. Reed before the Somalia Inquiry,
   transcript of policy hearings, 21 June 1995, p. 438.

3 Kellett, *Combat Motivation*, pp. 90, 137, 140. See generally, Desmond Morton, "The Supreme Penalty: Canadian Deaths by Firing Squad in the First World War" (1972) 79 *Queen's Quarterly* 345.

4 Kellett, *Combat Motivation*, pp. 137-140.

5 See Omer Bartov, *Hitler's Army: Soldiers, Nazis, and War in the Third Reich* (Oxford University Press, 1991). See also Kellett, *Combat Motivation*, p. 146, describing how the Germans placed minefields, barbed wire, and special guards behind their own lines.

6 *R. v. Généreux* (1992) 70 C.C.C. (3d) 1; [1992] 1 S.C.R. 259. See, to the same effect, the companion Supreme Court of Canada case, *Forster* (1992) 70 C.C.C. (3d) 59; [1992] 1 S.C.R. 339.

7 *Généreux*, p. 21 C.C.C. Section 11(d) states that "any person charged with an offence has the right...to be presumed innocent until proven guilty according to law in a fair and public hearing by an independent and impartial tribunal."

8 *Généreux*, p. 25 C.C.C.

9 *R. v. MacKay* (1980) 54 C.C.C. (2d) 129; [1980] 2 S.C.R. 370.

10 *MacKay*, p. 151 C.C.C.

11 *MacKay*, p. 153 C.C.C.

12 *MacKay*, pp. 137-138 C.C.C.

13 E.F. Sherman, "Military Justice Without Military Control" (1973) 82 *Yale L.J.* 1398, pp. 1409-1410.

14 Joseph W. Bishop, Jr., *Justice Under Fire: A Study of Military Law* (New York: Charterhouse, 1974), p. 21. See also R.A. McDonald, "The Trail of Discipline: The Historical Roots of Canadian Military Law" (1985) 1 *Canadian Forces JAG J.* 1, p. 28: "An undisciplined military force is a greater danger to Canada than to any foreign enemy."

15 Stat. Can. 1950, c. 43. See also s. 129(5): "No person may be charged under this section with any offence for which special provision is made in sections 73 to 128 but the conviction of a person so charged is not invalid by reason only of the charge being in contravention of this subsection unless it appears that an injustice has been done to the person charged by reason of the contravention."

16 See *Lunn* (1993) 19 C.R.R. (2d) 291, pp. 297-298 per Mahoney C.J.: "I find no merit in the argument that this provision is so vague as to be unconstitutional... What is, or is not, conduct or neglect to the prejudice of good order and discipline in the context of the Canadian Armed Forces is eminently amenable to legal debate." See to the same effect the U.S. Supreme Court case, *Parker* v. *Levy* 417 U.S. 733 (1974), holding that the Uniform Code of Military Justice, articles 133 ("conduct unbecoming

an officer and a gentleman") and 134 ("all disorders and neglects to the prejudice of good order and discipline"), are not unconstitutionally vague under the due process clause of the Fifth Amendment.

17 G. Herfst, "Meeting the Needs of Military Justice: The Advantages and Disadvantages of Codified Rules of Evidence — An Examination of the Military Rules of Evidence", LL.M thesis, Dalhousie University, 1995, pp. 68-69.

18 *Criminal Code*, s. 235(1) and s. 269.1.

19 Brief for the Commission of Inquiry into the Deployment of Canadian Forces to Somalia: Military Justice, p. 16 (hereafter, Military Justice Brief).

20 See also *National Defence Act*, s. 146.

21 *National Defence Act*, ss. 140(b), (c), (d) and (e).

22 *National Defence Act*, ss. 60(c), 60(f), 60(2), and 69.

23 See Military Justice Brief, p. 12. See also K.W. Watkin "Canadian Military Justice: Summary Proceedings and the Charter", LL.M thesis, Queen's University, 1990, p. 13: "In 1988, there were 4,245 summary trials and only 95 courts martial. Between 1986 and 1988, summary trials, on average, accounted for 98 per cent of the disciplinary proceedings conducted in the Canadian Forces." Data on summary awards of service tribunals are now collected under 1994 CFAO 114-2.

24 See generally L.B. Radine, *The Taming of the Troops: Social Control in the United States Army* (Westport, Conn.: Greenwood Press, 1977), p. 156.

25 Military Justice Brief, p. 12.

26 Military Justice Brief, p. 2.

27 *National Defence Act*, s. 167.

28 *National Defence Act*, s. 166; QR&O 111.16.

29 A general court martial cannot, however, pass a sentence that includes a minor punishment: QR&O 111.17.

30 Such a punishment requires the approval of cabinet. See *National Defence Act*, s. 206(1) and QR&O 114.07. In general, a superior officer is an officer of or above the rank of brigadier general who can try certain officers and NCOs who cannot be tried by a commanding officer.

31 See *National Defence Act*, s. 192(3); QR&O 112.06.

32 QR&O 111.22.

33 QR&O 111.60.

34 Military Justice Brief, p. 14.

35 See generally QR&O, chapter 112. QR&O provisions relating to the prosecutor can be found in QR&O 111.24, 111.43, 113.107 and 113.60.

See Rubson Ho, "A World That Has Walls: A *Charter* Analysis of Military Tribunals", (1996) 54 *U. of Toronto Faculty of Law Review* 149, for an argument that a simple majority decision by a court martial violates the Charter.

36 See QR&O 112.68. The rules are found in QR&O, volume 4, appendix 1.3.

37 QR&O 109.02. Will this procedure be found to be consistent with *Stinchcombe* (1991) 68 C.C.C. (3d); [1991] 3 S.C.R. 326?

38 A sentence of death, however, requires unanimity: *National Defence Act*, s. 193(1).

39 QR&O 112.41 and 112.50.

40 *National Defence Act*, s. 173.

41 QR&O 111.36.

42 QR&O 111.35.

43 QR&O, chapter 113.

44 *National Defence Act*, s. 177; QR&O 113.51.

45 QR&O 113.53.

46 See Memorandum from D Law/MJ, 15 November 1993, "Court Martial/ Appeal Statistics".

47 *National Defence Act*, s. 163(1); QR&O 108.25.

48 *National Defence Act*, s. 164(1); QR&O 110.01.

49 For summary trial of majors, see CFAO 110-2, "Summary Trial of Majors."

50 QR&O 102.19.

51 QR&O 110.03.

52 QR&O 108.27.

53 QR&O 108.33.

54 For summary trial by a superior commander, see QR&O 110.02ff.

55 QR&O 108.31. For Superior Commanders, see QR&O 110.055.

56 QR&O 108.31(2). The list also includes offences under s. 132 of the *National Defence Act*.

57 QR&O 108.31(3); CFAO 19-25, paragraph 18.

58 QR&O 108.03 and 108.29; CFAO 19-25, paragraph 3.

59 QR&O 108.03. See Watkin, "Canadian Military Justice", p. 20: "In practice the assisting officer is usually an officer holding the rank of lieutenant or captain and most often is the officer immediately in command of the accused."

60 QR&O 108.03, note (c). Legal duty counsel is available if the accused has been arrested or detained: CFAO 56-5-6(a).

61 QR&O 108.03(8). Redress of Grievance is, however, available for summary trials: *National Defence Act*, s. 29 and QR&O 19.26.

62 QR&O 108.32.

63 QR&O 108.30.

64 QR&O, chapter 108.

65 QR&O 108.10.

66 QR&O 108.11.

67 QR&O 108.12(2).

68 QR&O 108.12.

69 QR&O 108.10, note (b). A helpful document is Aide-Memoire on Conduct of Summary Trials for Commanding Officers and Delegated Officers Canadian Forces (DND, May 1991), revisions by Lt.-Col. D. Couture, office of the JAG.

70 See generally on U.S. military justice, David A. Schlueter, *Military Criminal Justice: Practice and Procedure*, third edition (Charlottesville, Va.: Michie, 1992); F.A. Gilligan and F.I. Lederer, *Court-Martial Procedure*, two volumes (Charlottesville, Va.: Michie, 1991); Army Regulation 27-10, Military Justice (Washington: Department of the Army, 1994); and Watkin, "Canadian Military Justice", p. 211ff.

71 Uniform Code of Military Justice (U.C.M.J.), Article 18; see Schlueter, *Military Criminal Justice*, p. 41.

72 Article 19; see Schlueter, *Military Criminal Justice*, p. 40.

73 Article 16; see Schlueter, *Military Criminal Justice*, pp. 39-40 and 599ff.

74 Article 15; see Schlueter, *Military Criminal Justice*, pp. 39 and 103ff.

75 Article 15(f): "The imposition and enforcement of disciplinary punishment under this article for any act or omission is not a bar to trial by court-martial for a serious crime or offense growing out of the same act or omission, and not properly punishable under this article; but the fact that a disciplinary punishment has been enforced may be shown by the accused upon trial, and when so shown shall be considered in determining the measure of punishment to be adjudged in the event of a finding of guilty." See Schlueter, *Military Criminal Justice*, p. 108ff, setting out the various provisions that attempt to distinguish between major and minor offences: "In practice, the commanding officer's authority is not limited to imposing punishment for only minor military offences", but if it is "major" it will not bar a court martial.

76 Army Regulation 27-10, paragraph 3-18(c).

77 U.C.M.J., Article 64.

78 See Schlueter, *Military Criminal Justice*, p. 115.

79   See Schlueter, *Military Criminal Justice*, p. 111ff; Army Regulation 27-10, paragraph 3-16 and 3-17.

80   See Schlueter, *Military Criminal Justice*, Appendix 5, pp. 810-813.

81   Watkin, "Canadian Military Justice", p. 220.

82   (1985) 1 *Canadian Forces JAG Journal* 1.

83   Stat. Can. 1944-45, c. 23.

84   McDonald, "The Trail of Discipline", p. 10.

85   *An Act respecting the Militia and Defence of the Dominion of Canada*, Stat. Can. 1868, c. 40, s. 64.

86   See *Militia Act*, Stat. Can. 1904, c. 23, ss. 24 and 25.

87   See McDonald, "The Trail of Discipline", p. 19.

88   McDonald, "The Trail of Discipline", p. 20. See *Royal Canadian Air Force Act*, Stat. Can. 1940, c. 15.

89   *Naval Service Act*, Stat. Can. 1909-10, c. 43.

90   McDonald, "The Trail of Discipline", p. 10.

91   *Naval Discipline Act*, 1866, c. 109, building on *Naval Discipline Act*, 1860, c. 123.

92   *Naval Discipline Act*, 1860, c. 124, s. 38.

93   McDonald "The Trail of Discipline", p. 7.

94   McDonald, "The Trail of Discipline", p. 8, citing the 1661 act, c. 9.

95   S. 33 of 1661 act, c. 9.

96   See McDonald, "Trails of Discipline", p. 11; M.L. Friedland, *Double Jeopardy* (Oxford: Clarendon Press, 1969), p. 343ff.

97   1 Wm. and Mary, c. 5.

98   See Friedland, *Double Jeopardy*, p. 342.

99   Friedland, *Double Jeopardy*, p. 343.

100 McDonald, "The Trail of Discipline", p. 16.

101 See generally W.J. Lawson, "Canadian Military Law" (1951) 29 *Can. Bar. Rev.* 241; NDHQ, *The National Defence Act: Explanatory Material* (November 1950).

102 Lawson, "Canadian Military Law", p. 249.

103 Andrew M. Ferris, "Military Justice: Removing the Probability of Unfairness" (1994) 63 *U. of Cincinnati L. Rev.* 439, p. 450. The committee, created by the secretary of defense in 1948, was chaired by Edmund H. Morgan, the distinguished Harvard professor of law. A similar commission was established in England; see J.H. Hollies, "Canadian Military Law" [1961] *Military Law Rev.* 69, p. 70.

104 McDonald, "The Trail of Discipline", p. 21. The navy, but not the other services, had "stoppage of grog" as a minor punishment, but this was removed from the regulations in 1982 (McDonald, p. 25).

105 McDonald, "The Trail of Discipline", p. 24. In the nineteenth century the commanding officer could order only seven days' imprisonment for all offences except absence without leave, in which case he could order 21 days (McDonald, p. 17).

106 McDonald, "The Trail of Discipline", p. 24.

107 S. 78(5) of the Army Act 1955.

108 *National Defence Act* 1950, s. 136(3).

109 *Canadian Forces Act*, 1952, Stat. Can. 1952, c. 6, ss. 2(8).

110 See Lawson, "Canadian Military Law", p. 253. At about this time, the United Kingdom, the United States, Australia and New Zealand established civilian courts of appeal from military tribunals. See Janet Walker, "Military Justice: From Oxymoron to Aspiration" (1994) 32 *Osgoode Hall L. J.* 1, p. 4ff. The board was replaced by the Court Martial Appeal Court in 1959; see Watkin, "Canadian Military Justice", p. 50. For a discussion of the Canadian Court Martial Appeal Court, see Walker, "Military Justice", p. 8ff.

111 Walker, "Military Justice", p. 4.

112 (1980) 54 C.C.C. (2d) 129; [1980] 2 S.C.R. 370.

113 See D.J. Corry, "Military Law under the Charter" (1986) 24 *Osgoode Hall L. J.* 67, p. 76. The three cases are *Platt* (1963) 2 C.M.A.R. 213; *Robinson* (1971) 3 C.M.A.R. 43; and *Nye* (1972) 3 C.M.A.R. 85.

114 The military also wanted, but did not get, an amendment to s. 10(b) of the Charter to make sure nothing in the section could be construed as giving the accused the right to counsel at a summary proceeding; see evidence before the National Defence Committee of the Senate, 19 May 1981, 17:12.

115 Judgement, 6 January 1995 (C.M.A.C. 372), p. 5.

116 1 June 1995 (Lamer C.J., Gonthier and Iacobucci JJ.).

117 See A.D. Heard, "Military Law and the Charter of Rights" (1988) 11 *Dalhousie L. J.* 514, p. 532.

118 See *Généreux* (1992) 70 C.C.C. (3d) 1; [1992] 1 S.C.R. 259.

119 Heard, "Military Law", p. 532.

120 See Watkin, "Canadian Military Justice", p. 53.

121 *Statute Law (Canadian Charter of Rights and Freedoms) Amendment Act*, Stat. Can. 1985, c. 31. Part III.

122 See General P.D. Manson, Notice of Amendments to QR&O Volumes I and II, Canadian Forces Supplementary Order 48/86 (DND, 19 September 1986), as cited in Major B. Bock, "Leadership, Command and the Canadian Charter of Rights and Freedoms" (Canadian Staff College, 1989).

123 See QR&O 108.31. See also Watkin, "Canadian Military Justice", p. 53; and McDonald, "The Trail of Discipline", p. 26.

124 See Watkin, "Canadian Military Justice", p. 52.

125 See McDonald, "The Trail of Discipline", p. 26: "This was done in order to better comply with the provisions of the Charter by expanding access to a lawyer in cases where detention or a substantial fine might be awarded as punishment." Only the CO could therefore impose these punishments, and the accused would have to be given an opportunity to elect a court martial. The delegated officer did not have the authority to offer the accused the right to elect trial by court martial. See also Watkin, "Canadian Military Justice", p. 53.

126 *Canadian Forces Act, 1952*, Stat. Can. 1952, c. 6.

127 Watkin, "Canadian Military Justice", p. 54.

128 See McDonald, "The Trail of Discipline", p. 26; and Heard "Military Law", p. 533.

129 *Statute Law (Canadian Charter of Rights and Freedoms) Amendment Act*, Stat. Can. 1985, c. 31.

130 House of Commons Debates, 27 March 1985, p. 3421.

131 Section 58, replacing subsections 252(2) and (3), and section 59, adding 273.1-273.5.

132 Section 48, replacing subsection 154(1); section 49, replacing paragraph 156(a); and section 50, replacing subsection 157(1).

133 Section 51, replacing section 158.

134 Section 57, adding sections 248.1-248.9.

135 Section 47, adding section 151.

136 Section 45, replacing section 66.

137 The *National Defence Act* was and is enabling; see s. 179: "In any proceedings before a service tribunal, the accused person has the right to be represented in such manner as is prescribed in regulations made by the Governor in Council." See QR&O 108.03(1), stating that "The accused has the right to be represented at a summary trial by an assisting officer."

138 Note (c) to QR&O 108.03 states: "An accused person does not have a right to be represented by legal counsel at a summary trial. However, if an accused requests such representation, the officer conducting the summary trial has the discretion to: (i) permit representation by legal counsel; (ii) proceed without representation by legal counsel; or (iii) apply for disposal of the charges against the accused by a court martial." See also QR&O 105.11, which provides that "a person who is arrested or detained shall, without delay, be informed:...(c) of the reason

for the arrest or detention; (d) that the person has the right to retain and instruct counsel without delay; (e) that the person has the right to have access to free and immediate advice from duty counsel; and (f) of the existence and availability of Legal Aid, where applicable." The latter two subsections were introduced after *Brydges* (1990) 53 C.C.C. (3d) 330; [1990] 1 S.C.R. 190.

139 Manson, Notice of Amendments, p. 4, as cited in Bock, "Leadership, Command and the Canadian Charter", p. 7.

140 R.S.C. 1950, c. 43, s. 57.

141 Section 45, replacing section 66.

142 "Service tribunal", as defined in section 2 of the *National Defence Act*, "means a court martial or a person presiding at a summary trial."

143 Section 162 of the *National Defence Act*. Note (c) to article 107.12 states: "Before dismissing any charge, the commanding officer should realize that if the charge is dismissed it cannot subsequently be preceded with by a service tribunal or a civil court since section 66 of the *National Defence Act* precludes a service tribunal or civil court from trying an accused upon a charge that has been dismissed." A delegated officer does not have the power to dismiss a charge (note (b) to 107.12).

144 *National Defence Act*, s. 230.1.

145 206 U.S. 333 (1907), p. 345 per Harlan J.: "If a court-martial has jurisdiction to try an officer or soldier for a crime, its judgment will be accorded the finality and conclusiveness as to the issues involved which attend the judgments of a civil court in a case of which it may legally take cognizance."

146 See Friedland, *Double Jeopardy*, p. 337.

147 See Friedland, *Double Jeopardy*, p. 335ff. See also the High Court of Australia cases, *Re Tracey; Ex parte Ryan* (1989) 63 *Aust. L.J.R.* 250; and *McWaters* v. *Day* (1989) 64 *Aust. L.J.R.* 41. In *Re Tracey* the court expressed the opinion that common law double jeopardy principles would apply. See the judgement of Mason C.J., Wilson and Dawson JJ., p. 258, citing *Grafton* and Friedland, *Double Jeopardy*: "there are cogent arguments why those [double jeopardy] principles should apply given that a court martial exercises, as we think it does, judicial power." See also the judgement of Brennan and Toohey JJ., p. 272: "subject to any common law protection from double jeopardy." The court struck down the sections in the *Defence Force Discipline Act 1982* (Commonwealth), which provided (s. 190(5)) that "where a person has been acquitted or convicted of a service offence, the person is not liable to be tried by a civil court for a civil court offence that is substantially the same offence."

The section was held to exceed the Commonwealth's power to bar state proceedings. See generally R.A. Brown, "Military Justice in Australia" (1989) 13 *Criminal Law J.* 263; Symposium issue, "The Constitution and Military Justice" (1990) 20 *U. Western Aust. L.R.* 4; and Walker, "Military Justice", p. 11, note 34.

148 See section 62 of *National Defence Act*, R.S.C. 1950, c. 43. Section 71 of the present act says "subject to section 66".

149 Watkin, "Canadian Military Justice", pp. 104-105. See also the transcript of the oral presentation of the military brief to the Somalia Inquiry, 21 June 1995, p. 455.

150 *Re Tracey*, p. 262 per Brennan and Toohey JJ.

151 See Friedland, *Double Jeopardy*, p. 336.

152 (1985) 23 C.C.C. (3d) 193; [1985] 2 S.C.R. 673.

153 *Généreux*, p. 21 C.C.C.

154 (1990) 5 C.M.A.R. 87, p. 101; (1990) 61 C.C.C. (3d) 541.

155 *Ingebrigtson*, p. 108 C.M.A.R.

156 See Captain C.F. Blair, "Military Efficiency and Military Justice: Peaceful Co-Existence" (1993) 42 *U.N.B.L.J.* 237, pp. 239-240.

157 Walker, "Military Justice", p. 24.

158 Following the earlier Court Martial Appeal Court case, *Schick* (1987) 4 C.M.A.R. 540.

159 *Ingebrigtson*, pp. 91, 92, 96 C.M.A.R.

160 The changes are conveniently summarized in Walker, "Military Justice", p. 21.

161 QR&Os 4.09(2), (3), (4) and (6); 15.01(6); 101.13-16; and 111.22. On the latter, see Lamer C.J. in *Généreux*, p. 34 C.C.C.

162 QR&O 26.10-11, 204.218, and 204.22.

163 Lamer C.J. in *Généreux*, pp. 34-35, 37 C.C.C.

164 Mary Collins for the Minister of National Defence, House of Commons Debate, 6 May 1992, p. 10255.

165 Stat. Can. 1992, c. 16, s. 2, adding section 165.1 to the *National Defence Act*. See also section 9, replacing section 187, which now gives the prosecutor, as well as the accused, the right to object to members and the judge advocate of the court martial.

166 QR&O 111.051(5).

167 CFAO 4-1.

168 See 41 *Halsbury's Laws of England*, fourth edition (London: Butterworths, 1983), pp. 438-439; and Annex E to Chapter 6 of the U.K. QRs. See also Sherman, "Military Justice Without Military Control", pp. 1403-1404.

169 *Halsbury's*, p. 471ff.

170 *Halsbury's*, p. 473.

171 John Mackenzie, (1995) *New Law Journal* 1624.

172 Report of the Commission on Human Rights Application No. 22107/93, Alexander Findlay. See Mackenzie, (1995) *New Law Journal* 48 and 208. The Commission found that the role of the convening officer was unsatisfactory, expressed some unease about the ad hoc nature of the membership of the court martial, and was concerned that an appeal against sentence by the convicted person to the Court Martial Appeal Court is not permitted.

173 See the draft document on the case prepared by the U.K. Judge Advocate General, Hon. J.W. Rant.

174 See *Engel*, 1976 Council of Europe *Yearbook of the European Convention on Human Rights* (The Hague: Martinus Nijhoff, 1977), p. 490.

175 *U.S.* v. *Thomas* M.J. 388, p. 393 (C.M.A., 1986), as cited in Schlueter, *Military Criminal Justice*, p. 256. See the many articles on command influence cited in Schlueter, note 1, p. 255. See also L.C. West, *They Call it Justice: Command Influence and the Court-Martial System* (New York: Viking Press, 1977), p. x: a commanding officer "may well usurp the independent judicial functions of the court-martial, and 'influence' his court members to render a verdict and sentence designed to reflect his own wishes, regardless of the merits of the individual case."

176 Schlueter, *Military Criminal Justice*, p. 256. See also Major D.M.C. Willis, "The Road to Hell is Paved with Good Intentions: Finding and Fixing Unlawful Command Influence", *The Army Lawyer*, August 1992, p. 3: "Unlawful command influence — direct and indirect, real and perceived — is one of the most persistent problems in military law."

177 Article 25(d)(2) of the Uniform Code of Military Justice.

178 See Schlueter, *Military Criminal Justice*, p. 261.

179 U.C.M.J., Article 37(a).

180 See *Weiss* v. *U.S.* 114 S. Ct. 752 (1994), p. 756.

181 *Weiss*, p. 756, affirming the Court of Military Appeal, which had discussed but rejected *Généreux*. *Généreux* was not cited by the U.S. Supreme Court, a matter commented upon with regret by counsel for Généreux: see Guy Cournoyer and Tiphaine Dickson, "How Canadian constitutional law could have tipped the scales of an independent military justice system in the United States" (1994) 41 *Federal Bar News and Journal* 270.

182 *Weiss*, pp. 760-761 per Rehnquist C.J.: "Judicial deference thus 'is at its apogee' when reviewing congressional decision making in this area."

183 *Weiss*, p. 761.
184 *Weiss*, p. 762.
185 See also Chapter 8 of Army Regulation 27-10, Military Justice, 8 August 1994.
186 *Weiss*, p. 762.
187 Schlueter, *Military Criminal Justice*, p. 271. Cf. Ferris, "Military Justice: Removing the Probability of Unfairness", p. 491, who states: "At a minimum, Congress should act to provide for terms of office of no less than five years for military trial judges and no less than ten years for military appellate judges."
188 F.A. Gilligan and F.I. Lederer, *Court Martial Procedure* (Charlottesville, Va.: Michie, 1991), 1994 Cumulative Supplement, volume 1, p. 81. Army trial judges are rated by senior members of the United States Army Trial Judiciary (see "Legal Operations", FM 27-100, 1-7), but those who do the rating may also have further career ambitions.
189 Note, however, that in *Ingebrigtson*, p. 101 C.M.A.R., Mahoney C.J. referred to "command influence" in relation to courts martial.
190 Transcript of Policy Hearings, 21 June 1995, p. 456. See also, to the same effect, G. Herfot, "Meeting the Needs of Military Justice — the Advantages and Disadvantages of Codified Rules of Evidence", LL.M thesis, Dalhousie University, 1995, p. 61.
191 Stat. Can. 1985, c. 27, s. 53, now s. 163(1.1) of the *National Defence Act*.
192 *MacKay* (1980) 54 C.C.C. (2d) 129, pp. 160-162; [1980] 2 S.C.R. 370.
193 *MacKay*, p. 162 C.C.C.
194 *Toth* v. *Quarles* 350 U.S. 11 (1955).
195 *Reid* v. *Covert* 354 U.S. 1 (1957).
196 *Grisham* v. *Hagan* 361 U.S. 278 (1960). See also *Billings* v. *Truesdell* 321 U.S. 542 (1944), holding that civilians could not be court martialled for resisting conscription.
197 395 U.S. 258 (1969), pp. 272, 265-266.
198 *Relford* v. *Commandant, U.S. Disciplinary Barracks* 401 U.S. 355 (1971).
199 *Solorio* v. *U.S.* 483 U.S. 435 (1987), pp. 449-450.
200 *Weiss* v. *U.S.* 114 S. Ct. 752 (1994).
201 Walker, "Military Justice: From Oxymoron to Aspiration", p. 12.
202 See Walker, "Military Justice", p. 13, note 43.
203 See the cases cited in Walker, "Military Justice", p. 14, note 44.
204 *Ionson* (1987) 4 C.M.A.C. number 432.
205 [1989] 2 S.C.R. 1073.

206 Judgement C.M.A.C. number 372, rendered 6 January 1995.
207 *Brown*, p. 6, citing *MacKay* (1980) 54 C.C.C. (2d) 129; *MacDonald* (1983) 4 C.M.A.R. 277; *Sullivan* (1986) 4 C.M.A.R. 414; and *Ionson* (1987) 4 C.M.A.R. 433.
208 *Brown*, p. 9.
209 Leave to appeal dismissed by Lamer C.J., Gonthier and Iacobucci JJ. on 1 June 1995.
210 Brief, p. 7; *National Defence Act*, s. 111(1)(b); QR&O 103.43.
211 Transcript of Policy Hearing, 21 June 1995, p. 455.
212 *National Defence Act*, ss. 60(2) and 69(1).
213 See Respondent's Factum (Mémoire de L'Intimée), p. 19.
214 Walker, "A Farewell Salute to the Military Nexus Doctrine" (1993) 2 *National J. of Constitutional Law* 366, published before, but probably written after, Walker, "Military Justice". Cf. R.D. Lunau, "Military Tribunals under the Charter" (1992) 2 *National J. of Constitutional Law* 197.
215 See *Rutherford* (1982) 4 C.M.A.R. 262.
216 See generally the affidavit by Captain (N.) C.F. Blair attached to Respondent's Factum in *Généreux*, p. 20:

>   61.   The exercise of Canadian military jurisdiction over our troops and dependents outside Canada serves the interests of both Canada and the host nation. Where Canadian tribunals are conducted close in both time and place to the occurrence of the offence charged, and in compliance with Canadian law, then the Canadian individual who is accused benefits from a trial in a language and judicial system which he or she understands, and which affords the safeguards of Canadian law. At the same time, local authorities and inhabitants can observe the trial, and be reassured that offences committed in their territory will be dealt with in a formal, fair, and visible manner.

> The U.K. established the Standing Civilian Court in 1976 to handle these situations (Respondent's Factum, p. 22).

217 The High Court of Australia could not agree on the solution in *Re Tracey; Ex parte Ryan*. Three members of the court adopted the *Solorio* approach (p. 257): "it is not possible to draw a clear and satisfactory line between offences committed by defence members which are of a military character and those which are not. The impossibility of doing so was recently accepted in the United States in *Solorio* v. *United States*." Two members of the court followed the *O'Callahan* approach, however (see pp. 267-270). Another member, Deane J. (p. 275) seems to support

O'Callahan, while the final member, Gaudron J., did not discuss the U.S. cases.

218   Military brief on Military Justice, p. 2.

219   Watkin, "Canadian Military Justice", p. 3.

220   Lockyer, "Charter Implications for Military Justice" (1993) 42 *U.N.B.L.J.* 243, p. 250.

221   Lockyer, "Charter Implications", p. 250.

222   Watkin, "Canadian Military Justice", pp. 285-289.

223   Conversations with JAG officers in Ottawa in August 1995 lead this writer to believe that Kenneth Watkin's thesis provides a good indication of the present thinking of the military.

224   See Major Barry Brock, "Leadership, Command and Canadian Charter of Rights and Freedoms" (Canadian Forces College, 1989), p. 12.

225   Brock, "Leadership, Command", p. 10, citing a paper by Major R. Jodoin, "The Code of Service Discipline after the Constitution" (Canadian Forces College, 1983).

226   See S.B. Flemming, *Civilianization Theory and Martial Discipline in the Canadian Forces in the Post-Korean War Period* (DND Operational Research and Analysis Establishment, Staff Note 2/89, 1989), pp. 7, 12.

227   See the preliminary draft of a study by Anthony Kellett for the military, "The Influence of the Regimental System on Group and Unit Cohesion", November 1991, p. 54, which shows a dramatic drop in detention barrack sentences from 1986 to 1991 in the Canadian land forces. The Royal Canadian Regiment had 232 days of detention per 1,000 members in 1986 and only 14 in 1991; the Princess Patricia's Canadian Light Infantry from which 2 Commando personnel were drawn went from 649 days detention per 1,000 persons in 1986 to 85 in 1991; and the Royal 22nd Regiment went from 660 days detention per 1,000 persons in 1986 to 178 in 1991. The Somalia Inquiry may want to update these figures, although it appears that current figures on summary proceedings are not kept by the military. Clearly, better statistics should be available to track trends in proceedings.

228   *Board of Inquiry*, p. 3309.

229   Hewson Report, p. 57.

230   Hewson Report, p. 21.

231   See QR&O 108.11, 108,12, 108.10 (note b), and 108.31(2).

232   See QR&O 108.03 and 108.13; CFAO 19-25-4, issued in 1994; QR&O 108.15; CFAO 114-2, issued in 1994; and QR&O 19.26.

233   *Shubley* v. *The Queen* (1990) 52 C.C.C. (3d) 481, pp. 494, 495; [1990] 1 S.C.R. 3.

234 *Wigglesworth* v. *The Queen* (1987) 37 C.C.C. (3d) 385; [1987] 2 S.C.R. 541. Both *Shubley* and *Wigglesworth* deal with the question of whether and when section 11(h) bars a prior disciplinary hearing. This is a different question from whether a particular disciplinary hearing comes within section 11 of the Charter. Nevertheless, the cases and the subsequent discussions treat the two questions as one.

235 *Wigglesworth*, p. 404 C.C.C.

236 *Shubley*, p. 500 C.C.C.

237 *Shubley*, p. 494 C.C.C.

238 *Shubley*, pp. 495-496 C.C.C.

239 *National Defence Act*, s. 66.

240 See *Oakes* (1986) 24 C.C.C. (3d) 321; [1986] 1 S.C.R. 103.

241 *Shubley*, p. 496 C.C.C.

242 Uniform Code of Military Justice, Article 20.

243 *Middendorf* v. *Henry*, 425 U.S. 25 (1976), p. 45. The court also held (p. 46) that a summary court martial is not a "criminal prosecution" within the meaning of the Sixth Amendment's right to counsel guarantee.

244 QR&O 108.03.

245 See Watkin, "Canadian Military Justice", p. 118, note 8 and Appendix III, showing that in 1988, for example, 674 elections were given by COs, but only 32 (or 5 per cent) of the accused exercised the election. In 1986 only 26 of 805 (2 per cent) exercised their right of election.

246 See Watkin, "Canadian Military Justice", p. 239. See also Schlueter, *Military Criminal Justice*, pp. 110-111, for the right to demand a court martial when faced with an Article 15 proceeding. Service members who are "attached to or embarked in a vessel" may not, however, demand trial. Summary courts martial also require the accused's consent; see Schlueter, p. 599. See also Watkin, p. 287.

247 Superior commanders can fine but cannot sentence a person to detention (QR&O 110.03).

248 *Généreux*, p. 17 C.C.C.

249 The potential penalty for the disciplinary offence in *Wigglesworth* was imprisonment for one year and as such was a "true penal consequence". A subsequent *Criminal Code* prosecution was permitted, however, because it was held to be for a different offence.

250 Cf. *Middendorf* v. *Henry*, p. 34, stating that "the summary court-martial...was not a 'criminal prosecution' within the meaning" of the Sixth Amendment.

251 (1985) 23 C.C.C. (3d) 193, [1985] 2 S.C.R. 673. See Corry, "Military Law under the Charter", pp. 88-89; and Heard, "Military Law and the

Charter of Rights", p. 526.

252 The CO has the discretion to permit counsel (QR&O 108.03, note (c)).

253 U.C.M.J., Article 20. See generally Schlueter, *Military Criminal Justice*, p. 599ff.

254 See 41 *Halsbury's Laws of England*, p. 436, note 5. Following a 1976 amendment, a field rank officer, under special procedures, can award 60 days' detention. See generally, Watkin, "Canadian Military Justice", p. 223ff. Naval COs, however, can award three months' detention.

255 See Watkin, "Canadian Military Justice", p. 42.

256 *National Defence Act 1950*, Stat. Can. 1950, s. 136(2).

257 Assuming that there can be a section 1 justification of a section 7 violation.

258 *National Defence Act*, s. 83. In the U.K., however, COs are limited to trying cases where the governing legislation imposes a penalty of two years or less; see Watkin, "Canadian Military Justice", p. 225.

259 *Narcotic Control Act*, R.S.C. 1985, c. N-1, s. 4.

260 QR&O 108.31(1)(b). The same applies to superior commanders; see QR&O 110.055.

261 *Korponey v. A.G. Canada* (1982) 65 C.C.C. (2d) 65; [1982] 1 S.C.R. 41.

262 (1986) 25 C.C.C. (3d) 207; [1986] 1 S.C.R. 383. There are a number of later Supreme Court of Canada cases on waiver: see, for example, on waiver of section 10(b) rights, *Manninen* (1987) 34 C.C.C. (3d) 385, [1987] 1 S.C.R. 1233; *Evans* (1991) 63 C.C.C. (3d) 289, [1991] 1 S.C.R. 869; on waiver under the *Young Offenders Act*, *Smith* (1991) 63 C.C.C. (3d) 313, [1991] 1 S.C.R. 714; *E.T.* v. *The Queen* (1993) 86 C.C.C. (3d) 289; [1993] 4 S.C.R. 504; and for the right to an interpreter under section 14 of the Charter, *Tran* v. *The Queen* (1994) 92 C.C.C. (3d) 218; [1994] 2 S.C.R. 951. The waiver requirement in *Tran* was very high and it had to be exercised personally by the accused. The standard seems to vary depending on the right involved.

263 *Korponey*, p. 74 C.C.C. (emphasis in original).

264 *Middendorf v. Henry*, pp. 46-48.

265 *Korponey*, p. 74 C.C.C.

266 QR&O 108.31(3); CFAO 19-25 paragraph 18.

267 See QR&O 105.11; CFAO 56-5 paragraph 6(a).

268 See the Summary Court-Martial Rights Notification/Waiver Statement in Army Regulation 27-10, *Military Justice* (1994).

269 See Flemming, *Civilianization Theory*, p. 12.

270 See the study by Kellett, "The Influence of the Regimental System on Group and Unit Cohesion", discussed earlier in the chapter.

271 Office of the Judge Advocate General Newsletter, January to June 1994, article 1.
272 Flemming, *Civilianization Theory*, p. 7.

CHAPTER SEVEN — CIVIL CONTROL, INTEGRATION, AND OVERSIGHT

1 See John Sweetman, ed., *Sword and Mace: Twentieth-century Civil-Military Relations in Britain* (London: Brassey's, 1986), p. xii. See also M.L. Friedland, *Double Jeopardy* (Oxford: Clarendon Press, 1969), p. 345.
2 See F.A. Johnson, *Defence by Committee* (Oxford University Press, 1960).
3 See Alex Danchev, "The Central Direction of War, 1940-41", in Sweetman, *Sword and Mace*, p. 57ff.
4 See John Sweetman, "A Process of Evolution: Command and Control in Peacetime", in Sweetman, *Sword and Mace*, p. 52.
5 See generally S.E. Finer, *The Man on Horseback: The Role of the Military in Politics*, second edition (London: Pinter, 1988).
6 Stephen Deakin, "British Civil-Military Relations in the 1990s", in Daniella Ashkenazy, *The Military in the Service of Society and Democracy* (Westport, Conn.: Greenwood, 1994), p. 122.
7 See QR&O 19.44. In Germany, by contrast, military personnel can run for parliament and other office and then return to the military. This came about because of the German desire to emphasize that a soldier is a "citizen in uniform". See Jurgen Oelrich, "The German Concept of the 'Citizen in Uniform'", in Ashkenazy, *The Military in the Service of Society and Democracy*, p. 136.
8 *Toronto Star*, 4 November 1995.
9 R.S.C. 1985, c. N-5, s. 4. See generally, Douglas Bland, *Chiefs of Defence: Government and the Unified Command of the Canadian Armed Forces* (Toronto: Canadian Institute of Strategic Studies, 1995), p. 127ff. Technically, the governor general is the commander-inchief of the armed forces, just as the Queen is in the U.K. (see Bland, pp. 130-132), but this is now a formal ceremonial relationship.
10 *National Defence Act*, s. 18(1) and (2).
11 As cited in Bland, *Chiefs of Defence*, p. 45. There is, and has been, however, obvious tension between the military and civilian control. See Major R.J. Walker, "Poles Apart: Civil-Military Relations in the Pursuit of a Canadian National Army", M.A. thesis, Royal Military College, 1991, who states in his abstract: "The history of Canadian civil-military

relations is highlighted by the government's immutable rejection of the concept of exclusive army control and its evolution revolves around the army's attempts to circumvent that immovable obstacle throughout the trials of peace and war."

12 Walker, "Poles Apart", pp. 147, 129, 145.

13 See Bland, *Chiefs of Defence*, p. 203, who points out that in the Gulf War "many observers thought that Parliament would have to be recalled to allow the CF to go on 'active service'" but that General de Chastelain, the chief of defence staff, stated that the government "has no legal obligation to get Parliament's approval to put the CF on the offensive... In my opinion, the government has all the authority it needs to proceed with whatever action it wants."

14 Stat. Can. 1988, c. 29.

15 Article II, section 2.

16 K. Kemp and C. Hudlin, "Civil Supremacy Over the Military: Its Nature and Limits" (1992) 19 *Armed Forces and Society* 7, p. 23.

17 Kemp and Hudlin, "Civil Supremacy", pp. 8, 22. See also David Segal, "Civil-Military Relations in Democratic Societies", in proceedings of a conference on the Role of the Military in Democratic Societies, sponsored by York University Centre for International and Strategic Studies, 1992, p. 10ff.

18 See John Hart Ely, *War and Responsibility: Constitutional Lessons of Vietnam and its Aftermath* (Princeton University Press, 1993), and a review of that work by Peter D. Coffman, "Power and Duty: The Language of the War Power" (1995) 80 *Cornell L. Rev.* 1236.

19 Article I, section 9. See generally, Jean Smith, *The Constitution and American Foreign Policy* (St. Paul, Minn.: West, 1989), p. 227ff.

20 See Jean Smith, *George Bush's War* (New York: Henry Holt, 1992), p. 5.

21 Public Law 93-148; 87 Stat. 555, ss. 3, 4 and 5.

22 Smith, *The Constitution and American Foreign Policy*, p. 235; Kemp and Hudlin, "Civil Supremacy", p. 10.

23 Smith, *The Constitution and American Foreign Policy*, p. 236. See U.S. Constitution, Article I, section 8, clause 12.

24 Critchley, "Civilianization", pp. 127-128. See also the Report of the Special Joint Committee on Canada's Defence Policy, *Security in a Changing World* (Ottawa, 1994), p. 2ff; and OPDP 2 1994/95, p. 1-1-8 (A-PD-050-0D1/PG-002).

25 *Final Report, Task Force on Review of Unification of the Canadian Forces, March 15, 1980* (Ottawa, 1980), p. 31.

26 Critchley, "Civilianization", pp. 127-128.

27 Management Review Group (MRG), *Report to the Minister of National Defence on the Management of Defence in Canada* (July 1972), p. ii, cited in Critchley, "Civilianization", p. 128.

28 CDS General Gerald Theriault, 1992, quoted by Douglas Bland.

29 Douglas Bland, *Chiefs of Defence*, pp. 161-162. See also P.C. Kasurak, "Civilianization and the Military Ethos: Civil-Military Relations in Canada" (1982) 25 *Can. Public Administration* 108, who points out (p. 109) that "a significant number of the members of the armed services have come to believe that the Canadian Forces have adopted civilian norms and standards to an unacceptable degree and that civilian public servants exercise undue influence over matters that are (or should be) exclusively military in nature...". See also a recent course paper by Lieutenant Commander R.V. Marsh, "NDHQ: Headquarters or Head Office" (Staff College, 1992), pp. 23-24: "The analysis in this paper demonstrates that NDHQ serves both as a headquarters and head office, but not well in either capacity. One solution is evident, the CDS and DM functions, which truly conform to a Headquarters and Head Office organization, need to be split and downsized. In so doing the impact of civilians on operational efficiency and effectiveness will be removed."

30 Critchley, "Civilianization", pp. 133-134.

31 *Security in a Changing World*, p. 44.

32 "The Organization of Canadian Defence", p. 8.

33 *Security in a Changing World*, p. 57.

34 Bland, *Chiefs of Defence*, p. 287. C.E.S. Franks argues for greater parliamentary involvement in security matters; see *Parliament and Security Matters* (Ottawa: Supply and Services, 1980); and "Accountability for Security Intelligence Agencies", in P. Hanks and J.D. McCamus, *National Security: Surveillance and Accountability in a Democratic Society* (Cowansville, Quebec: Éditions Yvon Blais, 1989), p. 19.

35 Bland, *Chiefs of Defence*, p. 7.

36 See A. Cox and S. Kirby, *Congress, Parliament and Defense* (New York: St. Martin's, 1986), pp. 292-293: "The problem with defense, however, is that unlike all other areas of government activity it is a highly sensitive area in which calls of national security and executive privilege can be used." This is not a significant hindrance in the United States, where "the problem of information overload can be just as important a restraint as the lack of information."

37 The same consideration applies to the security service. See Stuart Farson, "Accountable and Prepared? Reorganizing Canada's Intelligence

Community for the 21st Century" (1993) 1 *Canadian Foreign Policy* 43, p. 65.

38 D.C. Hendrickson, *Reforming Defense: The State of American Civil-Military Relations* (Baltimore: Johns Hopkins, 1988), p. 30. See also J.M. Lindsay, "Congressional Oversight of the Department of Defense: Reconsidering the Conventional Wisdom" (1990) 17 *Armed Forces and Society* 7.

39 Hendrickson, *Reforming Defense*, p. 33.

40 Cox and Kirby, *Congress, Parliament and Defense*, pp. 308-309. "Adequate accountability," they argue, "can only be achieved through the development of proportional representation in Britain. Under such an electoral system coalition governments would have to be formed and this would immediately ensure that Parliament was more actively involved in decision-making."

41 *Auditor General Act*, R.S.C. 1985, A-17, s. 7(1). See the discussion of the independence of the auditor general in M.L. Friedland, *A Place Apart: Judicial Independence and Accountability in Canada* (Ottawa: Canadian Judicial Council, 1995), pp. 214-216.

42 See *Statutory Instruments Act*, R.S.C. 1985, c. S-22, s. 20. The earlier *Regulations Act* (Stat. Can. 1950, c. 5, s. 9(2)) also allowed exemptions from the act; see *Third Report of the Special Committee on Statutory Instruments*, Mark MacGuigan, chair (1968-69), pp. 18-19. The Statutory Instruments Regulations, Consolidated Regulations of Canada, 1978, c. 1509, provides in section 7 that regulations made under the authority of section 12 of the *National Defence Act* are exempt from registration "due to the number of regulations". See also section 15(1) exempting the regulations from publication.

43 QR&O 21.01(2) and (3).

44 *National Defence Act*, R.S.C. 1985, s. 45(1).

45 QR&O 21.07ff.

46 See Terms of Reference of the Board of Inquiry, Appendix 4 to Annex A to the Statement by the BOI CARBG, Phase I, Vol. XI, 19 July 1993.

47 QR&O 21.08(4) and (5).

48 See Appendix 1 to Annex A to the Statement by the BOI CARBG, Phase I, Vol XI, 19 July 1993.

49 R.S.C. 1985, c. I-11.

50 QR&Os 21.46; 21.61; and 21.56(2).

51 Army Regulation 15-6, "Procedures for Investigating Officers and Boards of Officers", May 1988.

52 S.M. Hersh, *Cover-Up* (New York: Random House, 1972), p. 232.

53 *Report of the Auditor General of Canada to the House of Commons*, 1992, chapters 16, 17 and 18; and 1994, chapters 24, 25, 26 and 27.

54 See F.C. Mosher, *The G.A.O.: The Quest for Accountability in American Government* (Boulder, Colorado: Westview Press, 1979).

55 As we will see, there is an inspector general for the Canadian security service (*Canadian Security Intelligence Service Act, 1984*, c. 21, R.S.C. 1985, c. C-23). The closest Canada comes to a military inspector general is the chief, review services, set up in 1985. In the words of an official description (A-AE-D20-001/AG-001, 1993), the chief, review services, "is the Departmental advisor and functional authority on all aspects of review matters and is responsible and accountable for the planning and conduct of program evaluations, internal audits and examinations of all aspects of Departmental and military activities; and for providing independent, objective reports on the effectiveness, efficiency and economy of the Department of National Defence (DND) and the Canadian Forces." A description of the office was given in a private presentation to the Somalia Inquiry by a retired former chief, review services, Major General Marc Terreau (15 December 1995). It may be that this office could develop into a more full-fledged inspector general.

56 This historical material is drawn from the statement by Lieutenant-General R.H. Griffith, the inspector general, Department of the Army, before the Committee on Governmental Affairs, United States Senate, 26 February 1992, and from inspector general course material, "History of the IG" (Fort Belvoir, Virginia). See also W.M. Evan, "The Inspector-General in the U.S. Army", in D.C. Rowat, ed., *The Ombudsman: Citizen's Defender* (University of Toronto Press, 1965), p. 147ff.

57 See Army Regulation 20-1, "Inspector General Activities and Proce-dures", March 1994.

58 Griffith's statement to the Senate, p. 1.

59 OTIG Regulation 10-5, "Organizations and Functions", chapter 2.

60 Army Regulation 20-1, chapter 10-1.

61 "History of the IG", p. 8.

62 The Inspector General, "Information Bulletin", May 1995, p. III-6.

63 Griffith's statement to the Senate, p. 9.

64 "History of the IG", p. 4.

65 Griffith's statement to the Senate, p. 10.

66 See Army Regulation 20-1, set out in Chapter 3, note 25.

67 Army Regulation 20-1, figure 6-1.

68 See IG, DOD, "Organization and Functions Guide", January 1994.

69 *Inspector General Act*, 92 Stat. 1101 (1978). See generally P.C. Light, *Monitoring Government: Inspectors General and the Search for Accountability* (Washington, D.C.: Brookings Institution, 1993).
70 Light, *Monitoring Government*, p. 25.
71 Public Law 97-252, amending the *Inspector General Act of 1978.*
72 Light, *Monitoring Government*, p. 2.
73 Bernard Rosen, *Holding Government Bureaucracies Accountable*, second edition (New York: Praeger, 1989), p. 151.
74 Griffith's statement to the Senate, pp. 2, 3.
75 Griffith's statement to the Senate, p. 3.
76 "Organization and Functions Guide", p. 2-2.
77 Army Regulation 20-1, chapter 10-1.
78 "Organization and Functions Guide", 2.3 (s).
79 See Light, *Monitoring Government*, p. 97.
80 Rowat, *The Ombudsman*, includes a section on the U.S. military inspector general.
81 D.C. Rowat, "Time for a Federal Ombudsman", *Canadian Parliamentary Review*, forthcoming.
82 *Official Languages Act*, R.S.C. 1985, c. 31 (4th Supp.), s. 49.
83 *Corrections and Conditional Release Act*, Stat. Can. 1992, c. 20, ss. 157-198.
84 *Privacy Act*, R.S.C. 1985, c. P-21, s. 53.
85 *Access to Information Act*, R.S.C. 1985, c. A-1, s. 54.
86 *Royal Canadian Mounted Police Act*, R.S.C. 1985, c. 8 (2nd Supp.), s. 16, adding ss.45.29ff.
87 See Frank Stacey, *Ombudsmen Compared* (Oxford: Clarendon Press, 1978), pp. 45-46.
88 *Ombudsman Amendment Act* 1983, s. 20.
89 Australian Commonwealth Ombudsman, *Annual Report 1994-95*, p. 169.
90 *Annual Report 1994-95*, p. 176.
91 Stacey, *Ombudsmen Compared*, p. 40ff; and Rowat, *The Ombudsman*, p. 95ff.
92 D.C. Rowat, *The Ombudsman Plan* (Lanham, Md.: University Press of America, 1985), p. 41ff; and Stacey, *Ombudsmen Compared*, p. 46ff.
93 Stacey, *Ombudsmen Compared*, p. 46.
94 Rowat, *The Ombudsman Plan*, p. 42.
95 Stacey, *Ombudsmen Compared*, p. 47.
96 Rowat, *The Ombudsman Plan*, p. 119.
97 Rowat, *The Ombudsman Plan*, p. 43.
98 Rowat, *The Ombudsman Plan*, p. 43.

99   Rowat, *The Ombudsman Plan*, p. 45.
100 The next three people to hold the office after Heye were all civilians and significantly less controversial in performing their duties. Had the office become more accepted by the government of the day, or were Heye's successors chosen for their political discretion? See Stacey, *Ombudsmen Compared*, p. 47.
101 *Royal Canadian Mounted Police Act*, R.S.C. 1985, c. 8 (2nd Supp.), s. 16.
102 The media and the military is an important subject not covered in this paper. See, for example, W.A. Wilcox, "Media Coverage of Military Operations: OPLAW Meets the First Amendment", *The Army Lawyer*, May 1995, p. 42; Jo Groebel, "The Role of the Mass Media in Modern Wars", in R.A. Hinde and H.E. Watson, eds., *War: A Cruel Necessity?* (New York: Tauris Academic Studies, 1995), p. 143; and A. Kellett, *Combat Motivation: The Behavior of Soldiers in Battle* (The Hague: Kluwer Nijhoff, 1982), pp. 185-188. See also QR&O 19.375.
103 Lieutenant Commander G.M. Aikins, "An Ombudsman for the Canadian Forces: Reestablishing an Ethical Framework" (Canadian Forces Command and Staff College, 1993), pp. 19-20.
104 As stated earlier in discussing the role of the U.S. inspector general, the existing office of chief, review services, could possibly be expanded to take on this function.
105 See Lawrence Lustgarten, "Security Services, Constitutional Structure, and Varieties of Accountability in Canada and Australia", in P.C. Stenning, *Accountability for Criminal Justice: Selected Essays* (University of Toronto Press, 1995), p. 172ff; R.G. Atkey, "Accountability for Security Intelligence Activities in Canada: The New Structure", in Hanks and McCamus, *National Security*, p. 37; Franks, "Accountability of the Canadian Security Intelligence Service", in Hanks and McCamus, p. 19; Philip Rosen, *The Canadian Security Intelligence Service* (Ottawa: Library of Parliament, 1984, revised 1994); Security Intelligence Review Committee, *Annual Report 1994-95*; and Canadian Security Intelligence Service, *Public Report and Program Outlook* (Ottawa: Supply and Services, 1994). Note that DND is planning to introduce an oversight mechanism for the highly secret Communications Security Establishment, which monitors foreign communications; see *Globe and Mail*, 26 January 1996.
106 See Rowat, *The Ombudsman Plan*, p. 46. Redress of grievance procedures for the Canadian military are contained in the *National*

Defence Act, R.S.C. 1985, ss. 29 and 96; QR&O 19.26 and 19.27; and CFAO 19-32.

CHAPTER EIGHT — CONCLUSION

1 Major A.G. Hines, "Military Ethics: A Code for the Canadian Forces" (Canadian Staff College, 1992), p. 21.
2 Section 8 of the *Crown Liability and Proceedings Act*, R.S.C. 1985, c. C-50, as amended.
3 Hugh Arnold, "Sanctions and Rewards: an Organizational Perspective", in M.L. Friedland, *Sanctions and Rewards in the Legal System: A Multidisciplinary Approach* (University of Toronto Press, 1989), p. 152.
4 Colonel A.R. Wells, DG Secur, 12 October 1994, #001871, p. 3.
5 John Braithwaite, *Crime, Shame and Reintegration* (Cambridge University Press, 1989), p. 68.
6 *Korponey* v. *A.G. Canada* (1982) 65 C.C.C. (2d) 65, p. 74; [1982] 1 S.C.R. 41.
7 Section 66 of the *National Defence Act*, R.S.C. 1985, c. N-4, as amended.
8 Section 162 of the *National Defence Act*.
9 *U.S.* v. *Thomas* M.J. 388, p. 393 (C.M.A. 1986).
10 *Security in a Changing World* (Ottawa, 1994), p. 57.
11 See appendix H in the internal document by Jim Simpson and François Lareau, "Report of Visit to U.S. Army Headquarters — Washington, D.C.", 18 September 1995, p. 1.